# SHAKESPEARE: SEVEN TRAGEDIES

# SHAKESPEARE: SEVEN TRAGEDIES

## The dramatist's manipulation of response

E. A. J. HONIGMANN

First published 1976 by
THE MACMILLAN PRESS LTD
London and Basingstoke
Associated companies in New York
Dublin Melbourne Johannesburg and Madras

77·350080

SBN 333 19598 1

Printed in Great Britain by
WESTERN PRINTING SERVICES LTD
Bristol

# Contents

# Acknowledgements

I am grateful to the University of Newcastle upon Tyne for permission to reprint short passages from my lecture, *Shakespearian Tragedy and the Mixed Response* (Newcastle upon Tyne, 1971); and to Miss Kathleen O'Rawe, who managed to decipher my 'foul papers' and produced the typescript. I am also most grateful to an old friend, R. A. Foakes, who read through the typescript and suggested several corrections and improvements.

# A Note on Dates and Definitions

In his first ten years or so as a dramatist Shakespeare wrote a few tragedies (notably *Romeo and Juliet*) but specialised in comedy and the history-play. In his second decade he was pre-eminently a writer of tragedy, and composed the mature tragedies in the following order: *Julius Caesar* (1599), *Hamlet* (1600–1), *Othello* (1603), *King Lear* (1605), *Macbeth* (1606), *Antony and Cleopatra* (1606–7) and *Coriolanus* (1607–8). The order is now pretty well agreed, but the dates are not so certain.[1] Yet at much the same time, it should be remembered, he also produced other plays, most of them comedies: *As You Like It* (1599–1600), *Twelfth Night* (1599–1600), *The Merry Wives of Windsor* (1600–1), *Troilus and Cressida* (1601–2), *All's Well That Ends Well* (1602–3), *Measure for Measure* (1603–4) and *Timon of Athens* (1607–8). The dates, again, have to be regarded as conjectural.

The mature tragedies are traditionally divided into two groups, the 'Roman plays' (*Julius Caesar, Antony and Cleopatra, Coriolanus*), and the four to which I sometimes refer as 'the central tragedies' (*Hamlet, Othello, King Lear, Macbeth*). Each group has its distinctive features.[2] The Roman plays, all based on the same source – Plutarch's *Lives* in Sir Thomas North's translation (1579) – express Roman attitudes to the state, to religion, suicide, love and marriage, whereas the central tragedies are more 'Elizabethan' and Christian in outlook. The Roman plays examine political questions, the central tragedies have a more metaphysical bent. But these are rough and ready distinctions, for *King Lear* is less overtly Christian than the three other central tragedies, the Roman plays all include some Elizabethan (or Jacobean) elements, and the tragedies might be grouped quite differently. We might distinguish, for example, between those that exhibit supernatural phenomena (*Julius Caesar, Hamlet, Macbeth* and, perhaps, *Antony and Cleopatra*) and the rest, or between tragedies of thought (*Julius Caesar, Hamlet*) and the rest. I deal with the seven mature tragedies individually, in chronological order, without paying much attention to groups, and so I must stress that the two traditional groups also differ in their manipulation of audience-response. In the Roman plays the audience enters less completely into the hero's point of view than in the central tragedies, which no doubt contributes to our sense that we are here concerned with a different kind of play. Brutus, Antony and Coriolanus reveal less of their 'inner self' or have less to reveal, fall short of the four 'central' heroes in spiritual grandeur, and are less generously endowed with Shakespeare's finest poetry. For these and other reasons the spectator identifies himself less fully with the Roman heroes, and, I think, admires them less. In addition spectators are 'disengaged' from the Roman heroes, particularly Antony and Coriolanus, by the unusual number of comment-speeches; they know how the Roman heroes appear to others from the outside, but, paradoxically, this knowledge conceals the inner man and helps to keep him at a distance.

There is no discussion of *Timon of Athens* in this book. As I have explained elsewhere,[3] *Timon* differs profoundly from the tragedies of the same period and has more in common with *Troilus and Cressida*, another play whose genre is hard to define. If *Timon* was regarded by Shakespeare as properly finished and was ever performed in his lifetime, it must have aroused a unique response. Some scenes appear to steer towards tragic emotions, but very few can be said to be tragic, since alien emotions almost always intrude: Timon's rage cannot compare with Lear's, affecting us as spiteful and grotesque, even petty, where Lear's is, quite simply, sublime. The audience, I think, would have been so 'disengaged' from Timon that it might well have wondered, in many scenes, whether it was watching a tragedy or a freak-show.

There is an index of technical and unfamiliar terms on page 214.

All quotations from Shakespeare are taken from Peter Alexander's edition of *The Complete Works* (Tudor edition, 1951), unless otherwise specified.

# I

# Introduction: Shakespeare and the Study of Response

Although there are signs of a new 'movement' in literary and dramatic criticism, it has not so far made much progress. More and more books[1] now touch on the reader's or theatre-goer's response, yet even those who believe that we should pursue this new critical interest draw back, all too often, when they consider the dangers. If they wish to examine the response to Shakespeare, whose response should it be? An Elizabethan one (impossible) – or a modern one? If a modern one, ought it to be that of the most experienced Man of the Theatre, or of the most learned scholar – or their very own? We could only speak authoritatively about our own; and yet it's not easy to report accurately

> With shabby equipment always deteriorating
> In the general mess of imprecision of feeling.

And other dangers abound. The enthusiast who undertakes to record how he reacts to a play must know when his response is ripe, and ready for collecting. During a performance, immediately after it, a little later, or much later? Indeed, can he respond and observe his own response both at once?

An inward-looking approach leads inevitably to charges of subjectivism or crude egoismus ('All my I', as Coleridge so unkindly said of Fichte's ego-centred philosophy). We need not, however, give up in despair. We can proceed along different lines: instead of merely fingering our own pulses in the theatre, or plugging ourselves into a private galvanometer, we can study the dramatist's technical skills in guiding audience-response. As an audience watches a play it 'responds' from the first word to the last, and an experienced dramatist knows this and leaves as little as possible to chance: he adjusts his plotting, and much else besides, to ensure that the audience will respond as he wants. His manipulation of response is therefore one of the dramatist's basic skills, no less important than plotting, characterisation, use of imagery or ideas, and the like: and we can observe how it operates exactly as we come to grips with other points of crafts-manship, by studying the text.

I am not arguing that its 'response problems' are the only or necessarily the best avenue of approach to a tragedy: I merely urge that criticism ignores them at its peril, intimately intertwined as they are with a play's every other component. Shakespeare's earlier commentators lost their bearings partly because they were not suffi-ciently interested in these very problems, and, if we follow them, we may still go wrong today. 'The character of Iago is so conducted', said Dr Johnson, 'that he is from the first scene to the last hated and despised.' 'Lady Macbeth', he said, again, 'is merely detested; and though the courage of Macbeth preserves some esteem, yet every reader rejoices at his fall.'[2] Does such a summing-up tally with our experience of Shakespeare's complex characters? I find it unaccept-able, if only because Johnson assumed our response to character to be static, 'from the first scene to the last', and ignored the fluctuations of feeling that we expect from great drama. With few exceptions, Johnson's successors offered similar reductive statements, or, if they acknowledged that response changes as a play develops, failed to ask themselves how it was done.

The fluidity of response can be illustrated, very simply, from our response to a repeated word. 'Nuncle' in *King Lear* (I. 4. 103ff.) may be 'contracted from *mine uncle*, the customary appellation of the licensed fool to his superiors', as editors assure us, but, used as it is by the Fool in his first scene, always preluding a piece of acid wisdom, it becomes a pin-pricking weapon, the Fool's counterpart to Lear's whip, and is tainted by impudence, and possibly by malice. Thus 'nuncle', a term of endearment, soon turns into something very different; and our response must change as we learn to understand the word's function (which differs from its meaning, as glossed by the editors).

'In dramatic composition', Maurice Morgann explained long ago, 'the impression is the fact'.[3] An audience's response changes as the dramatist adjusts the play's impressions. Each spectator participates creatively: consciously or unconsciously he sifts all impressions, com-pares them with earlier ones, flashes back and forth to the present, revises his expectations. The spectator, that is, attends not only to the immediate speech or situation but simultaneously and unremit-tingly reassesses the play as a whole, its style, its shape, its prob-abilities: he responds in many different ways. Response problems therefore take us beyond character, beyond liking or not liking Hamlet, and require us to investigate the spectator's imaginative engagement with the play. How fully do we enter into Hamlet's point of view? How can we take account of 'secret motives', which are shown but not described in so many words, in *Othello*? How clear-cut has Shakespeare made the political issues and personal relationships in *Coriolanus*? These are some of the larger response problems that any general essay on one of the three plays would certainly mention. What is now required, however, is a more sharply focused discussion of the dramatist's control of response, bringing out the extraordinary variety of the problems and also the extraordinary variety of Shakespeare's solutions.

Inevitably, a subjective note will sometimes intrude. But I am chiefly concerned with the dramatist's technical skills, not with one person's response. (If I am told that the two cannot be separated, what is the reply? That when the dramatist pulls us in this direction or that, we may observe the fact that he pulls, and the means employed, without always thinking ourselves obliged to define exactly what we feel.) And Shakespeare exercised his skills, I repeat, as an 'impressionist' artist: like Bacon, he understood perfectly 'what things are to be laid open, and what to be secreted, and what to be showed at half-lights.' There can be no doubt about it that he studied the theatre-audience's engagement – at the very least, as vigilantly as Mark Antony watches and guides his audience in the Forum Scene. In the chapters that follow I try to show how an expert in half-lights nudged or dictated the audience-response in his greatest plays.

# 2
# Impressions of 'Character'

Response problems, as I have said, take us beyond character. But they all refer back to character, directly or indirectly, since a play's every word is channelled through a dramatic speaker. We must therefore consider the mode of existence of a dramatic character, and ask how an audience engages with a Hamlet or Lear. In this chapter I shall argue that in creating his tragic heroes Shakespeare often used impressionistic devices that leave the spectator in uncertainties. Just as Troilus exclaims 'this is, and is not, Cressid' (V. 2. 144), we are bewildered by the Hamlet or Lear that we think we know: I propose to examine our relationship with the characters, our special ways of 'knowing' them, after which we shall be ready to ask more searchingly how we respond. It will be assumed that the reader is familiar with recent work on dramatic character – with historical criticism and with the replies it provoked.[1] And, now that the historical dust has settled, I shall also assume that we may guardedly speak of Shakespeare's characters as life-like.

        *        *        *

Whilst no self-respecting critic will henceforth wish to place Shakespeare's stage-persons on a psychiatrist's couch, to fish in imagined minds for a past that never was, a psychological or 'natural' bias still remains appropriate when we discuss a play's insistently life-like characters. If Shakespeare invites us to attend to the motives and inner self of a stage Hamlet it behoves us so to attend, and, as generations of theatre-goers have found, we can do this without getting into philosophical difficulties. When the play begins we don't ask awkward either/or questions about the stage-person's ontological status ('Is it Hamlet?', 'Is it Burbage?'), we settle instinctively for a compromise ('It's Burbage-as-Hamlet'), and we willingly allow the unique stage-person to have as many gestures, speeches and motives as the dramatist chooses. In saying this I am not arguing that we think of Shakespeare's characters as 'real persons' but only that when so directed we may evaluate a Hamlet's behaviour very much as we do a next-door neighbour's, with certain obvious reservations.

Shakespeare's plays, and especially his tragedies, require us to take an interest in motive, and often say so.

> I do not know
> Why yet I live to say 'This thing's to do' (*Hamlet* IV. 4. 43–4)

> Will you, I pray, demand that demi-devil
> Why he hath thus ensnar'd my soul and body?
> > (*Othello* V. 2. 304–5)

> *Is there any cause in nature* that makes these hard hearts?
> > (*King Lear* III. 6. 76–8)

Even when the question 'Why?' is not so pointedly raised, an audience cannot fail to grasp that the most casual remark may illuminate a speaker's motives, since the dialogue never goes on for long without signalling some kind of self-betrayal. Shakespeare's language, whilst usually far from life-like, compels the audience to look beneath the verbal surface and suggests a life-like inwardness in the dramatic speaker.

This inwardness has caused a great deal of trouble.[2] May we reasonably ascribe an 'inner self' to Hamlet and contend, say, that conscientious scruples of which he himself remains unaware prevent him from killing Claudius? To look for such unconscious or secret motives, we are sometimes told, is to misunderstand a dramatic character's mode of being. 'We persist in digging for them', it has been said, 'but what happens usually is that our spade goes through the other side of the drama'.[3] In other words, in pursuing secret motives we go outside the play, and therefore waste everyone's time; we are guilty of critical loitering with intent. Yet we might argue that the merest hints that Othello suffers from a sense of social insecurity, or Iago from a grudge against upper-class privilege,[4] function as impressions, just as barely audible noises function as noises; and in dramatic composition 'the impression is the fact'. Even if Othello or Iago remains unaware of his own motive, and the other characters fail to detect it, a dramatist can still reveal it to the audience: and should this sound like a brazen assertion, one that cannot be proved or disproved, secret motives being too slippery to get hold of or to squeeze till they pop, let us remember that many motives in drama are kept secret *for a time* and yet the audience knows all about them.[5] Long before any of the *dramatis personae* say so, we know that Orsino loves 'Cesario', that Cassio admires Othello

as his 'dear general', that Macbeth will not grieve when Lady
Macbeth dies. Secret motives are a standard feature of Shakespeare's
plays. Though they work more deviously in tragedy than in comedy,
the fact that some are more secret than others need not mean that in
digging for them 'our spade goes through the other side of the drama'
but only that those who tunnel in dark places will occasionally lose
their way.

The argument about secret motives resembles another one which
also bears on our way of 'knowing' a dramatic character. The action
of the play is the only reality, we are sometimes warned, and to try
to go behind it is futile. What were the relations of Hamlet and
Ophelia before Act I? 'The answer is, there were none. Outside of the
play, previous to the opening of its action, Hamlet and Ophelia do
not exist'.[6] Like secret motives, the previous relations of Hamlet and
Ophelia are said to lie outside the play. How, then, do we define a
play's *inside*? If the action of a play is the only reality, what precisely do we mean by *action*? Ophelia describes a visit from Hamlet
which might be sited outside the play: 'My lord, as I was sewing in
my closet . . .' (III. 1. 77ff.) Yes, the visit supposedly took place off-
stage. But we hear Ophelia speak of it inside the play, and that makes
a difference. The outside can be brought inside; or, more accurately,
those inside may look outside and their statements about off-stage
events will nevertheless remain securely within the play. (Such
statements, moreover, could fairly count as part of the play's *action*,
like all the other dialogue, since speech is one kind of action, arguably
the most important kind in Shakespeare's tragedies.) Having heard
that Hamlet importuned Ophelia with love, gave her remembrances
and so on, spectators need not, after all, apologise if they catch themselves wondering about the couple's previous relations, as Shakespeare himself directs attention to the past *inside the play*. Unlicensed
speculation would be futile, but, on the other hand, to refuse to take
account of what is inside the play seems no less irresponsible.

As will have become clear, it is prudent to think of all outside
events reported in a play as *reports* rather than as off-stage *events*,
irrespective of their timing before the opening or between the acts or
scenes. The reports 'exist', exactly like the other dialogue, and
audiences respond to these reports as to other stage-impressions,
evaluating them in the light of all the available evidence. Ophelia
tells of Hamlet's frightening visit (II. 1. 75ff.): there are no reasons to
disbelieve the details (the doublet unbraced, stockings fouled, piteous

look) but, having heard less than a hundred lines earlier that Hamlet might 'put an antic disposition on', we cannot help wondering whether she misunderstood an antic happening. Claudius describes recent political upheavals (I. 2. 1ff.), Hamlet laments his mother's marriage (I. 2. 129ff.), the Ghost discloses a murder most foul (I. 5. 9ff.): in these and many other reports we sense the speaker's special interest in an off-stage event and only partly believe him; and when different reporters express very different attitudes to the same events, as in the three instances just mentioned, we evaluate even more cautiously. Listening to reports we don't dispute their validity within the imaginative structure, though we may still refuse to believe what we hear.

Shakespeare's characters are also life-like in being presented to us from many points of view, which we have to piece together. When we compare another great dramatist interested in 'natural' effects, say Ibsen, we observe that Shakespeare's secondary persons distort the image of the hero much more, that the hero sees himself in more variously distorted ways, and that consequently, having to work harder to synthesise our impressions, our reward is a more genuinely complex understanding of character. Take Ibsen's Halvard Solness and Shakespeare's Lear, two autocrats challenged and destroyed by the younger generation. Some of the master-builder's closest associates think him a self-willed tyrant (his wife, his employees Knut and Ragnar Brovik), whilst two young girls who know him less well worship him as a hero (Kaja Fosli and Hilde Wangel); he himself, aware of both views, believes the former to be correct, at least as far as his recent career is concerned, but, infected by Hilde's enthusiasm, tries to live up to his heroic image by climbing the new tower built by his men, and falls to his death. Though things are complicated by Solness' conviction that his wife thinks him mad, more or less all the images of Ibsen's hero belong to one of two kinds, each of which seems fixed and static until quite near the end, when Solness himself attempts to bring the two closer together. As seen by other characters, Lear also presents two kinds of image, favourable and unfavourable, but both change, and sometimes we switch from one to another at bewildering speed. Goneril and Regan describe him publicly as 'dearer than eyesight', then privately as rash, unruly, unconstant (I. 1); Goneril next complains that every hour 'he flashes into one gross crime or other' (I. 3). Progressive antagonism cannot go much farther, and the sisters thereafter talk of Lear from a 'fixed' point of

view, as old and foolish. The more interesting prismatic effects come
from those who are loosely considered Lear's friends, and from Lear
himself. Cordelia claims that she loves him according to her bond
(which her asides prove an understatement) (I. 1), and later thinks
him her 'poor father', treated worse than 'mine enemy's dog', yet
addresses him as 'my royal lord' (IV. 7). The split between her private
image of Lear and the one she publicly subscribes to thus creates a
double exposure similar to Goneril and Regan's at the beginning, a
not uncommon fragmentation in Shakespeare. Kent, himself a double
image as Kent-Caius, clings to his vision of 'royal Lear' in two
important scenes (III. 2, III. 4. 1–108) where no one else present sees
Lear steadily as he once was, and thus superimposes majesty on the
stage-image of the frantic, dishevelled old man. But if Cordelia's
private view of her 'dear father' and Kent's of his 'master' shed light
from two different directions that are not too far apart, the Fool,
scrambling together the oddest assortment of attitudes, views him
from another angle entirely. He refers to the king as one who put
down his own breeches, a pretty fellow, an O without a figure, a
sheal'd peascod, a hedge-sparrow, an obedient father (I. 4), and so on:
all derisive images, certainly, but each one presents a startlingly
original perception that we have to relate to Cordelia's dear father,
Kent's master and all other verbal and stage impressions. And as
well as these sharply individualised images of Lear seen from the
outside we must take into account the uncertainties of his inner
vision. 'Who is it that can tell me who I am?' he asks, and soon
projects himself in various mutually incompatible ways – as loving
father and irate king (II. 4. 99–100) or as one who kneels and curses
(II. 4. 144–51).

Others might wish to speak more positively for Ibsen; and Lear,
I readily admit, looks like a special case, in so far as he suffers from
more radical confusions than, for instance, Brutus or Macbeth.
Nevertheless, though Shakespeare exploits his prismatic technique
in special ways in King Lear, all his tragic heroes experience 'identity
problems' and all are presented in richly diversified images. The
spectator therefore constructs his own image of a Shakespearian
character much as he comes to know flesh-and-blood beings, forever
working at it as the play continues and as new impressions pour in.
Secret motives and outside events reported in the play have a technical function in contributing to this impressionistic knowledge of
character: precisely because we do not translate secret motives and

reports into certainties they enable us to know Hamlet in a medium of doubts, inferences, likes and dislikes, knowledge and half-knowledge, the normal medium when one mind makes contact with another. From this intricate criss-cross of impressions we come to know Hamlet more intimately than we could from an authorised biography or from the smell of his underclothes – or from any critical explication, however inspired.

*     *     *

Arguing that Shakespeare's characters appear to be life-like and that we feel we know them so well because he used impressionistic devices, I can say with Dr Johnson, when he had mildly and modestly defended the poet of nature for disregarding the unities, that 'I am almost frighted at my own temerity'. I have gone as far as I dare, and the time has come to express reservations. First of all, let us admit that whereas we know other human beings from outside and ourselves from inside,[7] we combine these two very different modes of perception in our relationship with most of Shakespeare's tragic heroes. Strictly speaking, our knowledge of dramatic character will be *sui generis*, and comparisons with our intimate knowledge of human beings must not be pressed too hard.

Next it would be as well to give up all pretence of knowing 'the whole character' or 'the true character' of a dramatic creature, even though good critics have thought that this was possible. We must remember that however lightly a dramatist skips from Sicily to Bohemia, no matter how cleverly he juggles with the law of re-entry or double-time schemes, he still has to cram all he wants to say about character into the two or three hours' traffic of the stage. He proceeds selectively, using only what will be relevant to his plot, and so silently passes over facts that an Appointments Board would wish to hear about when assessing a whole character: Hamlet's age, his qualifications and previous experience as a revenger, and the three referees' letters from Wittenberg. It could be countered, of course, that a tragedy provides more insightful information, but not that it presents a complete character (if that can be done at all and isn't a fallacy of definition, a point that I find so abstruse that I prefer to leave it to our O-level examiners). Rather than claim too much we should therefore frankly admit that we possess no more than fleeting impressions of Shakespeare's characters. They all move through time and 'develop' in mysterious ways (*Othello* is by no means the only tragedy with a double-time scheme), from which it follows that even though a tragic character hangs together in our imagination, we should not presume to explain it except in tentative, impressionistic terms.

Another life-like feature that has encouraged misplaced confidence is the tragic hero's 'role-playing'. In the last two hundred years Morgann and others have remarked on this, but only after the new sociology had arrived could 'character and role' storm effectively into dramatic criticism, trailing clouds of jargon and also some useful distinctions. The shift to the more modern attitude becomes clear when we compare Bradley and Leavis on *Othello*. Bradley, it will be recalled, admired Othello's noble and trusting nature and thought him 'a changed man' once Iago's poison had begun to work; Leavis, on the contrary, thought Othello an 'obtuse and brutal egotist' who projects an idealised image of himself in the play's opening scenes, but, put to the test, reveals himself to be very different.[8] Both Bradley and Leavis thus recognised two Othellos in the play, the real Othello and another; Bradley assumed that we meet the real Othello first, at the beginning of the play, and Leavis that the essential man emerges in Act III. And who is right? Othello's role-playing, or 'idealised conception of himself', figures much more prominently in Leavis's essay, as might have been expected from one who was free to benefit from modern sociology. ('No amount of it', he darkly acknowledged, 'can forward our knowledge or understanding of anything' – but that was of sociology in another country and besides, *mutatis mutandis*, the wench is dead.) Leavis had all the advantages, and certainly deepened our understanding of Othello; but it remains to be asked whether *either* of the two Othellos, the noble Moor or the brutal egotist, necessarily represents the 'true' character. Could there not be an element of 'role-playing' in both? I am reluctant to accept that the real Othello only finds himself under stress, in Act III, in so far as he then adopts a way of thinking (in animal images and so on) already powerfully established as Iago's; it seems at least a possibility that, instead of casting off a role and discovering his character, Othello merely takes on a new role in Act III, one that reflects Iago's character as much as his own.

Notice that as soon as we begin to speak about role-playing in drama, the character or 'ghost in the machine' becomes more ghost-like, and is in danger of disappearing altogether. In the end all behaviour may seem to be role-playing of one kind or another: the more role-conscious we grow the more difficult is it to locate that

poor, bare, forked animal, 'unaccommodated man'. Recognising this
difficulty we have to admit that if the older character-criticism of
Shakespeare confused character with role and mood, and no doubt
with other ill-assorted inner processes, our modern role-theories can
also mislead. If we feel tempted to conclude, with Peer Gynt, that
after shedding our roles we shall find no self underneath, that the
'Emperor of Self' could be an onion, without a heart, the time has
come to pause and to ask what we mean by character.

Different experts give different answers. The one that would
interest us most would be Shakespeare's – and, not surprisingly, there
are Big-Endians and Little-Endians who claim to have got inside the
dome-like head, and to know his thoughts. The historical critics
advise that Shakespeare must have pondered character in Elizabethan
terms to which, after all, he often alluded. Their opponents see
Shakespeare as 'not of an age but for all time', a thinker so far ahead
of his contemporaries that only the most modern psychology can
hope to explain character as he understood it. But some compromise
is surely possible when we recall that the wit and wisdom of many
centuries still circulated in Shakespeare's day, together with the
psychology of humours, and often anticipated our most advanced
discoveries. We investigate unified personality and 'self-consistency';
the Jacobeans read in their Bible that 'the good that I would, I do
not; but the evil which I would not, that I do' (Romans vii. 19), and
might have considered this a helpful gloss on Macbeth. We talk
glibly about character and role; in the sixteenth century the fashion-
able equivalent was 'all the world's a stage': 'All the world doth
practise stage-playing. Wee must play our parts duly, but as the part
of a borrowed personage. Of a visard and apparence, wee should not
make a real essence. . . . Wee cannot distinguish the skinne from the
shirt.'[9]

Though Elizabethan and modern psychological textbooks look very
different, general thinking about character need not have been quite
so far apart. Readers of Shakespeare, however, will not expect to find
his 'idea of character' in a textbook or in general thinking, Elizabethan or modern, trusting their overriding impression that his
psychology was intuitive, exploratory and highly original. If, as I
think, this is correct, how can we hope to unravel his idea of character?

One way might be to look into the future, from the sixteenth
century, not at this theorist or that but at the general movement of

ideas, on the assumption that Shakespeare helped to *create* the future. So many thinkers (including Freud) drew inspiration from the plays or had their theories tested in studies of the plays (by Morgann, Whiter, Ernest Jones and others) that later psychology may well throw light on Shakespeare's darker purposes. What general development, then, can we discern? We may safely say: a steady move away from the notion that character is fixed, defined, an object, a formula, an ascertainable humour, a ruling passion. Few, perhaps, would now go as far as Hume, an earlier Peer Gynt, who ridiculed the very idea of personal identity: 'I never can catch *myself* at any time without a perception, and never can observe anything but the perception.' According to Hume we are 'nothing but a bundle or collection of different perceptions, which succeed each other with an inconceivable rapidity'.[10] An alternative to Hume's scepticism was a pluralistic view of character, which may be illustrated from writers as far apart as Diderot (in *Le Neveu de Rameau*) or Walt Whitman:

> Of every hue and caste am I, of every rank and religion . . .
> I resist any thing better than my own diversity.[11]

Strindberg, in the Preface to *Miss Julie*, where he seems to have seen himself as an innovator, must therefore be regarded as the spokesman of a familiar idea, when he repudiated the 'bourgeois notion of the fixed state of the soul.'

> My souls are conglomerates of a past stage of civilisation and our present one, scraps from books and newspapers, pieces of humanity, torn-off tatters of holiday clothes that have disintegrated and become rags – exactly as the soul is patched together.

Whitman and Strindberg are not names likely to figure in heavy type in a *History of Psychology*. I have cited them to illustrate a general trend, away from a 'fixed' view of character, in which literature supported theory. By no means all of those who adopt the more modern alternative of a divided self would agree that theirs is a pluralistic view, nor do I seriously suggest that Shakespeare's was (though after reading Bradley and Leavis on *Othello* we may despairingly clutch at such straws). Shakespeare, it would be safer to say, anticipated the trend and indeed helped to bring it about by *stretching* character, so that Othello encompasses the roles of noble Moor

and brutal egotist, not necessarily with the same commitment, and
'royal Lear' coexists from first to last with 'a very foolish fond old
man', different scenes stressing different features of the same person.
'We know what we are, but know not what we may be.' Ophelia
speaks for the tragic heroes (except that they only think they know
what they are), each one being placed in a situation that activates
unsuspected inner forces, each one being therefore stretched till we
wonder whether he remains one person or has become another.

Was't Hamlet wrong'd Laertes? Never Hamlet. (v. 2. 225)

That's he that was Othello – here I am. (v. 2. 287)

It is not hard to understand why Shakespeare grew interested in
this new way of looking at character: the more he stretched the hero,
the more powerful the tragic effect. In his greatest tragedies the hero
is invaded or possessed by an alien personality, and, challenged in his
inmost being, appears to be 'taken over', sometimes briefly (Hamlet),
sometimes for longer spells (Othello). The formula worked well, and
it may be that Shakespeare actually thought of it as a kind of 'stretching' (in which case I need not apologise for this unpleasing word).[12]

Avaunt! be gone! Thou hast set me on the rack! (*Othello* III. 3. 339)

I am bound
Upon a wheel of fire . . . (*King Lear* IV. 7. 46–7)

Placing his tragic hero upon the rack, and thus making him act
against his nature (as it was previously exhibited), Shakespeare
achieved an effect that we may observe in his other plays as well. All
the complex comic characters behave incongruously, from Petruchio's
Kate to Caliban, as do the tragic heroes: arriving on the literary
scene just as English drama advanced from Everyman to Faustus,
from type to individual, Shakespeare stretched character by exploring
its inexhaustible diversity, and so prepared the way for later pluralistic theories. But, despite superficial resemblances, the tragic heroes
differ from all but a very small number of Shakespeare's other
characters in so far as their diversity and incongruity is taken to
quite extraordinary lengths, far beyond that of 'people we know'.

I have said that the tragic heroes affect us as life-like. It remains to
be emphasised that though we see them from inside and from outside,
and though they are presented in such a variety of character-revealing
situations, they also affect us as infinitely more mysterious than

Ibsen's life-like characters or Chekhov's. Our impressions become contradictory and cloudy: one might almost argue that we know too much about the tragic heroes, what with the emotional precision of their speech and the sheer turn-over of significant detail, to be able to penetrate beyond the verbal surface to the inner man. Hamlet plainly tells Guildenstern that he will not 'pluck out the heart of my mystery', and after nearly four hundred years of defeated criticism we must concede the point. Why then insist on his individuality, on a 'life-like' character, if it cannot be plucked out and analysed in detail? Because tragedy, affirming man's indomitable spirit in a hostile universe, particularly concerns itself with self-discovery, with the search for identity, with the uniqueness of the individual. As heat applied to metals burns away impurities, so the intensity of the tragic experience (to adapt Keats) 'makes all disagreeables evaporate' and reveals the quintessential man. Driven in upon himself and threatened in the very centre of his being, the hero, in tragedies of very different periods, asserts an inviolable sense of selfhood: 'I am Duchess of Malfi still!'; 'Ahab is for ever Ahab, man!'; 'I am not a dime a dozen! I am Willy Loman!' No tragedies make more of this sense of self than Shakespeare's, where the hero, looking 'in my heart's core, ay, in my heart of heart', sometimes seems to discover a 'deep self', the very life-principle of the individual.

> But there, where I have garner'd up my heart,
> Where either I must live or bear no life,
> The fountain from the which my current runs
> Or else dries up – to be discarded thence![13]

We also believe in Shakespeare's tragic characters as 'individuals' because there are moments when we think we glimpse the ghost in the machine: though unable to drag it to the light of day and explain it, we react with the conviction that we have encountered the ghost, that beneath all the roles there lurks an identifiable self. Granville-Barker called them moments of *spontaneous revelation*. 'We learn much about a man when we learn what qualities in other men or women he unaffectedly admires', he explained, and as an example he cited Hamlet's words to Horatio, which 'ring out like a true confession of faith':[14] 'Since my dear soul was mistress of her choice . . .' But this is not the best example. Hamlet has his reasons for making a confession of faith, and creates the situation by calling for Horatio. A more genuinely spontaneous revelation occurs when the situation overwhelms the speaker and wrings from him a confession of feeling – when Macbeth returns from murdering Duncan, when Lear kneels to Cordelia, or when Othello, discovering Desdemona, discovers himself:

> It gives me wonder great as my content
> To see you here before me. O my soul's joy!
> If after every tempest come such calms . . . (II. 1. 181–3)

In such passages of wonder we see beyond the noble posture and its rhetoric 'into the life of things': as Othello responds spontaneously to moral beauty we feel that he shares this beauty, that deep answers unto deep.

Yet, it should be added, even when revealed spontaneously the inward self only reaches us in refracted glimpses, inferred from the emotion that bodies it forth. And when the tragic hero unpacks his heart, turned inside out by that special instrument, the Shakespearian soliloquy, we again fail to see the inward self directly but only glimpse it through a haze of self-scolding and self-deception. This, therefore, is the paradox of character in Shakespeare: whereas we think we know Hamlet perfectly, our knowledge is also oddly restricted. We think we enjoy a god-like insight, and in a sense this is true: we have special access to his inwardness, at times we share his feelings and almost 'become Hamlet'. And yet Shakespeare also went to unusual lengths to make his tragic hero inaccessible: he gave him secret motives, he included reports of strange behaviour, he shrouded the inner man in all the life-like trappings (roles, relationships, self-deceptions, a misty personal past), he racked him and made him act against his nature, he surrounded him with plausible commentators who distort his image. A tragic hero thus exists in the spectator's mind in a swirl of conflicting impressions – which, as we shall see, the dramatist conjured forth and controlled with the utmost care.

# 3
# Response and Dramatic Perspective

I told him that I had dined lately at Foote's, who shewed me a letter which he had received from Tom Davies, telling him that he had not been able to sleep from the concern which he felt on account of 'This sad affair of Baretti,' begging of him to try if he could suggest any thing that might be of service; and, at the same time, recommending to him an industrious young man who kept a pickle-shop.

JOHNSON. 'Ay, Sir, here you have a *specimen of human sympathy*; a friend hanged, and a cucumber pickled. We know not whether Baretti or the pickle-man has kept Davies from sleep; nor does he know himself.' (Boswell, *Life of Johnson*)[1]

Sympathy in the theatre is even more difficult to understand than sympathy in everyday affairs. Johnson, invariably shrewd in his general remarks on human nature, now seems oddly and uncharacteristically blinkered when he comments on 'human sympathy' in drama. Here are three examples:

Juliet plays most of her pranks under the appearance of religion: perhaps Shakespeare meant to punish her hypocrisy. (On *Romeo and Juliet*, IV. 3. 2–3)

This speech, in which Hamlet, represented as a virtuous character, is not content with taking blood for blood, but contrives damnation for the man that he would punish, is too horrible to be read or to be uttered. (On *Hamlet*, III. 3. 94–5)

I know not well why Shakespeare gives the Steward, who is a mere factor of wickedness, so much fidelity. He now refuses the letter, and afterwards, when he is dying, thinks only how it may be safely delivered. (On *King Lear*, IV. 5. 22)[2]

These extracts, together with Johnson's remarks on Iago and Macbeth and Lady Macbeth, to which I have already referred,[3] suggest that in the theatre a largely moral response may be inappropriate. Charles Lamb thought so, and denounced the theatre-goers of his day because 'we must love or hate – acquit or condemn – censure or pity – exert our detestable coxcombry of moral judgment upon everything.'[4] Yet, though Lamb wished to except only the artificial comedies of Wycherley and Congreve from the strictures of morality, arguing that they are filled with characters 'for whom you absolutely care nothing' ('they are a world of themselves almost as much as fairy-land'), the moralists soon thundered a reply, in the person of Lord Macaulay.

> In the name of art, as well as in the name of virtue, we protest against the principle that the world of pure comedy is one into which no moral enters . . . Morality constantly enters into that world . . . The heroes and heroines . . . have a moral code of their own, an exceedingly bad one, but not, as Mr Charles Lamb seems to think, a code existing only in the imagination of dramatists. It is, on the contrary, a code actually received and obeyed by great numbers of people.[5]

Neither Lamb nor Macaulay really explained how moral prepossessions influence response in the theatre. Lamb went too far in one direction, and Macaulay as far in the other (returning to a position not unlike Johnson's). The more modern tendency is to explain response in terms of perspective. 'Without direction given to sympathy', Walter Raleigh observed, 'a play is not a play, but a chaos or patchwork.' The Greeks, he went on, employed

> the Chorus, which mediates between the actors and the spectators, bespeaking attention, interpreting events, and guiding the feelings. Shakespeare had no Chorus, but he attains the same end in another way. In almost all his plays there is a clear enough point of view; there is some character, or group of characters, through whose eyes the events of the play must be seen, if they are to be seen in right perspective.[6]

Yet a theory of perspective cannot solve our problems swiftly and painlessly for, as Robert Langbaum has shown, different kinds of perspective operate in Shakespeare, so that 'we have really to choose between reading the soliloquies from a particular or from the general perspective.' If we respond more powerfully to character than to a play's less visible elements, such as its plot or its moral scale, we are liable to sympathize with any character, regardless of his moral position in the plot, provided only that he is sufficiently central to claim our attention, and has a sufficiently definite point of view and sufficient power of intellect and will to hold our interest. Thus, sympathy is likely to be more important than moral judgment . . .

Appalled by this possibility, and by the danger that sympathy might become a law unto itself, Langbaum argued against 'giving unconditional sympathy to sheer vividness of character':

it destroys the moral principle which apportions sympathy among the characters according to their deserts. It leaves an anarchic free-for-all in which the characters compete for a sympathy that depends on the ability to command attention, with the strongest character able to assert his point of view against the general meaning.[7]

General perspective meant for Langbaum a moral scale that was recognised by hero and villain alike, and was brought into the play from outside. 'Apparently, the moral order was accepted as fixed in a way that we now accept only the natural order.' If it ceases to be fixed, Langbaum thought, 'dramatic structure dissolves along with belief in a single objective moral order. For once we stop judging by an external standard, we stop understanding the character by what he does and says. We start understanding him from inside, through sympathy.'[8] Prophetic words! While an Elizabethan 'single objective moral order' was still conceivable when Langbaum wrote, the Elizabethan World Picture has now been shown up as a copy from an unidentifiable original,[9] if not a complete fake, and a general perspective brought into the world of the play as an 'external standard' hardly recommends itself. Every play, it would be safer to suggest, creates its own general perspective, one that will be 'Elizabethan', certainly, but that will also be as unique to the play as its imagery or plot: and it rests with the spectator to feel his way into it, and to make the grand discovery that *Hamlet* is not *Tamburlaine*.

Langbaum fails to solve the problem of dramatic perspective, I think, for several reasons. He seems to believe that a play has a *general meaning* exclusive of the strong characters that oppose it, much as if *Othello* could have a general meaning that leaves out Iago. He advances very little beyond Johnson, as his *general meaning* and *general perspective* are both determined by 'the moral principle'. And, most important, when he talks of general perspective he looks at drama from outside, from the vantage-point of one who knows the complete story and its moral scale, and forgets that as we read or watch a play we only master its perspectives very gradually, while strong characters may bid for our sympathy long before we have found our bearings.

Sympathy, for Langbaum, has a 'technical meaning . . . it is a way of knowing, what I call romantic projectiveness, what the Germans call *Einfühlung*, what the psychologists call empathy'. Sympathy thus involves our understanding a dramatic character from inside, accepting his point of view as a valid one, for him though not necessarily for ourselves. 'It does not mean *love* or *approval*.'[10] There are difficulties here, to which I shall return by way of T. S. Eliot's idea of poetic assent.

> there is a difference . . . between philosophical *belief* and poetic *assent* . . . In reading Dante you must enter the world of thirteenth-century Catholicism: which is not the world of modern Catholicism. . . . You are not called upon to believe what Dante believed, for your belief will not give you a groat's worth more of understanding and appreciation; but you are called upon more and more to understand it.[11]

To paraphrase: in reading *Macbeth* you must enter the imaginative world of a murderer; you need not believe what Macbeth believes (e.g. that there are Weird Sisters) but you are called upon more and more to understand his point of view. And understanding brings its obligations. *Tout comprendre, c'est tout pardonner*: the better you understand Macbeth's position from inside, the more inclined you will be to forgive him his crimes. The killing of Duncan may not be right, and yet may be 'right for Macbeth'; given his character and situation, we accept that he acts plausibly – and if the tragedy extorts *poetic assent* we *approve*, and cannot extricate ourselves by describing our approval as purely aesthetic. Testing Macbeth upon our own pulses, validating his behaviour as we watch it, we give a form of approval that implicates us, turning every audience into 'guilty creatures, sitting at a play.' We approve in a no-man's land between moral engagement and aesthetic detachment, which may be called psychological assent:[12] and, if my argument holds, it follows that we have a much closer relationship with Shakespeare's immoralists than Johnson or Langbaum (or, for that matter, the main stream of criticism) would lead us to believe.

By immoralists I mean the technical villains, and also such heroes as Othello and Lear, more sinned against than sinning, who commit murder and other offences that outrage our moral sensibility. Do we cease to sympathise with Othello when he rages at Desdemona, or when he smothers her? If not, as I believe (because Othello has won our psychological assent, arrives first in the two scenes, IV.1 and V.2, leads Desdemona in the dialogue and therefore has all the advantage of the scene's perspective), is it so impossible for Iago to retain our sympathy when he forms his devilish plans, or stabs Roderigo? I am not suggesting that we lavish our sympathy with equal enthusiasm upon every kind of horror, but only that in the theatre moral considerations count for less than outside.

All the same, they count for something, and it would be unwise to pretend otherwise. Even if a tragedy appears to 'transcend morality', as we sometimes read, it still generates its own morality, and moral considerations can never be kept at bay for long, however artfully the dramatist juggles with perspective. Consider Arthur Sewell's argument that Shakespeare's tragedies 'are what they are just because social and political judgements (though never wholly abrogated) tend to break down.'

> We must say of Hamlet, Macbeth, Othello, and King Lear that in some part of their natures they belong not to the temporal world but to a world beyond the world, a universe outside time, and that in this way we must apprehend them. In other words, vision, fulfilling itself in these characters, is no longer contained within society, legal, moral, or political, but seeks, as it were, to transcend society, to judge the social judgement, to bring society and its judgements *sub specie aeternitatis*. So – Macbeth is a villain; but when Duncan lies dead in the next room we think not of the murder but of the horror of Macbeth's realization that he shall sleep no more . . . These tragedies, then, all imply a metaphysical world in which what matters is not what men do to society but what they do to themselves.[13]

Sewell, I believe, insulated himself too completely against social judgements, more so than Shakespeare required. Duncan lies dead elsewhere, and for a while Macbeth alone fills our minds; but Duncan's body is discovered and ('O horror, horror, horror!') traditional moral attitudes flood back into the play. It is a question, indeed, whether Macbeth himself, for all his efforts to transcend society, should not be regarded as the play's most deeply traditional moralist, to whom we cannot deny our sympathy, after he has killed Duncan, precisely because his *moral* nature reasserts itself so irresistibly.

'Except in a few scenes in A *Midsummer Night's Dream*', Alfred Harbage has said, 'there are not thirty consecutive lines in Shakespeare that do not levy upon the vocabulary of ethics, or relate in some way to standards of conduct'.[14] Shakespeare's characters live in a moral atmosphere quite indispensable to their existence, it being the air they breathe. And yet, as is generally admitted, a spectator's moral sensibility may be successfully anaesthetised, at least for a while, to allow him to 'sympathise' with Macbeth. And if with Macbeth why not with Iago? This question by no means implies 'giving unconditional sympathy to sheer vividness of character' and 'an anarchic free-for-all in which the characters compete for a sympathy that depends on the ability to command attention'.[15] The dramatist imposes conditions and prevents anarchy by manipulating the scenic perspective, and neither every soliloquising villain nor even every soul-searching Hamlet wins *unconditional* sympathy. Totally unrestricted though the dramatic speaker may appear to be, there can be invisible restraints: Claudius and Hamlet may each have the stage to himself and pray (some of Hamlet's soliloquies are akin to prayer), yet the impression they make will be utterly different. This is because scenic perspective involves not only the dramatic character's immediate physical relationship with the audience but also a time-dimension, the knowledge brought from earlier scenes that disposes an audience to look at the speaker in this way or that. A soliloquiser appears to be free, and everywhere he is in chains.

It is true, however, that a dramatist can grant almost unconditional sympathy to an immoralist if he wishes, especially at the beginning of a play. Iago or Falstaff may appeal to us as more sharp-sighted, more amusing, more alive than other characters, or as more richly endowed with Shakespeare's own irrepressible genius for manipulating men. These are formidable advantages, especially when Iago opposes a man far from clear-sighted and entirely without humour. And the villain can enjoy other advantages: he may be given superb poetry, he may be made physically attractive (as Edmund, Goneril and Regan probably should be), he may seem to deserve sympathy in resigning himself to misfortune or in resolutely facing up to physical danger. Almost always they are *temporary* advantages: and sympathy for every dramatic character, it cannot be stated too emphatically, fluctuates perpetually in obedience to these and similar devices. A Iago who 'is from the first scene to the last hated and despised' is as improbable as a concerto in which a soloist only plays two notes.

Yes, it will be said, but even though Shakespeare can adjust the scenic perspective in an immoralist's favour (by sending Edmund away before the blinding of Gloucester, by presenting not the actual stabbing of Duncan but only Macbeth's horrified recollection), how can we 'sympathise' with a demi-devil like Iago, whose monstrous acts are not screened from sight? Of all Shakespeare's villains Iago seems to be at the greatest disadvantage, torturing his victim quite pitilessly, in full view of the audience, and manifestly delighting in another's pain. And yet even Iago, as I shall try to show, never loses 'sympathy' completely, until the very last scene: exposed in all his inhumanity he maintains his hold on the audience, dividing the honours with Othello in two long scenes (III. 3, IV. 1) in which Shakespeare's manipulation of audience-response deserves to be admired no less than the ancient's gulling of his general. How was it done? We observe, first, that the audience knows Iago's intentions, from several soliloquies, and consequently brings Iago's expectations to the temptation-scene; it cannot so easily enter into Othello's point of view, since he allows himself to 'be led by th' nose/As asses are' (I. 3. 395–6). The scene's perspective makes us watch Iago watching Othello, and thus turns us into Iago's accomplices. Second, the temptation-scene has the appeal of a bull-fight, and gives to Iago all the advantages of the matador: he prods and stabs at his victim, feints, moves exactly as he wishes, perfectly in control of the situation and yet within a hair's breadth of death, expertly judging the effect of every thrust. How can we help thrilling to his cruel artistry? We may hate it, but must we not admire it as well? I wonder, indeed, whether Shakespeare could have created Iago's delicate skills without to some degree sharing his creature's artistic satisfaction, and without expecting the audience to share it too.

Although we never accept Iago's point of view completely, his incidental function as the play's 'presenter', coupled with his wit and intelligence, allows him to surprise us again and again with what seem to be legitimate perceptions, to which we have to give assent. Shakespeare seems to have been so convinced of Iago's continuing appeal that he went to quite unusual lengths to re-direct audience-response in Act V, where one character after another turns on Iago and denounces him as a slave, villain, viper, devil, dog. Here are just a few examples (v. 2. 182ff.): (i) You told a lie – an odious, damned lie. (ii) O monstrous act! (iii) Villainy, villainy, villainy! (iv) Precious villain! (v) 'Tis a notorious villain! (vi) Where is that viper? Bring the villain forth. (vii) If that thou be'st a devil, I cannot kill thee. (viii) This wretch hath part confess'd his villainy. (ix) demidevil . . . ! (x) O villain! (xi) Most heathenish and most gross! (xii) O thou pernicious caitiff! (xiii) O Spartan dog . . . ! Such unprecedented name-calling indicates that Shakespeare sensed that there was still a bond between Iago and the audience, and that it had to be broken. And broken it is, quite remorselessly.

\*          \*          \*

Sympathy, as I have described it, cannot be taken as the equivalent of love or approval, and yet should not be regarded as a purely impersonal, non-emotional self-projection. Sympathy in the theatre usually includes elements of approval, even where a villain is concerned. If this sounds too fanciful, let us remember that Keats, who touched on 'sympathy' and related problems in several of his most perceptive letters, came round to a similar conclusion. 'If a Sparrow come before by Window I take part in its existenct and pick about the Gravel', he wrote in 1817, a much-quoted sentence that really said nothing new (compare Burns, To a Mouse; or Montaigne, 'Of Cato the Younger', Essayes I, xxxvi. A year later, attempting to define 'the poetical character', he took an important step forward when he perceived that creative self-projection involves delight:

> As to the poetical Character itself (I mean that sort of which, if I am any thing, I am a Member; that sort distinguished from the wordsworthian or egotistical sublime; which is a thing per se and stands alone) it is not itself – it has no self – it is every thing and nothing – It has no character – it enjoys light and shade; it lives in gusto, be it foul or fair, high or low, rich or poor, mean or elevated – It has as much delight in conceiving an Iago as an Imogen. What shocks the virtuous philosopher, delights the camelion Poet.[16]

The creator of Iago delights in his villain's cleverness; and, Keats might have gone on to say, the audience shares his delight and 'sympathises' with wickedness.

\*          \*          \*

Should Keats's response to Iago seem too Romantic, the alternative is to believe that as spectators we cannot remain neutral, that we have

to take sides. I think of it as the 'two buckets' theory, which may be
illustrated from *Richard II* IV. 1. 184ff.

> Now is this golden crown like a deep well
> That owes two buckets, filling one another;
> The emptier ever dancing in the air,
> The other down, unseen, and full of water.
> The bucket down and full of tears am I,
> Drinking my griefs, whilst you mount up on high.

It may apply in politics, as Shakespeare evidently believed, without
being equally appropriate to drama. Dramatic critics, however, sometimes write as if there is only enough sympathy for one bucket, not
two, an error against which others have protested. 'If the question
were put categorically in this form: "On whose side was Shakespeare
in the conflict that played such an important part in his work,
between the simple man and the Machiavel?" it could not, of course,
be answered: or we should have to answer, if at all: "On neither
side." '[17] I prefer to say 'On both sides', since Shakespeare permitted
his complex characters to present their own view as propitiously as
they could, from inside (the villains soliloquise, from Cassius to
Claudius, Iago, Edmund). But it makes little difference, as these are
both ways of asserting the dramatist's impartiality – which only disappears near the end of the 'central' tragedies, where Shakespeare
usually felt it necessary to turn the response against his villains.
(Not so in the Roman plays, since the villains here have a different
function. Edmund in *King Lear* is an interesting exception.)

The 'two buckets' theory will always survive, as there are forms
of melodrama in which we have to take sides. But it need not apply
to tragedy, even though we may be drawn to it when two dramatic
characters have an almost symbiotic relationship: 'the pathos and
the brilliant poetizing of the falling Richard make sustained sympathy with Bolingbroke difficult . . . a shift in point of view towards
Richard inevitably entails one towards Bolingbroke.'[18]

We must ask ourselves whether the audience's sympathy must
necessarily follow the political ups and downs, even in a play as
symmetrical as *Richard II*. Richard and Bolingbroke, after all, excite
very different kinds of response: in good fortune or bad Richard's
character lies near the surface, he rarely conceals his feelings, and an
audience easily finds the appropriate response for all of his moods;
Bolingbroke, on the other hand, remains an enigma throughout, both

his motives and his feelings being shrouded, and we respond to him uncertainly. If, as I believe, we can only sympathise with what we know, or think we know, sustained sympathy with Bolingbroke is difficult not because of 'the brilliant poetizing of the falling Richard' but because, from start to finish, an impenetrable man's reserve begets reserve in the audience. The two sympathy systems, if I may call them that, work differently and more or less independently, and a shift in point of view towards Richard by no means entails a *corresponding* one towards Bolingbroke: pity for Richard grows steadily, whereas sympathy for Bolingbroke hardly changes throughout the play.

As Richard and Bolingbroke have only four scenes together, and their conflict in those scenes is depersonalised by ceremonial, it may seem that I have used a bad example to fudge the argument. What of Goneril and Regan's disgraceful treatment of Lear, or the blinding of Gloucester (*King Lear* II. 4, III. 7)? Do we not take sides in these scenes? I must repeat that the tragedies encourage us to take sides as they near their end, and add that there are many scenes (such as the blinding of Gloucester) that enlist all of our sympathy for a victim. It would be folly to argue that we never take sides in the tragedies: I merely suggest that Shakespeare can prevent us from doing so, when it suits him, by adjusting the perspective.

\*          \*          \*

Shakespeare's critics, trying to be helpful, have always been inclined to take sides, substituting a polarised response for a more bewildering but richer experience. Johnson ('I like a good hater') was succeeded by others who spoke out as uncompromisingly against Shakespeare's less attractive characters, some of whom should have known better. 'A great bad woman, *whom we hate*', Hazlitt said of Lady Macbeth, and recorded that in *Measure for Measure* 'our sympathies are repulsed and defeated in all directions', particularly by 'Angelo, *whom we hate*.'[19] Shylock, played by Macklin as a monster, was simplified by some nineteenth-century actors and critics as a tragic or pathetic character, then simplified differently by Stoll as a comic villain with 'nothing really and sincerely pathetic in him at all'.[20] The very same writers sometimes described a less one-sided response to other villains, without asking themselves whether they over-reacted to the ones they loved to hate, as when Hazlitt claimed that 'we never entirely lose our concern for Macbeth; and he calls back all our sympathy by that fine close of thoughtful melancholy, "My way of life/Is fallen into the sear, the yellow leaf." ' But although Hazlitt and others might veer towards a *mixed response* they failed to explore its further implications, and it remained a matter of merely passing interest until quite recently. If we now know more about it some of the credit must go to Shakespeare's own explicit statements about mixed emotions,[21] and to the many poets and novelists who picked up where he left off:

> you have shewn yourself so silly, and so wise; so young, and so old; so gentle, and so obstinate; so meek, and so violent; that never was there *so mixed a character*.

> And it was this *duality of feeling* which he created in her, that made a fine hate of him quicken in her bowels. There was his wonderful, desirable life-rapidity, the rare quality of an utterly desirable man; and there was at the same time this ridiculous, mean effacement into a . . . prig of the stiffest type.[22]

Some credit also belongs to Freud and post-Freudian psychologists, who investigated different kinds of love–hate relationship (including the 'Oedipus complex', with help from *Hamlet*). And let us not forget the cult of ambiguity, ambivalence and paradox of the Thirties and Forties, which brought about a new awareness of response processes, as when A. P. Rossiter wrote of *Henry IV* that

> the narrowly Tudor-political or 'moral' approach will most over-simplify, and thin, the true Shakespearian vintage . . . The double-ness of implicit values in those situations which are ambivalent; those which can be seen as serious *and* farcical: as pathetic *and* absurd: as abominable *and* laughable: as fine-and-admirable *and* as all-very-fine-and-large; all that centres on Falstaff.[23]

Since a mixed or divided response may be associated too exclu-sively with the Shakespearian 'problem play',[24] Rossiter's essay on ambivalence or 'doubleness of feeling' in the histories should be pondered carefully. There are good reasons, I think, for not appro-priating the mixed response to a single genre – for regarding it, rather, as related to Shakespeare's way of looking at character, and as equally suited to comedy, history and tragedy.[25] And, as I shall try to show, the tragic hero no less than the villain calls forth a mixed response, and will be improperly sentimentalised if we gloss over his savage and unnatural thoughts and deeds. It could even be that the tragic heroes continue to fascinate the world, more than any other fictional characters, just because they elicit the most intricately mixed response in our surviving literature.

*        *        *

There could hardly be better indirect support for a mixed response to Hamlet and Othello than the extraordinary diversity of critical interpretations, for the more 'mixed' the response to a dramatic character the more likely is it that readers and spectators will get into difficulties, and will be tempted to simplify. Shakespeare must have foreseen that he might be misunderstood, and took his precautions: whenever necessary he switched on the *stage-response*, verbal and non-verbal comments by other *dramatis personae* designed to influence audience-response, an important technical resource that can easily pass quite unnoticed.

Usually, having no chorus at his disposal, his simplest way of manipulating audience-response was to introduce anonymous lords, gentlemen, servants, messengers and the like, both to give information and to transmit emotion. Such minor figures guide audience-response more straightforwardly than major ones, as A. C. Sprague explained in a useful book, it being an almost invariable rule that 'the more dramatic should give place, as evidence, to the less'.[26] In Shakespeare, however, even the less dramatic will be dramatic, and what appear to be 'author-speaking' devices may express only a partial truth, quickly superseded by another stage-response that pulls in a different direction. 'That's a brave fellow, but he's vengeance proud', says First Officer of Coriolanus (II. 2. 1ff.). 'He hath deserved worthily of his country' retorts Second Officer, and expatiates until First Officer gives way – 'No more of him; he's a worthy man.' Such attitudes, if not determined by the speaker's known *character*, may still be influenced by the immediate *situation*, and should not be regarded as definitive.

Shakespeare used the stage-response for an immediate advantage, to swing the audience to this attitude or that, and even cheated when he could get away with it. In *Henry V*, one of the few plays with a chorus-figure, this 'reliable spokesman' (who really represents nothing more than common opinion) misleads the audience about the Battle of Agincourt, just before it begins, and stylises the mood of the moment, as always, adopting a point of view much more restricted than that of the play itself:

      The poor condemned English,
Like sacrifices, by their watchful fires
Sit patiently and inly ruminate
The morning's danger; and their gesture sad
Investing lank-lean cheeks and war-worn coats
Presenteth them unto the gazing moon
So many horrid ghosts. O, now, who will behold
The royal captain of this ruin'd band . . .

In the tragedies we are often expected to resist the spoken word,
when it simplifies or contradicts our previous impressions, and even
to resist the stage-response, though this may jostle us vigorously in
one direction. Shakespeare's ingenuity in making the stage-response
shape the audience-response varies, of course, from play to play, but
it works most deviously in the tragedies. In *Henry IV* our response
to Falstaff approximates quite closely, in Part I, to the appreciative
glow of his admirers, and in Part II we also allow Falstaff's stage-
audience to guide us, this time not so favourably. In the first Part
one character after another says, like Mrs Quickly in the tavern-
scene, 'O Jesu, this is excellent sport, i' faith', and we are swept
along by this current of feeling; in Part II the Lord Chief Justice
declares that Falstaff's impudence will not 'thrust me from a level
consideration', and his steady, disenchanted view of the old ruffian,
shared by several other characters, becomes the generalised stage-
response, and also ours. In *Henry IV*, then, Shakespeare used the
stage-audience to signal to us fairly accurately. In the tragedies the
stream of comment rarely coincides so satisfyingly with our impressions: instead of sinking ourselves willingly in the stage-comment, as
often as not we bounce off it. The Fool in *King Lear*, an obvious
response-regulator, never speaks for us directly, as do Mrs Quickly
and the Lord Chief Justice; we have to bounce back from his verbal
distortions, and this leaves something to chance. When Kent refers
to 'the old kind King' (III. 1. 28) we wonder at the phrase. And
when Lear himself speaks we never quite believe him, for contrary
impressions almost always interfere; he calls himself 'a poor, infirm,
weak and despised old man' (III. 2. 20), and we cannot help recalling
that a few lines earlier he had imperiously addressed hurricanoes and
oak-cleaving thunderbolts. In the tragedies the audience knows too
much to be easily satisfied with simplified evaluations or any single
channel of response.

The stage-response could be switched on to steady the audience, if it was in danger of being bewildered; it could express two or more attitudes to the same person or event, guiding the audience designedly to a mixed response; and it could even mislead, expressing an attitude that the audience was not expected to share, as when Iago tries to set Brabantio against Othello by describing him as 'an old black ram', 'a Barbary horse', and so on (*Othello* I, 1. 89ff.). Forever adjusting dramatic perspective and stage-response, Shakespeare wrote his tragedies for an audience that had to exert itself to keep up with new impressions in every scene – an audience that he asked to respond creatively, at the very highest level of participation.

# 4
# Sympathy for Brutus

When Shakespeare began to write *Julius Caesar*, in 1598 or 1599, he had not attempted a tragedy for several years. He could have looked back complacently to one of his earlier successes, *Titus Andronicus* or *Romeo and Juliet*, *Richard III* or *Richard II*, and simply repeated a formula that had already proved its worth.[1] But Shakespeare was not in the habit of looking back complacently: in *Julius Caesar* he moved decisively forward, and nowhere more so than in planning the audience-response to the tragic hero. Titus and Romeo had been presented largely as victims of malice or circumstance and, in their central scenes, appealed to the spectator's pity; Richard III and Richard II had both elicited first one response and then another, corresponding to the upward and downward thrust of Fortune's Wheel. Brutus, however, affects us differently. Whereas the early tragedies direct response firmly, so that we know exactly where we are (even in the Richard plays, where we move easily from one defined attitude to another, without losing our bearings), Shakespeare, as I have argued,[2] sought for a more intricately mixed response in his mature tragedies, and, if we may find fault with a great play by comparing it with the greater ones that succeeded it, seems to have got the mixture wrong in *Julius Caesar*, or very slightly wrong, thus weakening the tragic effect. 'Somewhat cold and unaffecting, compared with some other of Shakespeare's plays' was Johnson's verdict, with which few will disagree.[3]

Making a fresh start on tragedy, Shakespeare wished the audience to respond in an entirely new way to his hero. If this is correct it should be possible to trace some signs of his thinking in his remodelling of Plutarch's Brutus. I think it can be done; but first I have to confess that M. W. MacCallum, in his indispensable book on *Shakespeare's Roman Plays* (1910), interpreted the dramatist's intentions quite differently. According to MacCallum the play 'screens from view whatever in the career of Brutus might prejudice his claims to affection and respect; and carries much further a process of idealization that Plutarch had already begun. For to Plutarch Brutus is, so to speak, the model republican, the paragon of private and civic virtue.'

Shakespeare, he went on, purified Plutarch's idealised Brutus, allowing 'nothing to mar the graciousness and dignity of the picture': the
tragedy gave prominence to Brutus's 'winning courtesy', his
'affectionate nature', his 'humble-mindedness', and 'his amiable and
attractive virtues are saved from all taint of weakness by an heroic
strain'.[4]

Fortunately this one-sided view of the remodelling of Brutus has
been challenged. T. S. Dorsch has shown conclusively that, far from
'purifying' Plutarch's idealised portrait, Shakespeare introduced 'a
number of faults for which there is little or no warrant in Plutarch'.

> Shakespeare's Brutus is, with all his estimable qualities, pompous,
> opinionated and self-righteous. His judgement is not to be trusted.
> He is led by the nose by Cassius and gulled by Antony. At almost
> every crisis in his fortunes he makes decisions, against the advice
> of experienced men of the world, that contribute materially to the
> failure of his cause. He seems completely blind to reality, an in-
> effectual idealist whose idealism cannot prevent him from commit-
> ting a senseless and terrible crime.[5]

At the same time Dorsch also recognised that in the play 'the virtue
and nobility of Plutarch's Brutus are brought out.' Though not
specifically concerned with the spectator's response, Dorsch therefore
anticipated my first point – that in refashioning Plutarch's Brutus
Shakespeare made him both more and less attractive.

*          *          *

Comparing Plutarch's Marcus Brutus and Shakespeare's Brutus (hereafter Marcus Brutus and Brutus) one's first impression is that they
have much in common. Plutarch saw Marcus Brutus as one who
'framed his manners of life by the rules of vertue and studie of
Philosophie', and repeatedly returned to his love of philosophy and
learning in general. His own uncle, Cato the philosopher, was the
Roman whom Marcus Brutus 'studied most to follow'. 'Touching
the Graecian Philosophers, there was no sect nor Philosopher of them,
but he heard and liked it: but above all the rest, he loved Platoes sect
best.'[6] When he joined Pompey's army Marcus Brutus 'did nothing
but studie all day long'; at Athens, after the murder of Caesar, 'he
went daily to heare the lectures of Theomnestus Academick Philosopher, and of Cratippus the Peripatetick', so that 'it seemed he left
all other matters, and gave him selfe only unto studye'; and before

the Battle of Philippi 'he would read some booke till the third watche of the night'.[7]

Although Shakespeare could not make room for all of Plutarch's character-revealing anecdotes he gives a similar general impression of Brutus as an intellectual. The dramatic Brutus talks of Cato's philosophy and is himself told by Cassius –

> Of your philosophy you make no use
> If you give place to accidental evils.[8]

Brutus looks back twice to his school,[9] works late in his study (II. 1. 7), and reads at night before the Battle of Philippi. He is *homo praeoccupatus*, not only in mislaying his book and discovering it in the pocket of his gown (IV. 3. 250) but in everyday demeanour, especially in his first scenes with Cassius and Portia. Yet while the general impression is similar, Shakespeare changed many details, the effect of which is that Brutus becomes an intellectual who makes mistakes – far too many mistakes – until we question not merely his judgement but his motives. Dorsch felt that 'we may respect the motives for which he spares Antony's life, and later allows him to speak in Caesar's funeral . . . but on both occasions his decisions are foolish blunders'.[10] If we follow Brutus from one mistake to the next, however, his motives will strike us as less than respectable. Shakespeare leads up to his first and second fault (as Plutarch described them) – his opposing the killing of Antony, and his permitting Antony to speak at Caesar's funeral – by introducing two minor issues, which are changed from the source.

> they durst not acquaint Cicero with their conspiracie, although he was a man whome they loved dearlie, and trusted best: for they were affrayed that he being a coward . . . woulde quite turne and alter all their purpose . . .

> having never taken othes together, nor taken or geven any caution or assuraunce, nor binding them selves one to an other by any religious othes: they all kept the matter so secret to them selves . . .[11]

In the play we watch the conspirators reaching their decisions (II. 1. 114ff.): Cassius makes a proposal and Brutus, each time, immediately speaks against it, thrice imposing his will on his fellow-conspirators – so that before long we suspect that his declared motives are only half the story. It is tempting to think that his 'secret motive' betrays itself in his objection to Cicero –

> O, name him not! Let us not break with him;
> For he will never follow any thing
> That other men begin. (II. 1. 150–2)

– but, though there is unconscious irony here, the truth lies deeper. After all, Cassius began the conspiracy and Brutus followed him, and the play assumes that he also followed Julius Caesar happily, at least for a while. Quite as disturbing at Brutus' relationship with the conspirators is his relationship with himself, his conviction that he speaks for the beautiful lofty things of the world, knows them, is one of them. This, the prior motive, makes it difficult for us to respect his stated motives when he opposes the killing of Antony. He saves Antony, as he murders Caesar, thinking too much of Brutus – his own reputation, his own style – and this distracts his judgement and corrupts it.

*     *     *

Shakespeare turned Brutus into an intellectual hideously corrupted by high-mindedness. The play reveals his corruption so gradually that it is easy to accept Brutus' own view of himself, yet there comes a point when spectators who have sympathised with him must draw back, and must repudiate his idealism – after the murder of Caesar, when he again imposes his 'style' on the conspirators.

> Stoop, Romans, stoop,
> And let us bathe our hands in Caesar's blood
> Up to the elbows, and besmear our swords. (III. 1. 106–8)

Shakespeare added this episode[12] to put the finishing touch to his conception of Brutus, who, presumably, wishes to enforce his idea that they are 'sacrificers but not butchers' (II. 1. 166). Cassius agrees to humour Brutus once again, yet his reply ('Stoop then, and wash') suggests that the thought would never have occurred to him:[13] the insane logic of it belongs to Brutus alone, and the action that follows makes visible the inner corruption of one man – of 'gentle Brutus', who had said, not long before, 'Our course will seem too bloody, Caius Cassius' (II. 1. 162). And, just in case the audience gets carried away by the idealist's exaltation, and fails to feel the full horror of his action, Shakespeare added another twist that dispels all doubts.

When Antony brings himself to grasp Brutus' hand, dripping with
'the most noble blood of all this world'

> Let each man render me his bloody hand.
> First, Marcus Brutus, will I shake with you (III. 1. 184–5)

the audience in effect touches blood with him and shares his physical
revulsion.

Three series of impressions deal with the intellectual's corruption.
His mistakes as a conspirator, his muddled thinking in general, and
his dangerously high conceit of himself – all have a serial arrangement, leading by imperceptible stages to their appointed climaxes,
and all work together to influence response, more and more unfavourably.

1. *Brutus' mistakes.* Plutarch had noted Brutus' two most serious
mistakes or 'faults' as leader of the conspiracy,[14] and Shakespeare
decided to add to them: he made Brutus personally responsible for
excluding Cicero,[15] and his Brutus even begs the Romans to listen to
Antony's funeral-speech (III. 2. 60–1: not so in Plutarch). Of Brutus'
many mistakes, however, the one that works most insidiously against
him is the first, his being duped by the papers thrown in at his
windows.[16] Whereas Plutarch's hero receives 'many bills' (or letters)
from 'his frendes and contrie men', faked letters 'in several hands'
finally push Shakespeare's Brutus from self-questioning to a firm
resolve:

> O Rome, I make thee promise,
> If the redress will follow, thou receivest
> Thy full petition at the hand of Brutus! (II. 1. 56–8)

As Brutus' later mistakes all result from the ill-founded conviction
that 'Rome' supports him, the audience, having seen how he was
tricked into thinking this, can never trust his judgement thereafter.

As well as multiplying Brutus' mistakes, Shakespeare devised an
appropriate stage-response for each one, to cue the audience and to
harden its attitude. The first ('Well, Brutus, thou art noble', I. 2.
307ff.) immediately deflates Brutus as a man who has been 'seduc'd'.
In Act II the serial arrangement has a delayed-action effect: when
Cassius wants the conspirators to swear their resolution and Brutus
protests (II. 1. 113), the proposal sounds like a mere whim, and is
dropped without another word. Cassius next suggests, a little more

positively, that Cicero should be sounded, Casca and Metellus agree, but Brutus objects and the others give way deferentially, though he has scarcely met their arguments. ('*Cassius* Then leave him out. *Casca* Indeed, he is not fit.') Cassius presses even more strongly for the murder of Mark Antony, Brutus again objects, and this time Cassius is definitely not convinced ('Yet I fear him . . .'). The stage-response rises to a muted climax, and thus prepares for Cassius' much more alarmed response to Brutus' next, more fateful mistake:

> You know not what you do. Do not consent
> That Antony speak in his funeral. (III. 1. 233–4)

As Cassius reacted with admirable restraint before, when he disagreed with Brutus, we are bound to take him seriously now. The serial arrangement therefore helps to drive home the folly of the idealist's reply:

>                By your pardon –
> I will myself into the pulpit first
> And show the reason of our Caesar's death.

2. *Brutus' muddles.* There is also progression in Brutus' muddles – by which I mean several longer speeches that go through the motions of reasoning and yet fail to hang together. The earlier ones get by, at least in the theatre, without impressing us as manifest fumbling; the later ones sound very odd indeed. I shall comment on two of each kind.

(i) 'It must be by his death' (II. 1. 10ff.). Here, said MacCallum, Brutus 'seeks to find something that will satisfy his reason'.[17] Yet the soliloquy has also been called confused and 'a marvel of fanatical self-deception'.[18] The argument, starting with a foregone conclusion ('his death'), heaves and wrenches itself to reach that conclusion ('kill him in the shell'), and contrasts strikingly with Brutus' controlled utterance a little earlier ('That you do love me, I am nothing jealous . . .', I. 2. 162ff.). But as Brutus communes with himself alone his disjointed sentences affect us as stream-of-consciousness rather than as argument, and fail to destroy (though they modify) our earlier impression of Brutus as a dependable truth-seeker.

(ii) 'Romans, countrymen, and lovers!' (III. 2. 13ff.). Brutus' Forum speech makes a pretence of being reasonable, and turns out to be largely emotional. 'Rome before everything!' is a message calculated

to please, and the stage-response of Third Plebeian ('Let him be
Caesar!') suggests that for him the emotion succeeds, the argument
fails. Antony, thereafter, has no difficulty in showing that the argument consists of mere assertion, in so far as Brutus had not *proved*
that Caesar was ambitious. But listening to Brutus we may miss this
point, if only because we remember that when offered a crown
Caesar 'put it by thrice, *every time gentler than other*' (I. 2. 227–8).
It takes an Antony to exploit the opening: we waver with the
Plebeians, and our confidence in Brutus' reasoning is undermined.

(iii)   'I did send to you/For certain sums of gold' IV. 3. 69ff.. Even
MacCallum, who held that Shakespeare idealised Brutus, found his
self-righteousness here 'a little absurd': 'What does all this come to?
That the superfine Brutus will not be guilty of extortion, but that
Cassius may: and then Brutus will demand to share in the proceeds.'[19] Though this reading has been challenged the weight of
opinion is on MacCallum's side, except that Brutus strikes others as
astounding, not just a little absurd.[20] For the first time in the play
Brutus' reasoning seems wrong-headed as he speaks and, significantly,
his self-admiration offends us in the same speech.[21]

iv. 'Even by the rule of that philosophy' (V. 1. 100–12). Asked by
Cassius what he will do 'if we do lose this battle', Brutus first
answers that he will not commit suicide, then adds that he will not
'go bound to Rome', implying that he would sooner kill himself.
Shakespeare follows Plutarch closely, making one important change.
Marcus Brutus explains that he once disapproved of suicide, 'but
being nowe in the middest of the daunger, I am of a contrary mind'.[22]
Instead of seeing the light himself, Shakespeare's Brutus has to have
his eyes opened by Cassius ('You are contented to be led in
triumph . . .?'), which leads to his volte-face. Introducing Cassius'
question, Shakespeare intimates an intellectual failure in Brutus, and
again this coincides with an unpleasing, self-admiring tone:

> No, Cassius, no. Think not, thou noble Roman,
> That ever Brutus will go bound to Rome;
> He bears too great a mind.

3. *Brutus' opinion of himself*. It has been said, in defence of Brutus'
high opinion of himself, that

> one of Shakespeare's simplest – and habitual – methods of telling
> us what a person is really like is to let that person himself tell us.

We must be on our guard against judging Brutus's estimate of himself according to modern notions of how people should speak about themselves, and saying that . . . he is merely 'talking big'. Nevertheless, his manner at various points in the play does not give us as favourable an impression of him as his friends entertain.[23]

If we check up on those 'various points', using 'modern notions of how people should speak about themselves', we observe that they are all in the last two acts – which suggests that Brutus' self-explanations also contribute to our sense of the intellectual's gradual corruption.

Initially Brutus' 'honour' and 'honesty' speeches scarcely jar the spectator, being cushioned by the situation.

(i)  If it be aught toward the general good
    Set honour in one eye and death i' th' other . . . (I. 2. 85ff.)

Taken to the brink and asked to declare himself, Brutus has to give a clear signal: his turn of phrase, though it may seem extravagant, thus reflects on the situation as much as on the man. (Potentially boastful speeches are neutralised by the situation in other tragedies. Compare *Macbeth* III. 4. 99: 'What man dare, I dare . . .')

(ii)                      What other bond
Than secret Romans that have spoke the word
And will not palter? And what other oath
Than honesty to honesty engag'd . . . (II. 1. 124ff.)

                      O ye gods,
Render me worthy of this noble wife! (II. 1. 302–3)

Shakespeare resorts to such indirect self-description to remind us in passing of Brutus' high opinion of *himself*, yet we cannot convict the speaker of boastfulness when he seems less concerned to praise himself than to praise others.

(iii)  Believe me for mine honour, and have respect to mine honour,
      that you may believe. (III. 2. 15–16)

An orator normally reminds his listeners of what he stands for: in the special circumstances of the Forum Scene Brutus' self-description is entirely acceptable.

Before the end of Act III Brutus' high opinion of himself never irritates our sympathy; after it, it does so repeatedly. Either self-praise coincides with an intellectual muddle, so that he vaunts his 'honesty' as he rebukes Cassius for not sharing his corruptly acquired gold, and his 'great mind' just after Cassius has had to put him right on a fairly simple point of self-knowledge;[24] or he praises himself to scold others, thus introducing a note of lofty contemptuousness:

> Judge me, you gods! wrong I mine enemies?
> And, if not so, how should I wrong a brother? (IV. 2. 38–9)

> O, if thou wert the noblest of thy strain,
> Young man, thou couldst not die more honourable. (V. 1. 59–60)

\*        \*        \*

Brutus differs from Plutarch's Marcus Brutus in making many more political mistakes, in muddling his arguments and in thinking too well of himself. The more we learn to distrust his judgement the more confidently he speaks of his *reasons*, the masterstroke being his proposal to hasten to Philippi – 'Good reasons must, of force, give place to better.'[25] Whatever the intellectual's virtues, we cannot respect his thinking. And Shakespeare increased the play's anti-intellectual bias by surrounding his philosophical hero with men of learning, far more than he put into any other tragedy, and this also conditions our response to Brutus. The intellectuals wish to intervene in high affairs, all of them are cut off or ridiculed – and the ridicule was usually added by Shakespeare. 'A certaine Soothsayer . . . had geven Caesar warning long time affore, to take heede of the day of the Ides of Marche . . .'[26] Shakespeare added Caesar's dismissive 'He is a dreamer; let us leave him: pass' (I. 2. 24). Artemidorus, a doctor of rhetoric, tried to warn Caesar of his danger, as in the play, and pressed a 'memorial' upon him. 'Caesar tooke it of him, but coulde never reade it, though he many times attempted it, for the number of people that did salute him . . .'[27] Plutarch continued that, according to some, another man gave Caesar the memorial, since Artemidorus 'was alwayes repulsed by the people.' Neither version satisfied Shakespeare, whose Caesar snaps contemptuously – 'What, is the fellow mad?' (III. 1. 10). In Act IV the poet is treated as unceremoniously ('saucy fellow, hence', IV. 3. 132), whilst Cinna the poet, though he makes no attempt to influence state affairs, illustrates the intellectual's ineffectiveness even more frighteningly. Shakespeare also introduced Casca's sneer that, when Caesar was offered the crown, Cicero, the most distinguished intellectual of the play, rose to the occasion like an intellectual, by speaking Greek.

> *Cassius*   To what effect?
> *Casca*   Nay, and I tell you that, I'll ne'er look you i' th' face again. But those that understood him smiled . . . (I. 2. 279ff.)

As Shakespeare could not have failed to read in Plutarch that Casca, after stabbing Caesar, 'cried in Græke, and called his brother to helpe him', it has been suggested that his Casca 'pretended not to know Greek'.[28] Surely not: Casca, more probably, was deprived of Greek because all the play's intellectuals (including Cicero) are ineffective and he, the man of action who strikes the first blow against Caesar, was meant to contrast with them.

*   *   *

As the play proceeds we respond more and more unsympathetically to Brutus' intellectual pretensions. Comparing it with Plutarch's *Life* we can see how Shakespeare tried to channel our response – how Brutus' high-minded reflectiveness gradually shades off into self-righteousness, even arrogance, and how inevitably everything leads on to the quarrel-scene. Lacking in charm and entirely humourless, the would-be intellectual may seem sufficiently handicapped, yet Shakespeare thought of still more ways of enforcing a hostile response, one of the best being the short, sharp visual effect. I have already mentioned the blood-bathing episode and the bloody hand-shake,[29] two moments of physical horror. They are preceded in the murder-scene by two other visual effects of quite exceptional power.

(i) Brutus, ready to strike the fatal blow, kisses Caesar's hand – a most un-Roman gesture in the year 44 B.C. ('I kiss thy hand, but not in flattery, Caesar'). Are we to take this as an insignificant anachronism, like the striking clock (II. 1. 191)? I think not. And the usual alternatives, that Brutus offers either the kiss of Judas or 'a last tender farewell',[30] also fail to explain the peculiar effect of his kiss. But if we recall that Brutus believes that Caesar 'would be crown'd' (II. 1. 12), and that kings graciously allow their inferiors to kiss their hands, we may interpret the gesture as ironical – somewhat like that of the Roman soldiers who plaited a crown of thorns for a 'king' in the year A.D. 33. Shakespeare had dramatised such a mock corona-tion in 3 *Henry VI*, where the Duke of York's enemies honour his royal aspirations with a paper crown, then stab him to death (I. 4.

95ff.). The extravagant servility of Metellus Cimber and Cassius, throwing themselves at Caesar's feet before they stab him, acts out a similar victim-jeering ritual, less openly but quite as unpleasantly, which implicates Brutus as well, even though his tone and gesture are more gravely ironical.

(ii)  The Folio has no stage direction that helps us to visualise the killing of Caesar, but the dialogue shows that Shakespeare followed Plutarch in several points: Casca strikes the first blow, Caesar muffles his face and falls at the base of Pompey's statue. That being so, it seems reasonable to suppose that he may have followed Plutarch in other details.

> [The conspirators] compassed him on everie side with their swordes drawen in their handes, that Caesar turned him no where, but he was striken at by some, and still had naked swords in his face, and was hacked and mangeled amonge them, as a wilde beaste taken of hunters. For it was agreed among them, that every man should geve him a wound, bicause all their partes should be in this murther: and then Brutus him selfe gave him one wounde about his privities. Men reporte also, that Caesar did still defende him selfe . . . but when he sawe Brutus with his sworde drawen in his hande, then he pulled his gowne over his heade, and made no more resistaunce, and was driven . . . against the base whereupon Pompeys image stoode . . .[31]

Although the conspirators sometimes screen the killing from the audience in modern productions, Plutarch's visual detail suits the play and we can hardly improve on it, in the absence of authorial directions. Editors, however – even those who recognise that our best course is to follow Plutarch – do not care to spell out in so many words that Brutus stabs a defenceless man who has muffled his face, and wounds Caesar 'about his privities', though some of them print the direction that Brutus strikes 'the last blow', for which there is even less authority.[32] Is it because they think that such shocking actions would discredit Brutus? If so, let us repeat that Shakespeare added Brutus' kiss, the blood-bathing and the bloody handshake to this very scene – all actions designed to shock and antagonise the audience.

*          *          *

So much for the unattractiveness of Brutus, compared with Plutarch's original. Shakespeare, however, aiming at a complex response, also went to some trouble to drive the audience in the other direction – by heightening the attractiveness of his hero. He achieved a great deal in the simplest possible way, by mere assertion. Others refer to 'gentle Brutus', 'gentle' is one of Brutus' own favourite words, and in the end the word sticks. 'His life was gentle' says Antony, summing up, and the audience normally agrees, even though Brutus had butchered his benefactor and precipitated a civil war. True, when used by Brutus himself the word sometimes sounds inappropriate, and this reflects back on his own reputation for gentleness:

Tell us the manner of it, *gentle Casca* (I. 2. 233)

And, *gentle friends,*
*Let's kill* him boldly but not wrathfully (II. 1. 171–2)

But whereas other assertions in the play have a rough passage ('For Brutus is an honourable man'), the gentleness of Brutus survives as a general impression.

Something can be accomplished by sheer assertion. But unlike modern salesmen, suckled on the comfortable doctrine that the more often you tell a lie the more certainly it will be believed, a dramatist must back the assertion that Brutus is gentle with other kinds of evidence. As Maurice Morgann explained, Shakespeare steals impressions upon us, and these may act more effectively than assertions: heard melodies are sweet, but those unheard are sweeter.

A minor figure, the boy Lucius, serves as supporting evidence. Very nearly all the persons in the play except Lucius come from Plutarch: this fact, once observed, immediately raises a question – what special purpose could Shakespeare have had when he added a slave-boy or servant-boy to the story?[33] Comparing the two scenes in which Lucius appears with his master (II. 1 and IV. 3) we find the common factor to be that Brutus has to waken him from sleep in both: his little life is rounded with a sleep. Brutus, both times, treats him considerately, in the second scene with an almost paternal solicitude, and can thus demonstrate his own gentleness at the very time when his humanity seems about to desert him. For the first Lucius episode acts as a frame for that terrifyingly depersonalised meditation, 'It must be by his death', and the second follows Brutus' willed emotional aridity in the quarrel-scene. Lucius was added, it appears, to remind us of the hero's inner self just when we are in most danger of forgetting it. And for once Shakespeare resisted the temptation to create a 'pathetic boy', his stage stereotype, making something more genuinely affecting out of Lucius' uncomplaining service and assured relationship with his master.

Lucius sleeps soundly in Brutus' presence, as do Varro and Claudius, the two guards specially summoned to sleep on cushions in his tent (IV. 3. 241). There's meaning in their snores, and in the stage-tableau of the general surrounded by sleepers. Elsewhere in the tragedies to be caught napping by the hero can have fatal consequences – witness Duncan and Desdemona, Rosencrantz and Guildenstern – for the hero feels hemmed in and threatened as each story unfolds and becomes increasingly dangerous, a wounded beast that may suddenly lash out, at Polonius, at Cordelia's executioner, or turn in fury on innocent by-standers. 'I'd strike the sun if it insulted me!' cried Captain Ahab, speaking for the beast at bay, the tragic will that spends itself against the world at large. There are signs in the quarrel-scene (IV. 3) that Brutus can rage inwardly like the other tragic heroes, yet Shakespeare conceived him as essentially different – a man to be trusted, incapable of casual destructiveness, in whose company others may sleep. The most extraordinary glimpse of the trust inspired by gentle Brutus comes in the final scene, where one of his men sleeps on the battlefield while their enemies close in. 'A thick-skinned sort of fellow' commented Granville-Barker, which is no doubt true; but Shakespeare had a motive for adding a fourth sleeper to his story – and presumably a motive less concerned with the life-likeness of a minor character than with the audience's attitude to his tragic hero.

A dramatist, it goes without saying, can call upon more eloquent instruments than sleeping bodies strewn about the stage: he can always switch on the stage-response, if he thinks that his audience needs firm guidance. In *Julius Caesar* almost everyone loves or admires Brutus:

> O, he sits high in all the people's hearts;
> And that which would appear offence in us
> His countenance, like richest alchemy,
> Will change to virtue and to worthiness. (I. 3. 157–60)

Several characters express such feelings much more positively than in Plutarch's original, carrying the audience with them. Caius Ligarius, for example, has only a single admiring sentence in

Plutarch ('Brutus, sayed he, if thou hast any great enterprise in hande worthie of thy selfe, I am whole',[34] and Shakespeare blows it up as follows:

> By all the gods that Romans bow before
> I here discard my sickness. Soul of Rome!
> Brave son, deriv'd from honorable loins!
> Thou, like an exorcist, hast conjur'd up
> My mortified spirit . . . I follow you
> To do I know not what; but it sufficeth
> That Brutus leads me on. (II. 1. 320ff.)

The hundred lines in which Portia and Ligarius express their love and admiration are quite indispensable, enacting emotions that were merely described by Cassius and others. Later, in the quarrel-scene, Cassius' more purified and personal feeling for his 'dear brother' reconciles us to Brutus when he has been shown at his most unendearing; and in the last scene of all, the continuing loyalty of his defeated soldiers releases a wave of feeling that cannot leave an audience unmoved. These are some of the peaks, but there is also a never-ending stream of casual information to remind us that everyone loves and trusts the hero. Even Antony contributes to it, albeit with hostile intent, in the Forum scene. Giving the play's most explicit account of Caesar's love of Brutus he magically brings it to life, a love so powerfully felt that it seems more real than Brutus' treachery.

> Through this the well-beloved Brutus stabb'd,
> And as he pluck'd his cursed steel away
> Mark how the blood of Caesar follow'd it,
> As rushing out of doors, to be resolv'd
> If Brutus so unkindly knock'd or no;
> For Brutus, as you know, was Caesar's angel.
> Judge, O you gods, how dearly Caesar lov'd him!
> This was the most unkindest cut of all;
> For when the noble Caesar saw him stab,
> Ingratitude, more strong than traitors' arms,
> Quite vanquish'd him. Then burst his mighty heart . . .
>
> (III. 2. 176ff.)

\*        \*        \*

In these and other ways Shakespeare rehabilitates Brutus in our esteem. Yet it would be wrong to pretend that an audience feels strongly drawn to him: there are times when we very nearly identify ourselves with the other tragic heroes, but Brutus keeps us at a distance, and we enter into him less completely. This is not because he lacks an emotional nature that could buoy up our sympathy and float us past the barriers of murderous words and deeds, for there are signs enough of emotional depth:

> O ye gods
> Render me worthy of this noble wife! (II. 1. 302)

> That every like is not the same, O Caesar,
> The heart of Brutus earns to think upon! (II. 2. 128–9)

> I shall find time, Cassius, I shall find time! (V. 3. 103)

No: the stoical Brutus suppresses his emotions, as far as he can, and thus keeps everyone at arm's length, including Portia and Cassius – and the theatre-audience. His inner nature reveals itself in an aside about Caesar, in his farewell to the dead Cassius, in his words to a sleeping boy, and only very rarely in an exchange of mutual feeling. Only Portia breaks through his reserve in the first three acts, after the most intense pressure; and as soon as he gives way Shakespeare interrupts ('Hark, hark! one knocks. Portia, go in awhile', II. 1. 304), as if unwilling to over-expose his hero in an emotional situation.

The audience is also kept at a distance by the intellectual hero's preoccupation. At the very start, Brutus ('I am not gamesome') refuses to join the crowd when Caesar goes to the 'holy chase' of Lupercal (not so in Plutarch). And Brutus withdraws not only from the throng but from his friends. Cassius complains –

> I have not from your eyes that gentleness
> And show of love as I was wont to have (I. 2. 32–3)

In Plutarch the two men had been rivals for the chief praetorship, and had to make up their 'grudge' before joining together as conspirators. Shakespeare dropped this motive, so that Brutus' aloofness can only mean withdrawal into himself. Portia, too, complains of neglect, in a scene closely modelled upon Plutarch – except that Shakespeare changed Portia's general discovery 'that there was some marvelous great matter that troubled his minde'[35] to more pointed charges of impatience and anger.

And when I ask'd you what the matter was
You star'd upon me with ungentle looks.
I urg'd you further; then you scratch'd your head
And too impatiently stamp'd with your foot . . . (II. 1. 241ff.)

Like Hamlet in his first scene, Brutus shrinks from human contact; but whilst Hamlet welcomes Horatio and the Players and even Rosencrantz and Guildenstern, Brutus, unless he is cornered, never expresses warmth of feeling when face to face with others.

Two unusual technical features support the impression of a pre-occupied Brutus. At the beginning of Act II he has five soliloquies, interrupted by brief exchanges with Lucius, at least four of which continue the same thread of thought. Why so, rather than a single soliloquy covering much the same ground? Four times Lucius no sooner enters than he is sent out again, a human yo-yo, to see to practical necessities ('Get me a taper', 'Look in the calendar', 'Go to the gate', 'Let 'em enter'). Brutus relapses into thoughtfulness after each interruption as if into his natural element, like some creature of the deep that rises to the surface of practical affairs only to sink below again, back into himself. Between the five soliloquies he comes up for air, as it were, then retires from the practical to the reflective sphere – and this prepares for his mistakes in practical politics, three of which follow within the next hundred lines.

The other technical feature is the play's generalised mood. Like *Hamlet*, where doubt and uncertainty flow in all directions, *Julius Caesar* creates a mood of its own, one closely related to the hero's state of mind. Scene after scene presents characters anxiously strain-ing to hear or see off-stage events. Brutus only half-listens to Cassius (I. 2), preoccupied by the shouts he hears and by thoughts of 'new honours that are heap'd on Caesar.' Strange noises and flashes threaten during the storm-scenes (I. 3ff.), and Casca, sword in hand, evidently expects some sudden danger. (Shakespeare expanded Plutarch's list of portents, inventing the escaped lion (l. 20) as an immediate motive for Casca's unsheathed sword.) Straining to catch sounds from the far-away Capitol, and imagining that she hears a 'bustling rumour' (II. 4. 18), Portia adds to the play's anxious expectancy. When Antony's servant arrives and so exactly repeats his master's words and gestures (III. 1. 124ff.), he conducts the mind directly to Antony; present though absent, the shadowy Antony for the first time in the play comes to life in those measured sentences, a

genie issuing from his bottle, a threat that alarms Cassius – and the
conspirators thereupon look forward to Antony's personal arrival
as a momentous turning-point. Towards the play's end Pindarus
watches the capture of Titinius, as he thinks (V. 3), and Brutus
hears 'low alarums' (V. 5. 23) that grow louder as his enemies
approach. These are a few of the threatening off-stage events that
carry the mind into a world beyond immediate reach, a world
that cannot be controlled, and create a generalised mood of expectant
anxiety.

Of course mood and atmosphere play an even larger part in the
later tragedies. But in *Julius Caesar* off-stage events sometimes contribute more than readers will observe – as in the quarrel-scene (IV. 3),
where Brutus and Cassius retire into a tent, not wishing their two
armies to witness their wrangling. The scene's usual heading ('*The
Camp near Sardis. Within the tent of Brutus. Enter Brutus and
Cassius*') allows us to forget that the tent is guarded, a fact of which
Brutus and Cassius must remain at least half-aware, however the
scene is staged.[36] 'Speak your griefs softly' Brutus had warned,
before they begin; and during the quarrel they still cannot afford to
raise their voices, although they may do so involuntarily, for the
listening guards, though invisible to Brutus and Cassius, bring the
pressures of an outside world into the tent.

*          *          *

The quarrel-scene (IV. 3), the longest and perhaps the most wonderful
in the whole play, 'can hardly be defended on strictly dramatic
grounds', thought Bradley, except in so far as it indicates 'inward
changes'.[37] Others have disagreed, either because the scene 'lays bare
the significance of the story' or because in it Brutus' 'tragic disillusion is most fully revealed'.[38] It could also be defended as the very
heart of the play – as the natural culmination of its central relationship and conflict, that of Brutus and Cassius, the only relationship
that continues through the five acts, the only one that steadily
deepens. (*Julius Caesar* differs from the later tragedies in lacking
fully developed secondary relationships: Brutus–Caesar, Brutus–
Portia, Brutus–Lucius are shadowy affairs, partly because Shakespeare
conceived them as relationships *in absentia*.) The quarrel-scene,
where mighty opposites violently collide and claw at one another,
tearing off masks and coming as near to self-knowledge as the play
permits, can be defended 'on strictly dramatic grounds' as the climax
of its inner action, and as no less exciting than the climactic events

of the outer, political action of Act III. It also redefines and intensifies the audience's response to Brutus.

We cannot side with Brutus, it is commonly said, in the scene's opening clash with Cassius. 'No one who reads with care the first hundred lines of Act IV, Scene iii, could feel that Shakespeare meant us to have any sympathy with Brutus during this exchange'.[39] So Granville-Barker:

> But which of us might not side with [Cassius] against [Brutus], who . . . with things going desperately for his side, must needs stiffen his stiff conscience against some petty case of bribery? Is this a time for pride in one's principles? . . . is it a time to depreciate and dispirit your best friends, to refuse their apologies . . .? Brutus tries many of us as high as he tries Cassius . . . Supercilious, unforgiving, and in the right! And when anger does rise in him, it is such a cold, deadly anger that poor passionate Cassius only breaks himself against it. Yet there is a compelling power in the man, in his integrity of mind, his truth to himself, in his perfect simplicity.[40]

Without wishing to deny Brutus' pride, I believe that Shakespeare prevents us from siding against him, and attains his purpose in other ways. Who, for example, starts the quarrel? Cassius, crying out four times that he has been wronged, insists on quarrelling and at last strikes fire from Brutus. We must remember, too, that Cassius threatens physical violence, and that Brutus' most contemptuous remarks are flung back at a man whose hand is on his dagger, a choleric man who may forget himself and stab. Taunts such as 'Away, slight man!' or 'For your life you durst not!' can affect us as either admirable or hateful, depending on the distance between Brutus' throat and the point of Cassius' dagger.

Brutus' disillusion with his fellow-conspirators also acts in his favour. When he refers to the ideals with which the conspiracy started ('Remember March, the ides of March remember!', IV. 3. 18) Shakespeare reactivates the audience's awareness that Cassius kept quiet about his less creditable motives and tricked Brutus with forged letters (I. 2. 306ff.): the audience must respond favourably, knowing that Brutus has even stronger grounds for indignation than he suspects. It is also quickly apparent, from the untypical way in which he overreacts to Cassius, that exceptional pressures have brought him close to breaking-point, and so we respond more leniently to what would otherwise be unpardonable speeches, as with other tragic heroes when the heat is on.

To side with Brutus in the quarrel-scene is nevertheless impossible. Analysing the scene we must beware of isolating it from the rest of the play: Shakespeare prepared for it in the minor Brutus–Cassius collisions of Acts II and III, in suggesting that Cassius will stoop to bribery (III. 1. 178–9), and so on. The short bartering-scene of the triumvirs (IV. 1) also influences response to the quarrel-scene, by placing the issues in a larger perspective. Plutarch's view, that 'there was never a more horrible, unnatural, and crueller' exchange of 'murther for murther', perfectly expresses the effect of IV. 1. 1–6, when Antony and Lepidus haggle a nephew for a brother, except that Shakespeare made it even more unnatural by omitting all signs of reluctance in the triumvirs. ('But yet', Plutarch wrote, 'they could hardly agree whom they would put to death: for every one of them would kill their enemies, and save their kinsmen and friends'.)[41] Wishing to suggest that another view of the scene was permissible, T. S. Dorsch said that 'it is possible to interpret [Antony's] conduct [in IV. 1] as just and unsentimental . . . [for] Antony shows that he will not be swayed by family ties', and, again, that Antony's proposal to misappropriate the money bequeathed by Caesar 'appears to have the full concurrence of his colleagues, and there is no suggestion that he is to gain personally from the affair'.[42] But when was a proscription ever just? And is a thief any less a thief because he shares the loot? And who will benefit from the legacy fiddle, if not the triumvirs? The scene demonstrates how power corrupts – and prepares for the quarrel-scene by exhibiting an opportunism so degraded that it inoculates us against taking Cassius' 'itching palm' (IV. 3. 10) too seriously.

After we have seen the triumvirs, Cassius' 'corruption' seems understandable, a necessary evil 'in such a time as this' (IV. 3. 7), and Brutus' anger strikes us as excessive; and after witnessing Brutus' high-minded anger we find it all the more strange that he asks for his share of the takings. Each episode conditions a response against Brutus in the one that follows; and his condescension to Cassius also affects us disagreeably ('I will give you *audience*', '*chastisement* doth therefore hide his head', 'What *villain* touch'd his body . . .?',[43] since previously he had treated all the conspirators as *brothers* (III. 1. 176). Worst of all, whereas 'a general honest thought' had impelled him before, we cease to respect him as well-meaning during the quarrel, his unmistakable purpose being to wound Cassius. Even when Cassius begins to break down Brutus continues to plunge verbal daggers into him, so that Cassius, like Caesar in the assassination-scene, stares incredulously and reels from blow after blow: Brutus is merciless, and in some obscure way *enjoys* Cassius' pain and humiliation.

In the opening clash with Cassius, as elsewhere in the play, we simultaneously admire and dislike Brutus; he exacts a mixed response, but nowhere else are we so intensely concerned for him and so hostile. The same is true of our response to Cassius. We regret his corruption (he more or less concedes it, IV. 3. 7–8), we are disappointed by his bluster and his threats of violence; on the other hand, he seems more frank than Brutus, with whose slowly-burning anger his darting impetuousness contrasts not unfavourably, and, most important, he still loves Brutus, he accepts his rebukes, he feels all the pain of the quarrel. Unlike its immediate descendant in the line of quarrel-scenes, Hamlet's interview with Gertrude (where an idealist, whose high expectations have been let down, again lashes one who loves him and drives her to breaking-point), the quarrel in *Julius Caesar* by no means prompts us to take sides: the rights and wrongs are too evenly balanced, the participants are both shown at their best and worst.

Towards the end of the quarrel a poet intrudes, as in Plutarch, and unsettles the emotional temperature. If the play leaves us in any doubt about it, Plutarch helps to explain his function: the poet, something of a clown, on more than one occasion pushed in where he was not wanted and, with a 'frantick motion' of counterfeit scoffing and mocking 'made all the companye laugh at him'.[44] Shakespeare, groping for an effect like that of the Porter in *Macbeth*, inserted him between two emotional climaxes, not to arrest or bisect the scene with comic relief but, quite the contrary, to make it gather itself together and spring forward the more vigorously. The poet may seem to dispel the mood of the quarrel, yet really serves, like an electric conductor, to carry that mood into the next episode, confirming our impression of Brutus' irritability just before the secret motive for it is allowed to emerge. We hear a distant after-vibration of the earlier thunder –

Cassius   I did not think you could have been so angry.
Brutus   O Cassius, I am sick of many griefs.

– and then, very quietly, the news of Portia's death, three words that are so effective partly because they signify that Brutus has buried the quarrel.

Placed at this point by Shakespeare (not so in Plutarch) the news about Portia retroactively colours our impression of the quarrel and is undoubtedly 'the scene's great stroke', as Granville-Barker described it. I am not so sure, however, that it is also 'the winning stroke in Brutus' own cause with us',[45] for the simple reason that Brutus' self-concerned attitude is immediately dwarfed by Cassius' outgoing, more expansive emotion.

> Brutus   No man bears sorrow better. Portia is dead.
> Cassius   Ha! Portia?
> Brutus   She is dead.
> Cassius   How scap'd I killing when I cross'd you so?
> O insupportable and touching loss!

If, as some believe, Shakespeare wanted Portia's death to be reported twice (IV. 3. 141–57, IV. 3. 179–93), Brutus' concern for his public image almost insults the 'holiness of the heart's affections'; but even if Shakespeare deleted the second report and it was printed in error, as others have argued,[46] the undeleted remark that 'no man bears sorrow better' wins less than total sympathy, focusing as it does upon the loser not the loss. The scene's winning stroke comes later, when Lucius has fallen asleep:

> Gentle knave, good night.
> I will not do thee so much wrong to wake thee.
> If thou dost nod, thou break'st thy instrument;
> I'll take it from thee; and, good boy, good night.

\*          \*          \*

Intertwined with the response to Brutus in the quarrel-scene and throughout the play, the response to Cassius appears to improve steadily. He begins as a malcontent or tempter, the technical 'villain' who tricks Brutus into joining the conspiracy, but Shakespeare softens and ennobles him, and by the time he dies he may well be thought the play's most attractive character.[47] Though there is some truth in such a reading, it unfairly simplifies the Cassius of Act I.

To believe, with MacCallum, that 'resentment of pre-eminence' makes Cassius a malcontent we have to trust Caesar's judgement:

Such men as he be never at heart's ease
Whiles they behold a greater than themselves,
And therefore are they very dangerous. (I. 2. 208–10)

Shakespeare, however, had already undermined our confidence in
Caesar's judgement of men; Caesar had gazed intently at the Soothsayer ('Set him before me; *let me see his face*'), and had erred disas-
trously in weighing him up, as even the semi-educated spectator
could not fail to know:

*Soothsayer*  Beware the ides of March.
*Caesar*  *He is a dreamer*; let us leave him. Pass. (I. 2. 23–4)

And Caesar also errs about Cassius who, far from resenting pre-
eminence, needs someone greater than himself to lean upon, as he
candidly admits:

Him and his worth and our great need of him
You have right well conceited. (I. 3. 161–2)

In scene after scene he abases himself before Brutus and all but says
to him what Peter Verkhovensky tells Stavrogin in Dostoyevsky's
more sensationalised handling of a similar relationship: 'You're the
boss. You're a force. I shall only be at your side . . .', 'I, especially,
need a man like you . . . You're my leader, you're my sun, and I am
your worm.'[48] Cassius envies not pre-eminence in general, but only
one man's; and that one man, Julius Caesar, offends him not just
because as an 'envious malcontent [he] is obsessed with a sense of
his inferiority'[49] but for more admirable reasons as well – because he
loves freedom, he loves the glory that was Rome. There may be an
ulterior motive when he addresses Brutus and Casca, but there is
genuine feeling as well:

Age, thou art sham'd!
Rome, thou hast lost the breed of noble bloods! . . . (I. 2. 150–1)

Nor stony tower, nor walls of beaten brass,
Nor airless dungeon, nor strong links of iron,
Can be retentive to the strength of spirit . . . (I. 3. 93–5)

Exalted feelings coexist with lower ones in Cassius. Caesar polarises
one side of him, the envious malcontent, and Brutus the other ('The
last of all the Romans, fare thee well!', V. 3. 99); the audience, from
the beginning, responds to both.

In the first act we must resist the temptation to simplify Cassius; in the last, Shakespeare himself seems to simplify him, especially in his suicide. Such an efficient way to go, after all his big talk of suicide and fine flourishes! –

> [I] thus unbraced, Casca, as you see,
> Have bar'd my bosom to the thunderstone,
> And when the cross blue lightning seem'd to open
> The breast of heaven, I did present myself
> Even in the aim and very flash of it! (I. 3. 48–52)

> I know where I will wear this dagger then;
> Cassius from bondage will deliver Cassius. (I. 3. 89–90)

Thinking that the conspirators are betrayed he may mean it when he says, less melodramatically, that he will slay himself (III. 1. 21–2); he then descends to his most improbable gesture in the quarrel-scene, one strangely reminiscent of Caesar (who 'pluckt me open his doublet, and offered them his throat to cut', I. 2. 265):

> There is my dagger,
> And here my naked breast; within, a heart
> Dearer than Plutus' mine, richer than gold;
> If that thou be'st a Roman, take it forth. (IV. 3. 99–102)

When it comes to the point, however, he swiftly makes his decision, presses his sword upon Pindarus, covers his face (like Caesar again) – and all is over. In the fifth act a complicated man shrinks into 'the last of all the Romans', a mere husk of himself, perhaps because the whole act falls away, and the play itself contracts.

\*       \*       \*

Most modern theatre-goers learn their Roman history from Shakespeare (and there are worse teachers). Educated Elizabethans knew the age of Cicero and Caesar from other sources, and Shakespeare must have taken their expectations into account, especially in his handling of the principal historical figures. There are several surprises, some of which the modern theatre-goer may not savour as he should.

Take Cicero. Mentioned twice in I. 2, he meets Casca in I. 3 and speaks four times, merely as a 'feed', where anyone else would have done as well. Thereafter we hear of him (II. 1. 141ff., IV. 3. 176ff.) but never see him again. Why then introduce him, when he might just as well have figured as a magic name, like Pompey and Cato?

Presented in person Cicero raises expectations ('great spirits now on earth are sojourning') that Shakespeare chose not to meet, and thus helps to scale down his great contemporaries, even those who show real signs of greatness in the play.

Shakespeare also teased his audience, I think, in giving a one-sided view of Mark Antony before the assassination-scene. The historical Antony had already climbed too high to impress his fellow-Romans as 'but a limb of Caesar' or, at the worst, a 'shrewd contriver' who 'may well stretch so far/As to annoy us all'.[50] He had held many important offices, including that of general of the horsemen ('the second office of dignitie, when the Dictator is in the citie: but when he is abroad . . . the chiefest man', according to Plutarch).[51] At the time of the Lupercalia Antony was Consul, together with Caesar, and 'did stowtly withstand' him on at least one issue.[52] His deferential reply when told to touch Calphurnia –

I shall remember.
When Caesar says 'Do this', it is perform'd. (I. 2. 9–10)

– gives a totally different impression. Before Caesar's assassination the man about to emerge as one of the triumvirs seems little more than 'a masker and a reveller' (V. 1. 62), speaks just five times, and speaks only when spoken to (thirty-five words in all, his longest speech being one of two lines). Shakespeare reduced his stature in this part of the play, which must have puzzled some spectators – and thus made his metamorphosis in Act III all the more stunning, when Antony for the first time takes the initiative and (like the Silent Woman) finds his tongue.

The biggest surprise must have been the portrait of Caesar. Can we doubt that once again Shakespeare aimed at a divided response? We marvel at the public figure, and we smile at the private man – a simpler version of the divided response than in the case of Brutus, but similar in pulling the audience in different directions at once. Introducing so many unhistorical touches (Caesar's deafness, defence-lessness against flattery, self-deception, and so on) the dramatist repeated a process that we have observed throughout this chapter: he disregarded history wherever the alternative was a special dramatic effect. Here, and indeed in all of the plays, Shakespeare was much less interested in history than in audience-response.

# 5
# Hamlet as Observer and Consciousness

Why should Shakespeare re-write the tragedy of Brutus and call it *The Tragedy of Hamlet, Prince of Denmark*? The more we compare the two plays the more likely it seems that he felt dissatisfied with his first mature tragedy, and that he went over the same ground again because he recognised, too late, that he had not made the most of it. Advancing from Brutus to Hamlet he must have pondered many of the fundamental questions of tragedy – not least, I think, the tragic hero's relations with the audience.

Superficially the two 'tragedies of thought' are remarkably alike. The intellectual hero is summoned to the world of action; duty, he hears, requires him to commit a murder – and a peculiarly repulsive one, since the proposed victim is the head of state, surrounded by friends, who can only be killed by cunning. The victim, moreover, seems to be well-disposed towards the tragic hero, so that Brutus and Hamlet have to plot against a well-wisher, not an endearing task. And their reasons for doing so leave the audience uneasy: they are persuaded to attempt the murder by seeming friends (Cassius, the Ghost) whose motives are by no means above suspicion, and they believe that Caesar and Claudius corrupt the state, even though both men govern effectively. In each play the intellectual hero meditates confusedly about his duty, which attracts and repels him, and seems temperamentally unsuited for it, 'sweet Hamlet' no less than 'gentle Brutus'.[1] Without going farther we can see that the two stories have more in common than any two other tragedies: yet, similar as they are, Hamlet is endowed with a much wider appeal than Brutus, and this I regard as a fundamental difference. Who has ever confessed 'I have a smack of Brutus myself, if I may say so' or 'Brutus, *c'est moi*'? Hamlet has had this effect on men as unlike each other as Coleridge and Hazlitt,[2] and, no doubt, on Sarah Bernhardt and all the ladies who have so feelingly played the part. I cannot believe that it is merely a matter of chance, or of vanity; on the contrary, the hero's radically changed effect upon the audience could well have been Shakespeare's starting-point in planning his second mature tragedy.

The intellectual hero, this time, is far less solemn than Brutus; he has a sense of humour, which immensely expands his appeal. (Of the many tragic heroes to come, not one can compare with Hamlet in exuberant or savage humour; but despite his success with Hamlet, strange to say, Shakespeare later returned to the unsmiling hero.[3]) Further, whereas the Roman shrinks from human contact the Dane has an outgoing, all-embracing temperament, freely expressing his love, or, every so often, recalling how completely he used to love (his father, his mother, Ophelia, Yorick); where Brutus is tight and closed, Hamlet is open and even carelessly, breath-takingly self-exposed (he scarcely troubles to hide his dislike of Claudius). Further, Shakespeare gave Hamlet a priceless gift, again one that he denied to later heroes – the common touch. The prince remembers Marcellus' name and, though he may have forgotten Bernardo's, he speaks to him as a person, not as a mere sentry, a winning stroke at the very start of the play. 'Marcellus?' 'My good lord!' 'I am very glad to see you. – (To Bernardo) Good even, sir.'[4] He welcomes the players as 'good friends', and one with particular affection, 'O, my old friend!' (II. 1. 418); he immediately hits it off with the pirates ('these good fellows' he calls them in his letter), as also with the grave-digger. How might Shakespeare's version of history have changed course, one cannot help speculating, had Brutus addressed only one Marcellus personally in the Forum, or had he been able to think of the plebeians as 'good fellows'!

That was not to be. But, moving on to his next tragedy, Shakespeare decided at the outset that we are to *like* his hero, much more positively than we were ever encouraged to respond to Brutus. Not that Hamlet is to charm us equally in every scene – far from it. When he lashes the defenceless Ophelia (III. 1. 88ff.) or pursues Gertrude relentlessly into 'the rank sweat of an enseamed bed' (III. 4. 92) we cannot like him; perhaps we even hate him, briefly, when he goes too far. By the time we reach these scenes, however, he has so completely captured the audience that his almost unpardonable ferocity makes little difference and the momentum of goodwill carries him through.

In his second tragedy of thought Shakespeare therefore experimented with a new response-problem. He switched from the forbidding intellectual to one who, when he wants, has a winning way

with him, an irresistible hero as far as the audience is concerned
Shakespeare was now less interested in the mixed response (though
he found it unavoidable in some scenes, as I have indicated, and it
becomes important again in later tragedies); instead he returned to a
problem that had not deeply engaged him in *Julius Caesar* – the
audience's faith in what, initially, I shall call the hero's judgement
He had changed the historical Brutus, it will be recalled, by multiply
ing his political mistakes, inventing intellectual muddles and
accentuating Brutus' high opinion of himself.[5] Watching *Julius
Caesar* no one could doubt that Brutus' judgement was at fault, and
perhaps Shakespeare simplified his Roman too drastically. Be that as
it may, the audience's faith in Hamlet's judgement turns out to be
an altogether different affair.

Instead of attempting to list all Hamlet's many attractive qualities
or debating whether Shakespeare modelled the prince's character
upon his own, I propose to examine the audience's judgement of
Hamlet's judgement, which I take to be *the* response-problem of the
play. Hamlet assesses or judges the Ghost, Claudius, Gertrude and
society at large; the audience judges Hamlet judging the Ghost etc
and in doing so has in effect the same task as Hamlet, at one remove
It may be objected, of course, that the audience has precisely this
task in every tragedy. But has it really? *Hamlet* differs from Shake
speare's mature tragedies, and from other dramatic tragedies known
to me, in presenting a hero of the highest intelligence who spends
much of his time observing, weighing, thinking, judging. Faustus is
a child in comparison, and Vindice and others modelled upon the
Prince of Denmark fall far short of his intellectual range. Brutus and
Othello observe the wrong objects and formulate the wrong ques
tions: they fail to identify the tempter (Cassius and Iago), and
accordingly all their 'judgements' go awry, whereas Hamlet alone
suspects the credentials of his tempter (the Ghost). Shakespeare's
other heroes impress us in the middle acts as men who have been
tricked by cleverer opponents into a tragic dilemma, Hamlet seems at
least as clever as his human opponents, tries tricks of his own (his
antic disposition, the play within the play, the forged commission
and he alone, of all the tragic heroes, could have said with such
obvious relish

> For 'tis *the sport* to have the engineer
> Hoist with his own petar; and't shall go hard

But I will delve one yard below their mines
And blow them at the moon. O, 'tis most sweet
When in one line two crafts directly meet. (III. 4. 206ff.)

Hamlet observes and understands more efficiently than the other
tragic heroes, being usually on the right scent (though at times he
may feel confused, even lost). Accordingly the audience has a different task in observing the observer, judging the judge: it can rarely be
sure that Hamlet is mad (as it knows Lear to be mad), or that he is
deluded (as Brutus and Othello are deluded), or even that he is guilty
of an error of judgement (as when Antony agrees to marry Octavia).
Hamlet's point of view wins the audience's assent, more or less, and
this makes the task of judging the judge peculiarly difficult.

*          *          *

The Tragedy of Hamlet not only differs from Shakespeare's other
mature tragedies in having a keen observer as hero, it is also filled
with exceptionally watchful secondary characters. Everyone, as
R. A. Foakes has explained, spies on everyone else, and a 'mutual
observing reflects what seems to be a universal need to see in order
to believe . . . But what is seen has to be interpreted, and may still
not reveal the truth'.[7] Action-packed though it be, the play is above
all concerned with observers and interpreters, their various methods
and abilities, minor lights that revolve around its central sun, the
Prince of Denmark. The sentries keep 'strict and most observant
watch', Polonius tells Reynoldo to spy on Laertes, Claudius asks
Rosencrantz and Guildenstern to watch Hamlet, the 'observ'd of all
observers', Hamlet hopes to trap Claudius at the play ('I'll observe
his looks') and also requests Horatio to 'give him heedful note',
Claudius and Polonius bestow themselves as 'lawful espials', and so
forth. If it is helpful to think of Hamlet as a play about disease or
about death,[8] it could equally be called a play about observation.

Its observation is not only outward-looking. While Hamlet himself
catches our attention as the character most intensely preoccupied
with 'that within' ('But I have that within which passes show',
I. 2. 85), others also attempt this more difficult exercise, and we can
compare their success with his. Claudius harangues himself in
soliloquy ('O, my offence is rank, it smells to heaven', III. 3. 36ff.),
then, at the point of entry into a deeper inwardness, falls silent, and
finally confesses failure. The sequence is unusual: from soliloquy
(where he looks at himself from the outside), to another form of

self-communion that remains inaudible, and back to baffled soliloquy – which suggests that, quite apart from being unable to pray, he cannot reach the inner self, he cannot really look within. Gertrude only observes 'that within' when subjected to the most terrifying pressures, and we cannot tell whether she learns to see for herself or whether she merely sees what Hamlet describes to her (III. 4. 88ff.). Claudius and Gertrude, it is worth noting, attempt to look within just before and just after Hamlet's least convincing self-scrutiny, 'Now might I do it pat' (III. 3. 73ff.): as all three find their inward-looking so difficult, we pardon Hamlet's failure the more readily.

Elsewhere Hamlet, the prince of observers, has more success – perhaps because he has trained himself to look for 'that within', whether he observes himself, or another person, or natural phenomena. As the play's imagery confirms, his mind moves from the visible to the invisible, from the outer to the inner. 'That skull had a tongue in it, and could sing once' (V. 1. 75). His sense of his own inwardness may be revealed almost in passing ('O, it offends me to the soul to hear a robustious, periwig-pated fellow . . .', III. 2. 10), or with studied emphasis, as when he promises to wear Horatio 'In my heart's core, ay, in my heart of heart' (III. 2. 71). He assumes a similar inwardness in others and undertakes to 'catch the conscience of the King' (II. 2. 601), or tells Gertrude that he will set up a glass 'Where you may see the inmost part of you' (III. 4. 20). Though chiefly interested in the inwardness of the soul, he is also morbidly fascinated by the purely physical facts of inwardness: 'if the sun breed maggots in a dead dog . . .', 'a man may fish with the worm that hath eat of a king, and eat of the fish that hath fed of that worm'.[9] And if he discovers no maggots or worms he imagines some other form of rottenness or emptiness 'within': some vicious mole of nature, bad dreams, a foul and pestilent congregation of vapours, a quintessence of dust.[10]

Claudius achieves little by introspection but excels as an observer of others, as does Hamlet; and, not surprisingly, each observes and reacts in his own special way. Claudius weighs people as a politician, looking for an advantage, whereas Hamlet is interested in the other person's moral nature, and as often as not forgoes whatever advantage he might have seized. Each of them usually observes correctly and observes in character, as a few examples will show.

Claudius (1) I. 2. 112ff. Claudius 'beseeches' Hamlet not to return to Wittenberg, and Hamlet remains stubbornly silent. Gertrude intervenes, extracting a grudging promise, 'I shall in all my best obey you, madam', and Claudius immediately sees that, in Hamlet's present mood, it is the best bargain he can get, and makes the most of it. 'Why, 'tis a loving and a fair reply.' (2) III. 1. 162*ff*. Having eavesdropped on the nunnery-scene, Claudius abandons two theories previously advanced to explain Hamlet's strange behaviour (madness, love); he sees, correctly, that 'there's something in his soul/O'er which his melancholy sits on brood', and that the hatch and the disclose 'will be some danger'. No sooner has he observed the new facts than he determines on the best way to deal with them, by sending Hamlet to England; but neither Hamlet nor Ophelia interests him as a person, they are merely pawns in the game. (3) IV. 5. 109*ff*. Claudius gives his most consummate exhibition as an observer of men during the Laertes rebellion, biding his time, soothing, flattering, and finally converting an enemy into an ally.

*Hamlet*. When Hamlet observes that he has come to the cross-roads in his relations with another person he gives due warning, quite openly, and thus loses the advantage kept by Claudius, who pretends to be everyone's friend. (1) II. 2. 273*ff*. 'Were you not sent for? Is it your own inclining? Is it a free visitation?' He challenges Rosencrantz and Guildenstern directly. (2) III. 1. 130*ff*. 'Where is your father?' He warns Ophelia that he has noticed Polonius and, by his question, makes her declare herself for truth or falsehood, for the prince or the king. (3) III. 4. 27*ff*. 'Almost as bad, good mother,/ As kill a king and marry with his brother.' He bluntly states his suspicions to Gertrude.

Claudius, a 'smiling, damned villain', observes from behind a mask of goodwill or from behind some other form of screen, never revealing more than he must to the person observed; as far as possible he repeats the 'orchard' situation (I. 5. 59*ff*.), watching while his victim sleeps. Hamlet, on the contrary, pounces on his victim with direct questions or accusations, and observes the effect;[11] and, being more engrossed by the person observed than by the consequences, he gives himself away as he observes. The play-scene is the outstanding example: he publicly states his suspicions, so that Claudius at least must understand them ('"A poisons him i' th' garden for his estate . . . You shall see anon how the murderer gets the love of Gonzago's wife'), and, intent upon his victim, pays no heed to the fact that he has also exposed himself. Politically, Claudius is doubtless the shrewder; yet Hamlet's observation reaches into the depths, where

Claudius never attempts to go. Questioning or accusing others directly, Hamlet brings them to the shock of recognition, of *self-recognition*, and, his eyes fixed upon theirs, he tents them to the quick, he sees 'into the life of things'.

\*          \*          \*

Hamlet is a penetrating observer who, I have said, wins the audience's assent *more or less*. Before we continue let us consider two very different attitudes to his point of view, neither of which seems to me acceptable. 'Hamlet is the only tragedy in which the audience watches the whole action through the eyes of the hero. In *Julius Caesar* the point of view is continually changing . . . and in *Othello* there are scenes in which we are alienated from the Moor. But we watch Polonius, or Gertrude or Claudius, not as they see themselves but as Hamlet sees them.'[12] Something like this is often said, but it has only a limited truth. The eyes of the hero certainly influence the audience's seeing, and more pervasively than in the other tragedies. Can we, however, view the first scene through the eyes of the hero, before he appears? Or the crucial opening lines of the second scene, before he speaks? More serious objections will emerge in the next few pages, so I need not expand upon them now.

Just as we must not make too much of Hamlet's point of view, we should beware of reacting too positively against it. D. H. Lawrence disliked Hamlet as an 'unclean thing', which turns the traditional tragedy upside down.

> I had always felt an aversion from Hamlet: a creeping, unclean thing he seems, on the stage, whether he is Forbes Robertson or anybody else. His nasty poking and sniffing at his mother, his setting traps for the King, his conceited perversion with Ophelia make him always intolerable. The character is repulsive in its conception, based on self-dislike and a spirit of disintegration.[13]

A far cry from Bradley's prince with 'all the nobility and sweetness of his nature'![14] Surprisingly, there seems to have been a general movement against Hamlet in the post-war years, and in particular against his unhealthy sensibility.

> Hamlet (the man) is dominated by an emotion which is inexpressible, because it is in *excess* of the facts as they appear . . . [His] disgust is occasioned by his mother, but . . . his mother is not an adequate equivalent for it; his disgust envelops and exceeds her . . .

The intense feeling, ecstatic or terrible, without an object or exceeding its object, is something which every person of sensibility has
known; it is doubtless a subject of study for pathologists.
(T. S. Eliot)[15]

G. Wilson Knight attempted to state the case more fully against
'unhealthy' Hamlet, and to readjust the play's perspective, arguing,
in a celebrated essay, that 'though we instinctively tend at first to
adopt the view-point of Hamlet himself, we are not forced to do so
throughout.' 'Hamlet's soul is sick' (this was Wilson Knight's
refrain), he takes 'a devilish joy in cruelty towards the end of the
play', so we should be equally prepared to adopt the point of view
of the other side, of 'human' Claudius against 'inhuman' Hamlet.
Wilson Knight added, at a later date, that he would not 'retract
what I have elsewhere said concerning the evil in Hamlet, except to
admit a certain exaggeration.'[16]
    These essays and asides lie behind L. C. Knights's *An Approach to
'Hamlet'* (1960), a brilliant book that again dealt with Hamlet's
consciousness and the audience's response to it, and one that seems to
me right about individual passages and yet wrong about the play.
Leaping nimbly from one scene to the next, Knights argued that
Hamlet's 'god-like reason is clogged and impeded by the emotions of
disgust, revulsion and self-contempt', and that 'Shakespeare leaves
us in no doubt of the inadequacy – and worse – of Hamlet's basic
attitudes.' In 'To be or not to be', he said, there is no pretence of
following a logical sequence of thought, 'one idea blends with
another – killing Claudius, killing oneself, the well-nigh insupport-
able troubles of life, the fear of futurity – all carried by currents of
half-expressed emotion, so that the thoughts that the Prince is trying
to bring into some order are eroded and carried away on the stream
of feeling.' After the nunnery-scene Ophelia sums up ('O, what a
noble mind is here o'erthrown!') and 'that surely is quite explicit.'
The purpose of the last long soliloquy, 'How all occasions do inform
against me', 'can only be to define one further stage in the withdrawal of Hamlet's consciousness, a sacrifice of reason to a fantasy
of quite unreflective destructive action.'[17]
    It is a consistent reading but, I think, it distorts the play. To begin
with two small points: we may have doubts about Hamlet's reasoning
and yet, 'with thoughts beyond the reaches of our souls', still trust
his consciousness: and we cannot take Ophelia's opinion of Hamlet

too seriously when so much of the nunnery-scene goes above her head, and Claudius immediately contradicts it ('what he spake . . . Was not like madness', III. 1. 164). There are, however, larger questions to ponder. Knights argued from 'crucial points of the action', the soliloquies, the nunnery-scene and the like: it is important to notice, I believe, that as we experience the play these crucial points are carefully spaced, with passages of easy conversation in between that also affect our response. Shakespeare knew that he must not overwhelm the audience with too much anguish, and took his measures.

> Many a green isle needs must be
> In the deep wide sea of misery.

After the emotional altitudes of the first soliloquy Hamlet descends to everyday chat with Horatio and the sentries, then hears about the Ghost, and any doubts we may have had about his clogged reason swiftly vanish as it darts in pursuit of the facts. 'Arm'd, you say?' 'From top to toe?' 'Then saw you not his face?' 'What, looked he frowningly?' Immediately after the nunnery-scene there comes Hamlet's advice to the Players, where he views the torrent, tempest and whirlwind of passion from the outside, as it were, and identifies himself with *discretion* and *the judicious*; or, to put it another way, he talks shop and clearly knows what he is talking about, the professionals listen to him so respectfully. No sooner has he struggled with Laertes in or beside Ophelia's grave, one of his most hysterical outbursts, than he enters conversing rationally with Horatio, and his account of events at sea reveals a swift decisiveness totally unimpeded by emotion. These are all 'rehabilitation-scenes', in that they convince the audience that his mind works effectively and can still get at the truth, and they re-establish its faith in his judgement.

Granted, rehabilitation-scenes are not directly concerned with what Knights called Hamlet's 'basic attitudes'. But how clearly can basic attitudes be identified in the theatre? Knights, I believe, responded as a reader and not as a spectator when he so firmly and explicitly found fault with Hamlet's, and with his consciousness. A reader can scrutinise every word or speech at leisure, and may even persuade himself that he is more far-sighted than the philosopher-prince, and that Hamlet 'is a man who has given himself over to a false direction of consciousness'.[18] Not so a spectator: if Hamlet's exceptional mind has impressed him as it should in Acts I

and II, he will be altogether more slow to censure it when the prince
appears to make mistakes in Acts III and IV, if only because he has
no time to stand back from the play and puzzle things out. He will
mistrust his own consciousness as well as Hamlet's, and reserve his
judgement.

Hamlet makes two kinds of mistake in Acts III and IV, and they
must be distinguished. First, he blunders tactically, losing the initiative to Claudius. With the benefit of hindsight we are struck by a
series of such mistakes but, it must be stressed, their local effect is
different. Hamlet's manner in the nunnery-scene alarms the king,
who swiftly determines to send him to England (III. 1. 169): we may
say after the event that, knowing himself to be watched, Hamlet
behaved unwisely, especially when he announced 'those that are
married already, all but one, shall live' (III. 1. 147). As the action
unfolds, however, what chiefly impresses us is Hamlet's quickness in
identifying Polonius and in deciding to play the scene his own way:
he makes a mistake in failing to identify the king but we scarcely
notice it, being a mistake wrapped up in cleverness. So, too, when he
shows his hand more and more openly in the play-scene: after the
event we may again feel that he exposed himself unnecessarily but
while the scene lasts, up to Claudius' hurried departure, we are more
impressed by Hamlet's dazzling improvisations, and he seems to have
his enemy at his mercy.[19] His greatest tactical mistake follows in the
next scene, where he cannot bring himself to kill the praying king.
Unless we take his stated motives literally, which very few are now
inclined to do, we ought to draw the obvious conclusion from the
fact that criticism can make little or nothing of 'Up, sword, and
know thou a more horrid hent' (III. 3. 88ff.) – namely that, not
understanding Hamlet's judgement at this point, we ourselves have
to suspend judgement.

Whenever he is matched against Claudius in Act III Hamlet
always appears to be the more dangerous – in the eavesdropping
scene, the play-scene, the prayer-scene. Though he loses some ground
every time, giving his mighty opposite more room for manœuvre, he
impresses the audience locally as a winner; and let us not forget that,
but for the unlucky killing of Polonius instead of Claudius, he would
have been the winner. At the purely tactical level, in short, the
audience will scarcely fault Hamlet's judgement but, if anything,
will admire it.[20] At the same time, however, he makes another kind
of mistake, if that is the right word, to which the audience may react

less favourably – his treatment of Ophelia and Gertrude in the play's two most painful scenes. He speaks daggers to both, he intends to give pain, and he may be thought guilty of a failure of sensibility.

I now return to the 'unhealthy' Hamlet, and in particular to T. S. Eliot's prince 'dominated by an emotion which is . . . in excess of the facts as they appear'.[21] If, as is often said, his attitude to Ophelia and Gertrude is nasty, obsessive, excessive and so on, how are such things to be measured? Not with coffee spoons, we may impertinently reply, nor should we presume to fix Prince Hamlet in a formulated phrase. His situation is unusual (a father murdered by an uncle, a mother the murderer's doting wife, a ghost calling for revenge), so what would be the *appropriate* emotion? Unless we can cite a norm we have no right to accuse Hamlet of *excessive* emotion or of a failure of sensibility.

The point, of course, is debated several times in the play. And who speaks for emotion 'in excess of the facts'?

> But to persever
> In obstinate condolement is a course
> Of impious stubbornness; 'tis unmanly grief;
> It shows a will most incorrect to heaven,
> A heart unfortified, a mind impatient,
> An understanding simple and unschool'd . . . (I. 2. 92ff.)

Hamlet, when he understands the facts more fully, accuses himself of feeling too little rather than too much. What would the Player do, he asks,

> Had he the motive and the cue for passion
> That I have? He would drown the stage with tears . . . (II. 2. 554ff.)

Hamlet obviously exaggerates and Claudius, we soon realise, relates Hamlet's emotion to the wrong facts (to 'death of fathers', I. 2. 104, instead of Gertrude's most wicked speed in posting to incestuous sheets, I. 2. 156). The audience can accept neither point of view, and throughout the play has to measure Hamlet's sensibility for itself. There are times when it may seem to be an excessive and even an unhealthy sensibility yet, paradoxically, the audience will be the less inclined to take this view simply because the Claudius party so frequently insists upon it.

Hamlet's sensibility must not be regarded as fully knowable or all of a piece. In general, I think, the audience trusts it, though there are moments of doubt to which I shall return. When his 'nasty poking and sniffing at his mother'[22] reaches its climax, in the closet-scene, Shakespeare insures against a hostile audience-response by adopting two simple expedients. First, Gertrude's unconditional surrender, which implies that Hamlet was justified in all of his sexual detail and nasty emotion, and which also sets a kind of Q.E.D. upon the scene by echoing his earlier words. (The repetition reminds us that Hamlet has carried out his plan: he has not been swept away by 'the indulgence of an obsessive passion', as Knights would have it,[23] but has used his passion for a declared purpose.)

> You go not till I set you up a glass
> Where you may see the inmost part of you. (Hamlet, III. 4. 19–20)

> O Hamlet, speak no more!
> Thou turn'st my eyes into my very soul . . . (Gertrude, III. 4. 88ff.)

At this very point, admittedly, Hamlet cannot hold back the emotion that he had quite deliberately released to break Gertrude's will, and it threatens to gallop away with him. But now Shakespeare blocks a hostile response by resorting to his second expedient, the Ghost. Is it a 'real' Ghost, or the product of an overcharged sensibility? Is Hamlet mad, as Gertrude at first believes, or should we see him as the human target of intolerable supernatural pressures? Because we cannot know the answer[24] we are not entitled to accuse Hamlet of excessive emotion, unhealthy sensibility or the like.

The Ghost's arrival also complicates our response to Hamlet's emotion in another way. Speaking to Gertrude, Hamlet had compared her two husbands and the extraordinary differences between them ('look here upon this picture and on this', III. 4. 53ff.), exactly as the Ghost had done in I. 5; and he proceeded thence to the sexual detail and its 'obsessive passion', again following the Ghost. The resemblance is important:

> So lust, though to a radiant angel link'd
> Will sate itself in a celestial *bed*
> And prey on *garbage* . . .
> Let not the royal *bed* of Denmark be
> A *couch* for *luxury* and damned incest.

> In the rank sweat of an enseamed *bed*
> Stew'd in corruption, honeying and making love
> Over the *nasty sty*.[25]

In the closet-scene Hamlet speaks for the Ghost to Gertrude, recalling its thoughts and emotions. His obsessive interest in Gertrude's *bed* is as much the Ghost's as his own, either because every word of their first meeting is etched upon his memory (I. 5. 91ff.) or because a 'real' Ghost is near and influences him invisibly. The Ghost thus brings an exceptional factor into the scene which makes it difficult for us to fault Hamlet's sensibility.

Nevertheless there remain other episodes to which we may react more positively. His attitude to the death of Rosencrantz and Guildenstern, his callousness after he has killed Polonius[26] – are they not signs of moral coarsening, of a blunted sensibility? Hamlet certainly makes mistakes, even mistakes of sensibility; yet, we may say in his defence, all are more or less excusable in the circumstances. He had not concealed his dislike of Polonius, he had warned him to stop meddling ('Let the doors be shut upon him, that he may play the fool nowhere but in's own house', III. 1. 132), so why should he grieve? Like Rosencrantz and Guildenstern, Polonius 'did make love to this employment' (V. 2. 57), and has only himself to blame. And if Hamlet seems brutal in his attitude to dead Polonius it is largely because his sensibility is otherwise engaged. He has just learnt that Gertrude was not an accessory to her husband's murder, a discovery that means all the world to him and that anaesthetises him to other facts and contrary emotions. Later, when he recovers himself, his sensibility expresses itself appropriately enough, neither too little nor too much, restoring whatever confidence the audience may have lost: 'For this same lord/I *do repent*; but Heaven hath pleas'd it so . . .' (III. 4. 172–3). In the case of Rosencrantz and Guildenstern, of course, he describes the callous trick he played upon them after the event, and without regret. Has he therefore descended to the level of his enemies? Not really: the audience knows, though he himself does not, that while he has merely substituted one commission for another, a poisoned sword and chalice already await him. All the same, I find the forged commission more disturbing than his farewell to dead Polonius, since Hamlet has had time to reflect when he speaks to Horatio; and Shakespeare makes a bigger issue of it. What is more, we hear of it directly after Hamlet's ranting-match with Laertes, at Ophelia's funeral, another episode where Hamlet's sensibility seems disturbingly at fault. Towards the end, it seems, the thousand natural and unnatural shocks that he has suffered do affect his sensibility, a point also made when Horatio pulls away from him (for the first

time since Act 1) in quiet, gentle words that are strangely arresting.

> *Hamlet*   To what base uses we may return, Horatio! Why may
> not imagination trace the noble dust of Alexander till 'a find it
> stopping a bung-hole?
> *Horatio*   'Twere to consider too curiously to consider so.
>
> (V. 1. 196ff.)

By and large the audience trusts Hamlet's sensibility, more than it
trusts that of any other Shakespearian hero; and if he errs it blames
his opponents, or the Ghost, and tends to excuse *his* part in the affair.
Brutality is forced upon him, but, we are made to feel, against his
better nature. Rehabilitation-passages generally follow after he has
been shown at his worst. (Compare, too, the change of mood half-
way through the closet-scene, affording a glimpse of the son's *natural*
feeling for his mother, even though the strident note has not entirely
gone from his voice.) And nothing helps more to convince us of the
essential healthiness of Hamlet's sensibility than his hatred of insensibility, which expresses itself in many different ways. That a wife
as affectionate as his own mother should have remarried 'within a
month' – the idea sickens him, and Shakespeare devotes the first
soliloquy, where an audience for the first time enters fully into
Hamlet's consciousness, to his horror of 'things rank and gross in
nature' (I. 2. 136). Suspecting himself of insensibility Hamlet is just
as angry, in two other key-soliloquies;[27] and whatever subject is
touched upon, even in passing, he sides with sensibility against its
enemies – he denounces the 'heavy-headed revel' of the Danes
(I. 4. 13ff.), he mocks the false refinement of Osric (V. 2. 81ff.). (Why,
by the way, was Osric introduced so near the end, in the very last
scene, and given such prominence? The episode is the last of a series
that includes Hamlet's encounters with Polonius, and with Rosencrantz and Guildenstern, in all of which Shakespeare reminds us of
Hamlet's hatred of triviality and affectation. Even after Polonius and
the two school-fellows have disappeared, Shakespeare still felt the
need to define Hamlet's sensibility by contrast, and therefore inserted
his reflections upon 'the skull of a lawyer' (V. 1. 95ff.) and the Osric
dialogue.) The play's economy in establishing Hamlet's healthy
sensibility is at its most remarkable when he talks with the players
and reveals, again just in passing, his unyielding commitment to good
taste. He loved a play that pleased not the million, he flares up when

Polonius reacts with predictable bad taste to this very play, he cannot bear actors who tear a passion to tatters merely to split the ears of the groundlings, and so forth.[28]

By such means Shakespeare informs the audience, as often as he can, that his hero is not only heaven's scourge and minister but also a champion of sensibility in a world that has descended to the level of beasts.[29] This is not merely a matter of assertion, Hamlet's stated opposition to insensibility of every sort. It is demonstrated – by his shrinking from others into aside and soliloquy, by the anguish of his voice, and by his every turn of phrase. And it is also brought home to the audience when his mind darts into the future and, again and again, reads it correctly – an instinctive gift of an exceptional sensitivity reaching out into the unknown. Either he has premonitions about individuals or, more inexplicably, he feels vague presentiments of danger that the audience believes or knows to be fully justified:

My father's spirit in arms! All is not well.
I doubt some foul play. (I. 2. 254)

      O my prophetic soul!
My uncle! (I. 5. 40)

I will prophesy he comes to tell me of the players . . . (II. 2. 382)

There's letters seal'd; and my two school-fellows,
Whom I will trust as I will adders fang'd . . . (III. 4. 202)

Sir, in my heart there was a kind of fighting
That would not let me sleep . . . (V. 2. 4)

Thou wouldst not think how ill all's here about my heart . . .
(V. 2. 203)

His instinct proves sound every time, and is it not the same instinct that guides his consciousness throughout the play?

I have argued that Hamlet stands for sensibility in the world of the play, and I may be told that the point is not at issue. I have also urged that the audience continues to believe in his sensibility, despite all that happens in his most unpleasant scenes, and that Shakespeare enforces this response, even if moments of doubt are allowed to interrupt it – and here we come to the critical divide. Do we turn against the play's central consciousness as an 'unclean thing' and condemn the prince's 'basic attitudes'? The alternative is to think of

Hamlet, the passionate opponent of things rank and gross in nature, as a scourge and minister slightly damaged by 'the uses of this world':

> In *Hamlet*, Shakespeare draws a complete character, not for the comparatively barren purpose of 'creating' a Hamlet for our admiration, but in order to show how he, like the others, is inevitably engulfed by the evil that has been set in motion, and how he himself becomes the cause of further ruin. The conception . . . may be said to be this: evil, once started on its course, will so work as to attack and overthrow impartially the good and bad.[30]

Engulfed and overthrown – yes, in so far as evil kills him at last. Yet the miracle is that he is not completely overthrown within himself (as are Othello, Lear, Macbeth, in the middle acts); though the audience experiences moments of doubt he recovers himself every time, he remains what he always was to the end, certainly in Horatio's eyes – 'Now cracks a noble heart. Good night, sweet prince.' If we give our assent to that *sweet prince*, as we are surely meant to do, what becomes of the 'creeping unclean thing' that has haunted modern *Hamlet* criticism?

*     *     *

In Shakespeare every tragic hero's sensibility expresses itself in its own way, an idiom that the audience quickly adjusts to and evaluates instinctively. The Othello music, Lear's curses, Macbeth's hallucinations – all are expressive of the hero's character, revealing much more than the purely local message. In Hamlet's case his habit of idealisation is equally significant, although we notice it more at the beginning of the play than at the end. We may even think, when he first soliloquises, that his mother's o'erhasty marriage has destroyed it before the play commences, and has changed his thinking about woman (especially Gertrude and Ophelia) and *all* the uses of this world. If so we are wrong, for the idealising habit continues: he worshipped his father as much as his mother and, though he flippantly addresses the Ghost as 'old truepenny' and the like, he almost makes a god of him when he speaks of him as Hyperion, Hercules, Hyperion again, Jove, Mars, Mercury –

> A combination and a form indeed
> Where every god did seem to set his seal.[31]

He rates Horatio just as highly, a perfect Stoic, an ideal friend who

may be worn in the 'heart's core' (III. 2. 6off.); and a similar attitude
also survives when he looks back, in Act V, to his earlier delight in
Yorick, 'a fellow of infinite jest' (V. 1. 179). The habit continues,
and not only in his thinking about individuals: he treasures honesty,
honour and dignity, sweet religion and god-like reason; the speech
he calls for when the players arrive comes from the perfect play, 'an
excellent play, well digested in the scenes, set down with as much
modesty as cunning' (II. 2. 428ff.); his love for Ophelia was such that
forty thousand brothers could not make up his sum (V. 1. 264ff.).

Apart from the idealising passages assigned to Hamlet himself
there are others that also reflect back upon his sensibility, more or
less obliquely. Polonius' advice to Laertes (I. 3. 59ff.), like the 'order'
speeches in *Troilus and Cressida*, *Coriolanus* and so on,[32] consists of
commonplaces that serve as a clearly defined landmark at the beginning of the play, from which the story pushes off into the deeps. The
'order' speeches launch a political interest, Polonius gives prudential
advice about personal behaviour (what a man owes to himself, his
relations with friends and enemies), and similarly points forward to
the play's special concern. He describes the Elizabethans' ideal
gentleman, an ideal that has to be firmly stated because it asserts
itself, in one disguise or another, in so many scenes.[33]

> Sir, here is newly come to court Laertes; believe me, an absolute
> gentleman ...

> The concernancy, sir? Why do we wrap the gentleman in our
> more rawer breath? ...

> Give me your pardon, sir. I have done you wrong;
> But pardon 't, as you are a gentleman. (V. 2. 106–219)

The ideal is public property, and can be debased by a Polonius or an
Osric; Hamlet nevertheless accepts it and measures himself against it,
and others measure him with the same yard-stick.

> O, what a noble mind is here o'erthrown!
> The courtier's, soldier's, scholar's, eye, tongue, sword ...
>
> (III. 1. 150ff.)

The world of the play presents an ideal-conscious society; and even
those who only pay lip-service to this way of thinking usually direct
our minds back to the idealist Hamlet and what he stands for. To
praise Laertes as an 'absolute gentleman' is to praise Hamlet, who

will compete with him in gentlemanly exercise. When Claudius remembers Lamord ('Here was a gentleman of Normandy', IV. 7. 81ff.), Hamlet is similarly characterised by association: Claudius more or less equates Lamord and Laertes, one perfect gentleman vouched for by another, claims that Hamlet wished to match himself against Laertes, and thus implicitly measures Hamlet against Lamord, the 'gem of all the nation'. The audience of course recognises that the king overpraises Lamord to butter up Laertes, and that he no doubt lies about Hamlet as well. What may not be so readily apparent is that once again an 'ideal' has been pointed towards Hamlet.

Returning now to Hamlet's own speeches, we must add that his sensibility not only distorts by its habit of idealisation, it can also pull the other way. Man is either infinite in faculties or a quintessence of dust (II. 2. 307). In the closet-scene Hamlet compares his father and uncle, the one god-like and the other a mildewed ear blasting his wholesome brother (III. 4. 64). Almost every time he thinks of his uncle or mother his imagination interferes with what he observes (and producers, I think, should not take his words too literally, as 'indirect stage directions', when he speaks of Claudius paddling in the queen's neck with his damned fingers, and so on, III. 4. 182ff.). The same distortion is at work when he lashes himself in the soliloquies, and in the nunnery-scene, the grave-yard meditations, and in many passing remarks.

The audience, I have said, learns to evaluate the tragic hero's sensibility quite instinctively; it recognises his habit of distortion and adjusts to it. Experience shows that this is not always true – the outstanding example of failure being the prayer-scene (III. 3). Hamlet has his opportunity to kill Claudius, announces 'now I'll do it', then promptly talks himself out of it. And why? The different answers to this question suggest that we cannot rationalise all the impressions conjured forth by Shakespeare, though it would not be misleading to say that those who have discussed the passage have mostly distrusted Hamlet's stated explanation, the wish to 'trip him that his heels may kick at heaven' (III. 3. 93). Being concerned with Hamlet's consciousness rather than his motives, and with the audience's 'judgement' of it, I note that he idealises again, but not as before. He imagines the ideal revenge, which only makes sense in a Christian context – and yet is entirely unChristian. Taken aback by the suddenness of his opportunity Hamlet falters, his sensibility fails him; and the audience finds itself trapped in his confusion, more than at any other point in the play, and (if we are honest with ourselves) for once cannot tell how seriously he means what he says.[34]

*      *      *

'The Hamlet formula', said C. S. Lewis, pleading for what he called a 'childish response' in one of the wisest essays on the play, 'the Hamlet formula, so to speak, is not "a man who has to avenge his father" but "a man who has been given a task by a ghost." Everything else about him is less important than that.'

> This ghost is different from any other ghost in Elizabethan drama. . . . It is permanently ambiguous. Indeed the very word 'ghost', by putting it into the same class with the 'ghosts' of Kyd and Chapman, nay by classifying it at all, puts us on the wrong track. It is 'this thing', 'this dreaded sight', an 'illusion', a 'spirit of health or goblin damn'd', liable at any moment to assume 'some horrible form' which reason could not survive the vision of.[35]

The keenest observer of Shakespeare's variously gifted tragic heroes, Hamlet is placed in a situation that, above all, tests his observation and his consciousness. He meets something quite outside his previous experience, a Ghost that can harrow up his soul and 'Make thy two eyes like stars start from their spheres' (I. 5. 17); apart from observing Claudius and Gertrude, a comparatively simple matter, he has to evaluate the Ghost and its effect upon himself, two tasks that continue to occupy him throughout the play. At first his consciousness focuses upon the Ghost, trying to decide whether or not 'it is a damned ghost that we have seen' (III. 2. 80); later it is more thoughtfully concerned with the rights and wrongs of revenge – and all the while he also observes himself, his inability to do what he thinks he wants to do, the impression he makes upon others, and so on. None of his problems seems to him to admit of an easy solution, and the theatre-audience, being largely guided by him, necessarily shares his uncertainties as it responds to the play's unfolding.

Whatever the audiences may make of Hamlet's unusual problems, too many critics abhor uncertainty and feel obliged to answer the play's every question: some, for instance, happily 'take the ghost's word for a thousand pound' and, being men of peace, approve of Hamlet's unwillingness to exact revenge. If the play were really so simple these two popular solutions should hardly go together, for a good ghost would be unlikely to bring a wicked message. Yet while

Hamlet himself reaches, at various times, more or less clear-cut decisions about the Ghost and about revenge, an audience cannot shake off his own earlier hesitations and, I think, will wish to reserve its judgement as long as possible. To take an obvious example – once the Ghost's story has been proved true, in the play-scene, Hamlet ceases to think that it 'may be a devil' (II. 2. 595), and even addresses it in the closet-scene as if he believes it to be his father ('Do you not come your tardy son to chide?', III. 4. 106), which, consciously or unconsciously, he had refused to do at their first meeting.[36] The audience, though tempted to agree with Hamlet, will nevertheless remember that 'the devil hath power/T'assume a pleasing shape' (II. 2. 595): the devil can cite scripture for his purpose, or, as Banquo even more pertinently tells Macbeth –

> oftentimes to win us to our harm
> The instruments of darkness tell us truths,
> Win us with honest trifles, to betray's
> In deepest consequence. (*Macbeth* I. 3. 123–6)

As an Elizabethan audience would be quick to recognise, the fact that the Ghost's story turns out to be true, as far as it can be checked, by no means proves it to be Hamlet's father's spirit. The special pressures of his situation make Hamlet think so; the audience, being more detached, and enjoying an overall view denied to the tragic hero, sees that the Ghost's call for revenge brings about the deaths of Claudius, Gertrude, Polonius, Laertes, Ophelia, Rosencrantz and Guildenstern, and of Hamlet himself; all of them sudden deaths, unhousel'd, disappointed, unanel'd. The Ghost's story, though true, could still be the work of the devil.

Others have made this elementary point before. It is worth repeating because it reminds us that the Ghost remains (in C. S. Lewis's phrase) 'permanently ambiguous', not just till Act III but to the very end. Hamlet, having to make a decision after the play-scene, concludes that he may take the Ghost's word; yet when his opportunity comes, in the prayer-scene, he still resists the Ghost's influence. Later, when he has outlined Claudius' various crimes to Horatio, he asks 'is't not perfect conscience/To quit [i.e. requite] him with this arm?' and then talks of 'special providence in the fall of a sparrow', which implicitly contradicts the idea of personal revenge.[37] On both occasions his consciousness resists his own reasoning, presumably because it is not completely satisfied about the Ghost and its message:[38]

he still feels the ambiguity, and so cannot act. Some of the commentators, however, think it possible to pluck out the heart of the
mystery by using a more delicate instrument than Hamlet's consciousness – the 'historical method', which can solve every problem.

Let us compare Hamlet's consciousness with that of a recent
historical critic, Eleanor Prosser, who has explained in detail how
she judges the Ghost. 'Both Protestants and Catholics agreed',
according to Miss Prosser, 'that a soul could not return from Heaven
or Hell. By banishing Purgatory, the Reformation thus eliminated
any possibility that the soul of the dead could return to earth.' And
again: 'Since a ghost could not be a human soul, it could be only a
good or evil spirit, an angel or a devil'.[39] Having reduced the possibilities to two, Miss Prosser could the more readily conclude that
'the Ghost is probably malignant', i.e. the Devil.[40] She cites her
theological authorities, but what one would prefer to know is how
the average Elizabethan thought about ghost-lore, especially a play-
goer, whose mind might be confused by Senecan ghosts and, indeed,
by popular superstition. We cannot know; yet Shakespeare certainly
felt free to assume that a departed person's spirit could return to this
world as 'an honest ghost' (I. 5. 138), a point granted by Horatio as
well as Hamlet and, we may safely insist, a premise of the play.

The Ghost tells Hamlet 'I am thy father's spirit'; in the world of
the play it is at least a possibility, and has to be taken seriously. The
play's alternative, that the Ghost is the Devil or an evil spirit, seems
less likely to Hamlet but more so to Miss Prosser – and since Miss
Prosser tries to clinch her argument from the text we must look at
the detail. She has the advantage of Hamlet in seeing the Ghost first,
in the opening scene, and here already makes up her mind. When
Horatio adjures it to speak ('By heaven I charge thee, speak!'), this
'firmly establishes one point: this Ghost is forced to leave when
Heaven is invoked'.[41] Others have said the same, but must it be so?
It seems just as plausible that the Ghost, 'being so majestical', resents
being charged (or commanded) by a mere commoner, or that it takes
offence because told that it *usurps* the fair and warlike form of buried
Denmark: as the Ghost itself later says 'leave her to heaven' (I. 5. 86),
I think it rash to assume that Horatio's 'by heaven' offends it. Again,
Miss Prosser holds that the Ghost 'is meant to react as suddenly to
the voice of the cock as it did to Horatio's invocation of Heaven',[42]
citing the popular belief that roving demons scattered in fear at
cock-crow. Now the text appears to give some support –

> It was about to speak, when the cock crew.
> And then it started like a guilty thing
> Upon a fearful summons.

Horatio, however, merely guesses, and the Ghost soon offers a different explanation. It is not guilty as a devil or witch might be, being only

> Doom'd for a certain term to walk the night,
> And for the day confin'd to fast in fires. (I. 5. 10–11)

Contrary impressions neutralise whatever evidence appears to point to a malignant ghost; and the same is true of the later scenes with Hamlet. Miss Prosser makes much of the fact that when it actually speaks the Ghost fails to pass the usual religious tests: it comes to command revenge, it 'paints a series of obscene pictures', its appeal 'is entirely to the senses' and not to Hamlet's love of virtue, and it relentlessly aggravates his anguish and pain.[43] 'Throughout the cellerage scene', Miss Prosser goes on, 'the Ghost is acting like a devil.'

> Demons were believed to frequent mines, and Hamlet echoes this belief when he hails the 'old mole' as a 'worthy pioneer' that works in the earth . . . Moreover, 'hic et ubique' cannot refer to an 'honest ghost', for only God and the Devil can be both here and everywhere at the same time.[44]

All these arguments have some force, though less than is claimed. For if we approach 'this thing', 'this dreaded sight', with an open mind, as Hamlet and the audience are asked to do, its insistently Christian attitudes will have at least an equal effect. It laments the 'foul crimes done in my days of nature', it believes in love and 'the vow/I made to her in marriage', it condemns shameful lust and damned incest, and its longest speech comes to a climax in a passage of intense religious feeling.

> Cut off even in the blossoms of my sin,
> Unhous'led, disappointed, unanel'd;
> No reck'ning made, but sent to my account
> With all my imperfections on my head.
> O, horrible! O, horrible! most horrible!

Religious feeling, in short, seems so pervasively and powerfully present throughout the Ghost's interview with Hamlet that, despite all the evidence cited by Miss Prosser, it becomes more and more difficult to think of it as a devil. So, too, in the 'cellarage' passage, where the Ghost repeatedly exhorts Horatio, Marcellus and Bernado to swear by Hamlet's sword, which is tantamount to swearing upon a cross – another undevilish touch that neutralises all the suggestions of malignity.[45]

Whichever side we take in looking at the Ghost, contrary impressions quickly rekindle our original doubts. If, like Hamlet, we believe it to be an honest Ghost after the play within the play, we are troubled by the realisation that it lures him on to 'bloody and unnatural acts' and 'casual slaughters'; if we think we can prove it to be malignant, we overlook its quite extraordinary Christian feeling. In the circumstances we can scarcely fault Hamlet's judgement as he contemplates a Ghost 'in such a questionable shape', and the problems it brings. Like Hamlet, we tend to believe in the Ghost when we see it, and to distrust it when we have time to reflect; like Hamlet again, we first believe in the rightness of revenge, then, prompted by the play, we grow uneasy about it. We may not agree with all of Hamlet's interim decisions, as the flow of impressions tempts him this way and that, but we share his uncertainty and sympathise with his reluctance to commit himself to irrevocable action. Had Shakespeare created a recognisably malignant Ghost we would have had to judge Hamlet's judgement differently: but here, I believe, as in judging Hamlet's attitude to Gertrude or dead Polonius, we are in general accord with his consciousness, not opposed to it.[46]

# 6

# Secret Motives in *Othello*

Those who look for 'secret motives' in Shakespeare are sometimes treated as well-meaning lunatics, prospectors panning for fairy gold. To credit Hamlet with motives of which he himself remains unaware or, worse still, with impulses that contradict his stated motives, is, we are told, to confuse two different modes of being: a dramatic character has no past and no inwardness corresponding to yours or mine. As I have already argued, these are slippery ideas and general-isation can be dangerous.[1] In Shakespeare the boundaries between past and present, inner and outer, will not always be firmly marked; indeed, unless a play begins with a clear statement of intent (for example *Richard III*), it often obliges the audience to assume a life-like character's inwardness and to speculate about his 'motives' until he declares himself, and thus it positively encourages the habit of 'secret motive hunting'. Even before Hamlet speaks (in I. 2) we are expected to wonder why he alone wears black and behaves so oddly; after he has soliloquised several times we wonder (with Hamlet) why his stated motives and actions fail to tally; and throughout the play one passing remark after another challenges us to spot the motive. 'Art thou there, truepenny?' A strange phrase – what can be the reason for it? 'Buzz, buzz' (to Polonius) – the reason? 'Now could I drink hot blood' – the reason? The fact that Hamlet may later prove to be entirely 'unaware' of some of the motives imputed to him by no means invalidates the spectator's 'secret motive hunting' as such, a semi-conscious activity inseparable from a proper attentiveness to Shakespeare's dramatic language.

Naturally we only give this kind of attention to characters (or plays) that demand it. Hamlet's inwardness being manifestly more accessible than Osric's, we take it more seriously. And Hamlet's differs from Othello's, and this must affect the quality of the two plays as fundamentally as differences in imagery, tempo, ideas and so forth. Yet important as the subject undoubtedly is, we know next to nothing about the spectator's response to secret motives, thanks to all the frogs that croaked at Bradley. If we wish to examine the pos-sibilities we could do worse than turn to *Othello*, a tragedy in which the presenter, Iago, forever nudges the audience towards questions of character and motive, the only one in which the same questions still have their urgency in the closing moments, the only one in which a leading figure (and also Shakespeare) ostentatiously announces that his motives will not be divulged.

> *Othello*   Will you, I pray, demand that demi-devil
> Why he hath thus ensnar'd my soul and body?
> *Iago*   Demand me nothing. What you know, you know.
> From this time forth I never will speak word. (v 2. 304–7)

Even those who are not hostile to character-criticism sometimes write as if only clearly expressed motives deserve critical attention. 'From Johnson onwards', said Helen Gardner, 'the striking merit of *Othello* has always been recognized to lie in the individuality and vitality of the characters and the closeness of the interplay among them'; but, she went on, 'the play cannot be regarded as an attempt to objectify obscure and dark feelings that have not found full and clear expression, which it is left to the genius of the critic to expose'.[2] The collective genius of Shakespeare's best critics has nevertheless had its successes, and has exposed much more in *Othello* than I can summarise here. In what follows I shall therefore proceed selectively, my purpose being not so much to explain any single character in exhaustive detail as to drag a few secret motives into the open and to show how the audience responds to them.

*     *     *

If we may trust the most widely admired Shakespeare critics we have an outstanding example of 'secret motives' in Iago. Coleridge's phrase for the soliloquy at the end of Act I, 'the motive-hunting of motiveless malignity', whatever it means,[3] records a reluctance to accept Iago's *stated* motives; and Bradley seems now to have established that 'most of Iago's reasons for action are no more the real ones than Hamlet's reasons for delay were the real ones' – or so it seems, since later writers (such as Granville-Barker and W. H. Auden) have paid him the compliment of echoing his words without acknowledgement, and Helen Gardner herself declared that Bradley's study of Iago 'is perhaps his masterpiece'.[4] Provided that Iago's action is intelligible, which most actors and students of the play have taken for granted,[5] we must accordingly look for his other reasons for action, of which Iago himself remains unconscious. And they are not hard to find. Bradley made much of Iago's keen sense of intellectual superiority, and concluded that three closely related motives drove him on: his 'longing to satisfy the sense of power'; his pleasure in action that is perilous and therefore exciting; and his being an artist, 'a consummate schemer', who is infatuated by a drama that goes out of control. These are 'the chief ingredients of the force which, liberated by his resentment at Cassio's promotion, drives Iago from inactivity into action.'[6]

So far so good. Bradley may be said to follow the main stream of criticism, especially in his remarks on Iago as an artist, where he quotes Hazlitt and Swinburne. Yet the play also generates other potent impressions quite distinct from the ones mentioned by Bradley, and we distort it if we pass them over in silence. For example, those concerned with Iago's sexual imagery.

Let me begin by disposing of an impression attested independently by two experts in psychology: 'From the psycho-analytic point of view, Othello . . . turns upon sexual inversion, there being no possible motive for Iago's behaviour in destroying Othello and Desdemona except the rancour of the rejected and jealous lover of the Moor.'[7] Laurence Olivier tried to play Iago thus in 1938 and, according to Marvin Rosenberg, who has studied the reviews, 'hardly anyone could tell what Olivier's Iago was doing, and why'.[8] The proper answer to 'the psycho-analytic point of view' comes from L. C. Knights, commenting on the theory of 'repressed homosexuality' in *The Winter's Tale*: within the context of the play such information, even if correct, is irrelevant, since it is 'something that we *know about* instead of something we *respond to*'.[9] And most of us, I imagine, don't even know about it, unless we carry to the theatre a head stuffed with footnotes.

But there are other sexual implications that the audience may not consciously know about but certainly responds to. In the very first scene Shakespeare resorted to the most provocative imagery to introduce one of Iago's characteristic manœuvres, a central factor in all that ensues. 'You'll have your daughter cover'd with a Barbary horse', he tells Brabantio. 'Your daughter and the Moor are now making the beast with two backs . . .' It is a good, attention-catching opening, but it achieves far more than bustle and noise. For fifty lines the 'spotlight' is on Iago ('Call up her father' to 'You are – a Senator'), Brabantio remaining a shadowy figure in his bewildered replies: and in this brilliant sequence the medium almost obscures the message. For as long as possible the audience (and Brabantio) is kept in the dark as to precisely what has happened and it is Iago's gusto that transfixes us.

These fifty lines serve as a paradigm for Iago's later behaviour. To press distasteful sexual images upon unwilling listeners – he can never resist it. Preferably images that soil the listener's idea of a loved person, his daughter, mistress or wife. 'Poison his delight' (I. 1. 69) is the general formula, but as far as possible Iago employs one particular poison. For Roderigo's benefit he conjures up Desdemona 'sated' with Othello's body, and 'th' incorporate conclusion';[10] with Cassio he proceeds more cautiously, feeling his way ('she is sport for Jove') before he risks 'Well, happiness to their sheets!'[11] He plays a similar trick on Desdemona: speaking initially of Emilia ('She puts her tongue a little in her heart', II. 1. 106), he changes direction to include all women ('you are pictures out a-doors'), which permits him to say, to Emilia *and Desdemona*, 'you are . . . huswives in your beds', and, even more personally to Desdemona, because she took up his last remark, 'You rise to play, and go to bed to work.' Again, explaining the drunken brawl to Othello, who had just retired to bed for the first time with his wife, he has the impudence to say

> I do not know. Friends all but now, even now,
> In quarter, and in terms, *like bride and groom*
> *Divesting them for bed* . . . (II. 3. 171–3)

There could be a connection between the drive to fasten unwelcome sexual images upon others and Iago's self-inflicted pain, the suspicion that the lustful Moor, and also Cassio, 'hath leap'd into my seat'.[12]

The impression, not mentioned by Bradley, that Iago can never resist an opportunity to assault others in their imagination, affects my response to his central scenes with Othello. Here I am less conscious of malignancy (though this is present) than of an artist–explorer who sets out into uncharted territories, Othello's innermost being, thinking himself free to twist and turn in all directions, who slips unconsciously into a dangerous groove – a fixed behaviour-pattern. When Othello exclaims, 'Would I were satisfied!' (III. 3. 394) Iago cannot resist torturing him with detailed sexual imagery ('I lay with Cassio lately', and so on), and this becomes the play's turning-point. Had he wished, Iago could have explained away all the hints that went before as misunderstandings: after his description of Cassio's dream he can no longer go back, he has to go forward. At this crucial point he takes a tremendous risk, an unnecessary risk, insured by nothing more substantial than Desdemona's handkerchief: he cannot help taking it, I feel, being impelled by an imperious devil within demanding his own kinky satisfaction.

As in addressing Brabantio, Cassio, Roderigo and Desdemona, but with infinitely greater caution, Iago inches his victim to the brink of the verbally permissible. Despite his wonderful control of Othello's every reaction, however, Iago lacks perfect self-control, being carried away, as the scene grows to its crisis, by the impulse to make his sexual imagery more and more specific. In short, he indulges himself. Bradley sensed this weakness, without properly identifying it, when he described Iago as advancing 'to conclusions of which at the outset he did not dream', and as one who appears 'for moments . . . absolutely infatuated'.[13] Edging Othello from question to supposition, from the general to the particular, Iago's delight is unmistakable.

> Would you, the supervisor, grossly gape on . . .?
>                     Damn them, then,
> If ever mortal eyes do see them bolster . . .
> Were they as prime as goats, as hot as monkeys . . . (III. 3. 399–407)

At this point, of course, it is still a masked delight. But as he invents and describes Cassio's dream, and feels his hold upon Othello tightening, he gives his imagination free rein; and by the beginning of Act IV he can enjoy his favourite form of sadism with scarcely any need for preparation.

> *Iago*   Will you think so? *Othello*   Think so, Iago? *Iago*   What,
> To kiss in private? *Othello*   An unauthoriz'd kiss.
> *Iago*   Or to be naked with her friend abed
> An hour or more, not meaning any harm? (IV. 1. 1–4)

Bradley observed 'Iago's longing to satisfy the sense of power' and pleasure in perilous action, and added – 'his happiness was greater if the action was destructive'.[14] I think that we can define Iago's pleasure more exactly, and that it gives a very special colouring to some of the speeches with which he worms his way into Othello's mind. It remains a secret motive, in so far as Iago himself never consciously refers to it. Yet while not *discussed* in the play it is *exhibited*, in one dramatic episode after another, and sheer repetition cannot fail to have its effect. By the time the temptation-scene begins the audience knows Iago, even if it has not defined his 'pleasure' in so many words: and to equate Iago's self-knowledge with the audience's knowledge would be the most elementary of blunders, the more unpardonable since his half-hearted 'motive hunting' has been exhibited as well.

I must not conceal the fact that R. B. Heilman has proposed a very different reading of some of the passages cited above – namely, that Iago himself lusts after Desdemona and that sex rivalry drives him on. 'Beneath Iago's freely acknowledged hate there struggles a half-buried impulse', hence Iago constantly imagines Othello and Cassio experiencing sexual favours and he repeatedly 'undresses' Desdemona in imagination, because he 'can't stop nagging himself with his own torment'.[15] I find this hard to believe – but how are we to weigh 'a half-buried impulse' against 'a secret motive'? I would make the same point as before: when Iago 'undresses' Desdemona what is *exhibited* is not self-torment but his delight as he torments the listener.[16] Again: when he soliloquises about his 'love' of Desdemona, on a single occasion, he throws out the thought as part of a general review of the tactical possibilities (II. 1. 280ff.), and there is not the slightest sign that it matters to him or that he takes it seriously.[17] Without wishing to deny the impulse altogether, I would consign it to the dusty drawer of motives that we may know about (because Iago tells us) but cannot respond to (because Iago's 'pleasure' is more visible).

A second set of impressions, most of them duly noted by Bradley, also seems to me to work together and to produce another effect that he missed. 'Unless I am mistaken', said Bradley, of Iago, 'he was not of gentle birth or breeding . . . for all his great powers, he is vulgar, and his probable want of military science may well be significant'.[18] This, he added in a footnote, is merely 'a general impression', for there is no 'specific evidence'. The impression, as William Empson has shown, is more pervasive than Bradley realised. 'The posts of ancient and gentlewoman-in-waiting might be held by people of very varying status; the audience must use its own judgement': nevertheless 'an obscure social insult' often goes with the phrase 'honest Iago', a phrase repeatedly used by the socially superior Othello, Desdemona and Cassio; and even when they call him 'good Iago' this implies 'a less obtrusive form of the same trick of patronage'.[19] That others look down on Iago seems beyond dispute: what now needs to be stressed is his semi-secret response, and its connection with his stated motives. Why, for example, should he rage as he does when Cassio pays his respects to the ladies? Because any display of gentlemanliness touches him on the raw and Cassio, unluckily, enjoys preening himself.

> Let it not gall your patience, good Iago,
> That I extend my *manners*; 'tis my *breeding*
> That gives me this bold show of *courtesy*. (II. 1. 97–9)

Between that condescending 'good Iago' and the word 'Sir', with which the ancient replies, an Elizabethan audience must have recognised a familiar class-barrier. But what would it make of Iago's private reply, which follows seventy lines later? This comes in an aside of such bottled venom that it must have seemed quite out of proportion, had it not been carefully prepared for by other impressions.

> He takes her by the palm. Ay, well said, whisper. With as little a web as this will I ensnare as great a fly as Cassio. Ay, smile upon her, do; I will gyve thee in thine own *courtship*. You say true; 'tis so, indeed. If such tricks as these strip you out of your lieutenantry, it had been better you had not kiss'd your three fingers so oft, which now again *you are most apt to play the sir in*. Very good; well kissed! and *excellent courtesy*! 'Tis so, indeed. Yet again your fingers to your lips? Would they were clyster-pipes for your sake! (II. 1. 166ff.)

Iago proves equally sensitive later when the two noble Venetians, Gratiano and Lodovico, fail to treat him as an equal in Cyprus.

> *Gratiano*   This is Othello's ancient, as I take it.
> *Lodovico*   The same indeed; a very valiant fellow. (V. 1. 51–2)

Iago remembers their names, but they have forgotten his:

> *Iago*   Signior Lodovico?
> *Lodovico*   He, sir.

A cool greeting! Iago tries again, more insinuatingly:

> *Iago*   Signior Gratiano? I cry you gentle pardon;
> These bloody accidents must excuse my manners
> That so neglected you. *Gratiano*   I am glad to see you.

Not much better. Iago nevertheless continues to caress the Venetians with the word 'gentlemen' ('Light, gentlemen'; 'Gentlemen all, I do suspect this trash'; 'Stay you, good gentlemen'; 'Do you see, gentle-men?'; 'Kind gentlemen, let's go see poor Cassio dress'd');[20] and, as soon as he hears that Gratiano knows Roderigo he claims social equality by referring to the young snipe as his 'dear friend'. He even dares to address Cassio (who is in no condition to protest) as 'brother', a word as character-revealing as Othello's 'uncle'.[21] Throughout this episode the ancient's eagerness to be accepted as an equal by gentlemen is as manifest as Othello's elsewhere to be thought a Christian and a Venetian – and as isolating.

One of the puzzles in Iago's behaviour, according to Bradley, is that his motives appear and disappear in the most extraordinary manner. 'Resentment at Cassio's appointment is expressed in the first conversation with Roderigo, and from that moment is never once mentioned again in the whole play'.[22] Before we agree that Iago's motives disappear we must ask whether Bradley has correctly described the one in the opening conversation with Roderigo. It could be that Iago's initial feelings about Cassio's appointment form part of a much larger resentment, which floods into the play's open-ing scene and thereafter never disappears. Class-hatred, envy of privilege: it shows through when he contrasts Cassio's 'bookish theoric' with his own military 'practice' in the field, becomes clearer as he expatiates upon masters and servants (I. 1. 41–66), adds relish to his unprovoked attack upon wealthy Brabantio, and snarls un-disguisedly in 'You are – a Senator!' (I. 1. 119). Again I feel quite close to Bradley's general account of Iago's character, since he stressed the ancient's 'Keen sense of superiority' and contempt of others, added that 'his thwarted sense of superiority wants satis-faction', and elsewhere mentioned the impression that Iago was not of gentle birth.[23] As long as we fail to connect these impressions, however, we miss the logic of his motives: they are connected, I believe, by his class feeling, which gives a special edge to many of his best scenes. In performance, of course, Iago's accent and general deportment should help to bring such impressions into the open, though this has not always happened. The *Morning Chronicle* described Fechter's Iago as 'a bland and polished courtier, whose manner and appearance would grace the gondola of a princess or the levee of a Doge'; and Edwin Booth advised that 'to portray Iago properly you must seem to be what all the characters think, and say you are, not what the spectators know you to be . . . Be genial, some-times jovial, always gentlemanly'.[24] The other characters think of him as 'honest Iago', 'this fellow' and so on, Iago himself is aware of it – so the actor should rather suggest that Iago *would like to be gentlemanly* and that the mask sometimes slips.

Before we leave Iago's secret motives I must mention one more that has long been known to criticism. As Coleridge put it, Roderigo's complaint in the play's opening lines 'elicits a true feeling of Iago's – the dread of contempt habitual to those who encourage in themselves and have their keenest pleasure in the feeling and expression of contempt for others'.[25] The first scene, indeed, gives Iago so many different opportunities to express contempt that one might easily suppose that Shakespeare devised it for no other purpose. We hear that Othello, loving his own pride and purposes, has chosen a new lieutenant – and what was he? Forsooth, a great arithmetician, who knows no more about battles than a spinster, whose soldiership adds up to mere prattle without practice:

> this counter-caster
> He, in good time, must his lieutenant be,
> And I, God bless the mark! his Moorship's ancient. (I. 1. 31–3)

Notice how Iago's generalised feeling carries all before it, so that even he himself suddenly turns into that most contemptible thing, the lowest of the low, 'his Moorship's ancient'. A few lines later it transforms him again, though only hypothetically, when he sees himself wearing his heart upon his sleeve 'for daws to peck at'. But inevitably it is directed chiefly against others, the counter-caster, his Moorship, 'duteous' servants, Desdemona as the 'white ewe' tupped by an old black ram, Brabantio as a ridiculous, rich old man whose daughter has been stolen away. In later scenes the same contempt lavishes itself upon Roderigo who, again, seems to have been specially devised by Shakespeare to bring out this side of Iago, and upon Emilia, and it is never long from view.[26] We may call it conscious contempt, not really a secret motive – except that the audience knows more about it than Iago. His gaze is outward-looking, and he declares that he despises various individuals: yet for all his soliloquies he cannot look within, and he fails to realise that what impels him is not only contempt for Roderigo, Othello and others but contemptuousness as such, a corruption of the mind.

Let us now return to Iago's motiveless malignity and observe how it competes with his contemptuousness. As often as not his malignity is a stated fact, surprisingly void of feeling, whereas he feels his contemptuousness 'as immediately as the odour of a rose'.

> I hate the Moor;
> And it is thought abroad that 'twixt my sheets
> 'Has done my office. I know not if't be true; . . .
> The Moor is of a free and open nature
> That thinks men honest that but seem to be so;
> And will as tenderly be led by th' nose
> As asses are.
> I ha't – it is engender'd. (I. 3. 380–97)

He pursues his thoughts until he reaches a comfortable contemptuousness, breaking off when he gets 'home'. In the next soliloquy he again states his hatred ('The Moor, howbeit that I endure him not'), his mind again slides away towards contemptuousness and, having arrived there, rests: he will

> Make the Moor thank me, love me, and reward me,
> For making him egregiously an ass,
> And practising upon his peace and quiet
> Even to madness. 'Tis here, but yet confus'd . . . (II. 1. 302ff.)

In Iago's later soliloquies the hatred drops out, and contempt seems to be the only feeling he has for his principal victim: 'Work on/My medicine, work. Thus credulous fools are caught . . .'[27]

Iago's stated motives fail to be completely convincing because contrary impressions almost invariably interfere and undercut them. Too often they are stated rather than felt. If stated with feeling, we may sense a secondary motive apart from the one stated, as when Iago insists 'Though I do hate him as I do hell pains' (I. 1. 155): Roderigo had complained, 'Thou told'st me thou didst hold him in thy hate' (I. 1. 7), and his doubts have to be quietened. Some of the stated motives first appear as afterthoughts, or matter so little to him that he quickly forgets them.[28] We may observe how Shakespeare sets up contrary impressions from the soliloquy at the end of II. 1, where Iago's 'motives' enter his mind and declare themselves very strangely.

> That Cassio loves her, I do well believe it;
> That she loves him, 'tis apt and of great credit.
> The Moor, howbeit that I endure him not,

Is of a constant, loving, noble nature;
And I dare think he'll prove to Desdemona
A most dear husband. Now I do love her too,
Not out of absolute lust . . .

Trying to persuade himself that his plot will work Iago sees that it
all depends on the universality of lust, concerning which he had
just held forth to Roderigo (II. 1. 218ff.), sometimes loosely referring
to *lust* as *love*. That Cassio lusts for Desdemona seems plausible,
Iago thinks, that she lusts for him, "'tis apt and *of great credit'* (notice
the wishful thinking); the Moor will go on obeying the Law of Lust
as a doting husband; and come to think of it, Iago continues, snatch-
ing another example out of the air, 'I do love her too!' (the unspoken
thought being that this is reassuring, since it proves that the Law of
Lust applies generally, therefore Desdemona and Cassio must 'love',
therefore Iago's plot will work). Having adopted the position that
everyone lusts after everyone else he cites five hypothetical examples,
each more improbable than the last, and so two of the soliloquy's
three 'motives' (Iago's lust for Desdemona, his suspicion that Cassio
is Emilia's lover) enter his mind not so much as reasons for action
but as illustrations of the Law of Lust, that is, as by-products of a
fantasy. Only one of the three is supported by feeling –

I do suspect the lustful Moor
Hath leap'd into my seat; the thought whereof
Doth like a poisonous mineral gnaw my inwards

– and, as we know from other passages,[29] this is the only one of the
soliloquy's three 'motives' that Iago himself is inclined to take
seriously. The audience, however, cannot attach the same importance
to his jealousy, since it is contextually discredited: Iago feels his pang
just as he demonstrates that he can momentarily talk (or think) himself into believing anything, and the next instant he backs away
from the very feeling he has talked into existence:

. . . Doth like a poisonous mineral gnaw my inwards,
And nothing can nor shall content my soul
Till I am even'd with him, wife for wife;
*Or failing so*, yet that I put the Moor
At least into a jealousy so strong . . .

For various reasons Iago's stated motives fail to be completely convincing. The stated motives are concerned with other individuals, and too many of his grievances against Othello and Cassio seem to lack substance (hence the appeal of Coleridge's phrase, 'the motive-hunting of motiveless malignity'). That being so, the audience has to look elsewhere, away from Iago's malignity against other individuals: and his 'secret' motives, it now remains to be said, do in fact point elsewhere. They are all self-centred, being emotions expressive of personality, emotions that he radiates upon the world at large: sadistic pleasure in tormenting others (whoever they may be), envy of class privilege, contemptuousness, as well as more familiar Iago-symptoms such as self-delight as an artist.

In Iago's case, secret motives are not only exhibited again and again, much more often than his other motives are stated, they also support one another, each one being the more probable in so far as there are other signs of inner corruption. It would be wrong to suggest that they cancel all the stated motives (we have no reason to doubt that Iago resented Cassio's promotion, or that he hated the Moor). But, as the great majority of critics since Coleridge has acknowledged, they make their presence felt; and, I repeat, Shakespeare addressed a final question to Iago because he wanted the audience to think again about his motives, which had been a central preoccupation of the play.

Will you, I pray, demand that demi-devil
Why he hath thus ensnar'd my soul and body? (V. 2. 304–5)

\*          \*          \*

Although there is still argument about details, Iago's secret motives have the support of a long-standing critical tradition. It is as well to remind ourselves of this before we move on to Othello, who twins in so many scenes with Iago, whose gestation in Shakespeare's mind must have coincided with Iago's – and whose right to secret motives is still hotly disputed. Why should there be such a difference? Largely for one reason, I think: because F. R. Leavis reformulated the case for Othello and overstated it. Yet, as most recent commentators have found, Leavis cannot be ignored: he has asked important questions, he has changed our understanding of Othello.

First, then, a quick summary of Leavis's well-known essay (which, if possible, the reader should consult for himself.)[30] Leavis was dissatisfied with the traditional view of the play according to which the Moor 'is purely noble, strong, generous, and trusting, and as tragic hero is . . . merely a victim.' The truth is not so simple, he thought: Iago's power in the temptation-scene 'is that he represents something that is in Othello – in Othello the husband of Desdemona: the essential traitor is within the gates', and 'Iago is subordinate and merely ancillary'. For confirmation he pointed to a peculiarity of Othello's verse, his 'habit of self-approving self-dramatization', a form of self-idealisation which serves at times as 'the disguise of an obtuse and brutal egotism'. Leavis's general thinking about Othello's character therefore grew out of his response to the grand style (and, it should be noted in passing, he was always inclined to overstate the case against this kind of poetry).[31] The centre-piece of his argument is that, contrary to what is specifically asserted at the end of the play, Othello proved to be too easily jealous. 'As for the justice of this view that Othello yields with extraordinary promptness to suggestion, with such promptness as to make it plain that the mind that undoes him is not Iago's but his own, it does not seem to need arguing.'

Well, others have continued to argue; and in so far as they are concerned with 'something that is in Othello', an 'essential traitor' within the gates and Othello's 'self-deception' (all Leavis's words), they are arguing about secret motives. But, it should now be added, Leavis was by no means the first to interpret Othello in this way, and his general approach must not be brushed aside as newfangledness, or as merely polemical. Schlegel in 1815 wrote that 'the Moor *seems* noble, frank, confiding . . . but the mere physical force of passion puts to flight in one moment all his acquired and mere habitual virtues, and gives the upper hand to the savage over the moral man'.[32] Here we have the savage whose nobility is not all it seems, an idea that directly or indirectly influenced many critics and at least two of the most successful stage performances upon record, Salvini's and Olivier's. The *Athenaeum* described Salvini as a 'barbarian whose instincts, savage and passionate, are concealed behind a veneer of civilization so thick *that he is himself scarcely conscious he can be other than he appears*' (10 April 1875);[33] Olivier also played Othello with many primitive overtones, an interpretation that could point back to either Salvini or Leavis, or to both.

The theatre and earlier criticism give Leavis some support. But the weight of opinion has probably always been on the other side, regarding Othello as 'the noble Moor', more or less as he sees himself, 'fall'n in the practice of a damned slave' (v. 2. 295); and this was also the considered verdict of a great literary psychologist, one of the very few whose instinct in such matters rivals Shakespeare's own. Dostoyevsky, in *The Brothers Karamazov*, chose a subject somewhat like Shakespeare's and offered an interpretation of *Othello* in which the two points of view debated by Leavis are already embattled.

> 'Othello was not jealous, he was trustful,' observed Pushkin. And that remark alone is enough to show the deep insight of our great poet. Othello's soul was shattered and his whole outlook clouded simply because *his ideal was destroyed*. But Othello did not begin hiding, spying, peeping. He was trustful, on the contrary. He had to be led up, pushed on, excited with great difficulty before he could entertain the idea of deceit. The truly jealous man is not like that.[34]

Othello's trustfulness, though it may not by itself prove Leavis wrong, deserves a further comment. Othello not only trusts Desdemona but has a generally trusting nature.[35] When his confidence in Desdemona is undermined his trust attaches itself to Iago, it clings to him with an almost child-like surrender of intelligence. So, too, his trust in Venice, in the state to which he dedicated his life, seems ill-considered (from Othello's point of view), for it was a total trust and dangerously romantic. And his attitude to the magic handkerchief also seems too trusting, not to say superstitious, placed as it is after Brabantio's talk of spells and witchcraft, which was given such a cool reception in Act I.

There are good reasons for the traditional view of Othello as a trusting, loving, noble nature; and yet I am disturbed by Leavis's essay and think it would be wrong to refuse to learn from it. Must we really choose between the two? Leavis, I believe, overstated his case when he insisted that Iago is merely ancillary because 'the essential traitor is within the gates', thus making Othello more of a self-traitor than Adam's other descendants.

> But O, self-traitor, I do bring
> The spider love, which transubstantiates all,
>     And can convert manna to gall,
> And that this place may thoroughly be thought
>     True Paradise, I have the serpent brought.

What distinguishes Othello from mankind at large is not so much the traitor within the gates (we all have our private serpent), as a very special – and secret – sense of insecurity.

R. B. Heilman once argued along these lines, attempting to re-concile conflicting impressions of Othello's personality, the noble Moor and the brutal egotist – only to be told, alas, that it won't work in the theatre. 'It is difficult to see', said Helen Gardner, 'how any actor could present this "secretly unsure" Othello as he declaims Othello's magnificently confident lines.'[36] We must return, then, to Leavis's starting-point, Othello's style and the spectator's response to it, asking ourselves whether it sounds magnificently confident or magniloquent. Instead of listening first to the 'Othello music',[37] the well-known speeches that immediately spring to mind when we think of Shakespeare's Moor, let us begin with his other mode of speech, his 'business' voice.

> So please your Grace, my ancient;
> A man he is of honesty and trust.
> To his conveyance I assign my wife,
> With what else needful your good Grace shall think
> To be sent after me. . . .
> > Come, let us to the castle.
> News, friends: our wars are done; the Turks are drown'd.
> How do our old acquaintance of the isle?
> Honey, you shall be well desir'd in Cyprus . . .[38]

It has been said that Shakespeare had to find for Othello 'an idiom and vocabulary which distinguished him from the Europeans'.[39] The odd thing is that he can also speak like the Europeans, and only uses his special idiom on special occasions.

> Most potent, grave, and reverend signiors . . .

> Her father lov'd me, oft invited me . . .

> > O, now for ever
> Farewell the tranquil mind! farewell content! . . .[40]

Listening to these great dramatic arias I am conscious of Othello switching himself on and off, a feature that was disturbingly exaggerated in Paul Robeson's playing of the part. (Robeson spluttered and rasped out the 'business' dialogue, and more or less *sang* the great speeches.)

What makes the occasion special when Othello switches himself on, and what can be the secret motive? In a famous aside T. S. Eliot commented on the motive behind Othello's swan-song ('Soft you; a word or two before you go', v. 2. 341), and it may be that his perception has a wider relevance.

> What Othello seems to me to be doing in making this speech is *cheering himself up*. He is endeavouring to escape reality, he has ceased to think about Desdemona, and is thinking about himself . . . He takes in the spectator, but the human motive is primarily to take in himself. I do not believe that any writer has ever exposed this *bovarysme*, the human will to see things as they are not, more clearly than Shakespeare.[41]

It could be that the Othello music has the same function throughout the play. It is not Othello's 'natural' or only voice; he turns it on in certain situations, unconsciously, when he feels threatened, to cheer himself up. We have all known those who hum to themselves out of nervous habit: Othello *sings* defensively, and sings always the same cheering, invigorating song, the 'song of myself'.

Read out of context the Othello music may well impress us as magnificently confident. Yet as one 'song' succeeds another, usually in the same kind of context, the repeating situation acquires significance, as with Iago's secret motives, and we recognise that Othello merely puts on a parade of confidence (he idealises himself, as Leavis would say), sinking back into his 'business' voice when the danger has passed. The contrast between his two modes of speech is all-important in achieving this effect, and the context of the first few instances of the Othello music conditions and then fixes the response. In his first scene Othello no sooner hears that Brabantio will try to divorce him than he intones (and his confidence comes close to *boasting*, as he himself admits) –

> Let him do his spite.
> My services which I have done the signiory
> Shall out-tongue his complaints. 'Tis yet to know –
> Which, when I know that boasting is an honour,
> I shall promulgate – I fetch my life and being
> From men of royal siege . . . (I. 2. 17ff.)

When he defends himself before the senators of Venice (I. 3) the danger is clear enough, but not, perhaps, when he next switches on the Othello music, on his arrival in Cyprus.

It gives me wonder great as my content
To see you here before me. O my soul's joy!
If after every tempest come such calms,
May the winds blow till they have waken'd death . . . (II. 1. 181ff.)

This speech is more than just a wonderful expression of love if Othello
makes it a public demonstration, before the assembled Cypriot leaders,
in order to establish the fact of his (at that time) very strange marriage. There is an element of stylistic inflation, partly because the
Moor, though Governor of Cyprus, senses a threat as he claims his
wife, who is surrounded by white Cypriots.

In these early scenes of the play Othello covers up pretty well, and
perhaps, as Eliot said of the suicide-speech, 'he takes in the spectator'.
Notice, however, that as well as being placed in situations in which
any man must feel secretly unsure of himself (a stranger in Venice,
threatened by a magnifico and surrounded by men of another race),
Othello actually describes himself as a lover far from magnificently
confident. He saw that Desdemona listened to him with 'a greedy
ear' (I. 3. 149), he consented to tell her his life-story a second time,
was aware that it moved her to tears, and yet, though he loved her,
what did he do? Apparently nothing; poor Desdemona had to exert
herself to bring him to the point.

> My story being done,
> She gave me for my pains a world of sighs;
> She swore, in faith, 'twas strange, 'twas passing strange;
> 'Twas pitiful, 'twas wondrous pitiful.
> She wish'd she had not heard it; yet she wish'd
> That heaven had made her such a man. She thank'd me;
> And bade me, if I had a friend that lov'd her,
> I should but teach him how to tell my story,
> And that would woo her. Upon this hint I spake.

He never directly explains why Desdemona had to be 'half the wooer'
(I. 3. 176) and why so many hints were necessary, but the secret
motive is not far to seek. That Desdemona should run to the sooty
bosom of such a thing as Othello seems to Brabantio 'preposterous'
and, as he says three times, 'against all rules of nature'.[42] Othello,
we are left to infer, was secretly unsure of himself as a lover because
he too was conscious of the difference of race. And his insecurity in
later scenes (to which I shall return in a moment) points to the same
secret motive.

Othello's 'Moorishness' has been played down by many of those who try to explain the tragedy. 'In regard to the essentials of his character it is not important', said Bradley, while others have called it merely 'symbolic'.[43] An early student of Othello, perhaps the most gifted instinctive psychologist of them all, thought otherwise. With his uncanny genius for locating psychic wounds, Iago made as much as he dared of Othello's Moorishness, and the play as a whole confirms its importance.

Othello differs from Shakespeare's other tragic heroes in suffering from an ethnic and cultural split – the only other example being Cleopatra's Antony who, however, embraces his two cultures more comfortably, without strain. We can see what is distinctively Moorish in Othello when we compare his cry, 'O blood, blood, blood!' with Lear's 'Kill, kill, kill . . .!'[44] In Othello's case, a primitive blood-lust is supported by other barbaric desires – 'I'll tear her all to pieces!', 'O, I see that nose of yours, but not that dog I shall throw it to', 'I will chop her into messes!'[45] The desire to rip and slash and mutilate would have little significance on its own, but combined as it is with Othello's monumental dignity elsewhere it sets him apart from the other tragic heroes, reminding us of portraits of the noble savage (such as Melville's Queequeg), and helps to identify him as, inalienably, a Moor.

A Moor, yet one that desperately wants to be a Venetian. As in some of Shakespeare's other tragedies, signs of the hero's 'secret' are there from the start, and in Act v a single word forces it into the open. 'Name not the god, thou boy of tears'.[46] We hear Othello's give-away word twice: 'I scarce did know you, uncle', 'Uncle, I must come forth'.[47] Since the audience had not been informed of Gratiano's connection with Desdemona it is a double surprise that the Moor should claim kinship with him after Desdemona's death, and this throws a sudden light on his tragic need to be accepted as a Venetian. In his very last moments the same secret motive surfaces again, when he recalls an incident that sums up his life:

in Aleppo once,
Where a malignant and a turban'd Turk
Beat a Venetian and traduc'd the state,
I took by th' throat the circumcis'd dog
And smote him – thus.

Among other things, the 'turban'd Turk' stands for the pagan part of himself that survives beneath his Christianity, the 'Moorishness' that Othello had tried to renounce.[48]

There is some evidence, then, for an Othello secretly unsure of himself in his switching on of his 'music', his account of himself as a lover, his desire to be accepted as a Venetian. We may not notice it in Act I, but in Act III the signs cannot be ignored, particularly those connected with his Moorishness. To illustrate what I mean, let us glance at Henry James's masterpiece, *The Golden Bowl*, where Maggie, the heroine, knows that her husband and her friend Charlotte have a special relationship, and needs no proof. She knows of no technical infidelity but, as Mrs Assingham remarks, 'It isn't a question of . . . proof, absent or present; it's inevitably, with her, a question of natural perception, of insurmountable feeling. She irresistibly *knows* that there's something between them'.[49] Othello lacks the insurmountable feeling that ties lovers together and that should have shored up his faith in Desdemona; he lacks it because of the racial gap between them, which is such that his instinct cannot reassure him that he truly and profoundly *knows* Desdemona. Iago perceives this insecurity, and stresses that Othello cannot know how loosely Venetian women live, how strangely Desdemona loves – and Othello has no answer; or rather, he concedes the point. 'I know our country disposition well', Iago begins (he implies '*you* don't know it, as you don't belong to *our country*'):

> In Venice they do let God see the pranks
> They dare not show their husbands; their best conscience
> Is not to leave't undone, but keep't unknown.
> *Othello*   Dost thou say so?
> *Iago*   She did deceive her father, marrying you;
> And when she seem'd to shake and fear your looks
> She lov'd them most. *Othello*   And so she did! (III. 3. 206ff.)

As Helen Gardner has finely observed, 'the tragic experience with which this play is concerned is loss of faith'.[50] The first phase of the 'temptation' draws to its crisis when Iago dares to point a slow, unmoving finger at Othello's secret insecurity, his Moorishness (III. 3. 232ff.), which severely damages his faith in Desdemona, and also his faith in himself. Now, reminded of his own distance from Desdemona in 'clime, complexion and degree', he admits to himself in so many words that Iago *knows more*, and his inner timbers begin to part.

Farewell, farewell.
If more thou dost perceive, let me know more . . .

Why did I marry? This honest creature doubtless
Sees and knows more – much more than he unfolds . . .

This fellow's of exceeding honesty,
And knows all qualities, with a learned spirit,
Of human dealing. (III. 3. 242–64)

Looking at Othello as a noble Moor overthrown by Iago's devilish
cunning *and* by his own secret insecurity as a Moor (especially in his
relations with Desdemona), I am struck by the fact that the play's
two principal characters, who repeat each other in their stated
motives, as jealous husbands bent on revenge, also resemble each
other in their secret motives. Iago's resentment of class privilege
makes him as much the outsider in society as Othello's Moorishness;
both men want to be accepted, and both react with a quite irrational
'malignity' when they think themselves rejected. But of course there
are important differences as well: Iago's secret motives are paraded
from the very first scene, Othello's are scarcely observed at the beginning and never insist on our noticing them, as do Iago's. If secret
motives help to determine the depth and quality of a play, as I have
rashly assumed (not without moral support from Coleridge, Bradley
and other perceptive readers), we must not imagine that they all
work in the same way, or that they are all equally 'secret' as far as
the audience is concerned.

*          *          *

So far I have dealt with selected motives that appear to run right
through the play, and I have discussed only two characters. As we
watch a performance, however, we are usually obliged to fill in for
ourselves the unacknowledged motives of all the characters actively
engaged in a scene, including some that have a purely local significance. At one extreme we ask ourselves 'What makes Iago tick?',
and at the other 'Why should Roderigo stand so limply?' (a sign of
vacuity? or perhaps just a tired actor?). In between there will be a
huge variety of statements and actions that each spectator has to
explain to himself, more or less consciously, for in Shakespeare's
plays as in other old masters we are invited to contemplate the full-
ness of life –

Where the dogs go on with their doggy life and the torturer's horse
Scratches its innocent behind on a tree –

and we have to account for every detail. The impact of the plays, I
believe, will be partly a product of our 'secret motive' hunting, a
creative responsibility assigned to every spectator.

To illustrate a few of the tasks left to the spectator let us consider
a transition-sequence in which, we may mistakenly think, very little
happens. The short episode of Desdemona's arrival in Cyprus
(II. 1. 67–180) has been admired (by Granville-Barker), and also
deplored (by M. R. Ridley) as 'one of the most unsatisfactory passages
in Shakespeare'.[51] It is distasteful, the latter complained, to watch
Desdemona 'engaged in a long piece of cheap backchat with Iago,
and so adept at it that one wonders how much time on the voyage
was spent in the same way.'

The first point to notice is that Shakespeare invented the episode.
In his source, Cinthio's tale from *Hecatommithi*, the Moor 'embarked
on board the galley with his wife', as one would expect, and he and
she sailed together. Not so in the play – but why not? Partly, we
must conclude, because Shakespeare wanted to exhibit his supporting
characters in just such a scene, and not only to stimulate suspense
about Othello's safety, as Granville-Barker would have it. The play
slows down, Desdemona and the rest are left with little to do – and
so the spectator observes the more closely what they do, and has time
to ask himself why. Is Cassio too enthusiastic about 'the divine
Desdemona' and perhaps in love with her, as Iago had hinted?
Shakespeare suggests this thought, then eliminates it when Cassio
speaks with equal enthusiasm of Othello, and quite unenviously.

> Great Jove, Othello guard,
> And swell his sail with thine own powerful breath,
> That he may bless this bay with his tall ship,
> Make love's quick pants in Desdemona's arms,
> Give renew'd fire to our extincted spirits ...

The spectator notes, too, that all may not be well between Iago and
Emilia (provided that she shows some resentment in 'You ha little
cause to say so'; otherwise the passage, II. 1. 100ff., could be misunderstood as domestic comedy). And what is the ensign's precise
social position, and his attitude to it? He 'crowds' Cassio out of the
conversation (and easy-going Cassio seems not to mind); on the face

of it Iago entertains Desdemona, his social superior, yet he 'crowds' her as well, when he says 'You rise to play, and go to bed to work' and when he keeps on teasing her with the same sex-joke.[52] How cleverly he steers the dialogue, and with what wonderful facility he can improvise, making up his doggerel as he goes along! And how galling, when he has exhibited all his 'gentlemanly' graces (implicitly claiming something close to sexual and social equality), to be so nonchalantly put in his place by Cassio: 'He speaks home, madam. You may relish him more in the soldier than in the scholar.'

Much as we learn about Iago,[53] however, Shakespeare also needed the episode to place Desdemona, and in particular to reveal her 'secret' attitude to men. An extravagantly romantic young lady, who has lived too sheltered a life to know the way of the world? Othello's account of his wooing gave her that image, and Shakespeare now modifies it. The 'maiden never bold' who married the Moor knows enough about men and their attitudes to women to participate competently, if reluctantly, in a game of innuendo.[54] (Perhaps Cassio listens silently because this comes as a surprise to him.) The impression still lingers in Act III, where we are left to infer that Desdemona fails to control her fate not out of a general ignorance of men but because she does not know her husband. If there is some truth in Leavis's view of Othello as ignorant of Desdemona, she, to the same extent, is also 'obtuse' about his reactions. Later, when she asks Emilia whether she thinks, in conscience, 'that there be women do abuse their husbands' (IV. 3. 60), she returns with a quickened curiosity to the same area of conversation, social gossip about sexual behaviour, since her former knowledge has been superseded by her experience.

In this short conversational interlude the spectator fills in unspoken motives (only a few of which I have mentioned), and adjusts his image of the characters. Yet although secret motives exert some pressure here (especially Iago's wish to perform well as a 'gentleman'), they raise more urgent questions in some later scenes, where the spectator has to attend to them more consciously. Take Iago's last meeting with Desdemona (IV. 2. 107–72): why, we wonder, should she send for him at all? And, when he arrives, why can she not speak? Is it that her instinct warns her against him, or can she not bring herself to talk to another man about her husband, or is she merely reluctant to repeat Othello's words? And why should Emilia suddenly scent the truth ('I will be hang'd if some eternal villain . . .

Have not devis'd this slander'), and having got so near, fail to recognise the eternal villain whom she so accurately describes? A few of the secret motives are soon to be disclosed, though not before the spectator has tried to guess them (for example when Desdemona cries 'O God! Iago,/What shall I do to win my lord again?'), but observe that we have to interest ourselves in Desdemona's and Emilia's unacknowledged thoughts and motives just as the play turns round upon itself and also compels us to speculate afresh about Iago's. For, intensely moved as we are by Desdemona's anguish, the episode's stress-lines converge of course upon Iago, and we are interested above all in *his* unspoken thoughts. Can he avoid being moved as well? How pleased is he with what he has done? Face to face at last with 'love' in its purest form, a love that pardons him though he has not confessed (IV. 2. 136), a love that kneels though wrongly accused and that exerts an almost irresistible moral pressure, can 'malignity' hold out?

Actors and producers have always understood that the audience will be keenly interested in Iago's secret motives in this episode, and have tried to help in various ways. Too many, regrettably, choose to 'tell all', as did John Vandenhoff in 1839. 'He here advanced to the front, and his features disclosed alternate emotions of rage and fear; at length, overpowering both, cunning resumes its sway, as he answers – "Fye! there is no such man."' Wilson Knight, on the other hand, proposed that the actor should give nothing away.

> The effect on Iago is left by Shakespeare unregistered. To follow Shakespeare, let Iago turn up-stage after Desdemona's exit and stand with his back to the audience. Iago must not be shown as positively callous of her pathetic position, nor as deeply moved by it. He speaks courteously enough to her. It is just outside his inhuman attention. I do not think that the producer should commit himself.[55]

Yet in the Globe theatre Iago could not have turned his back to the audience, which more or less surrounded the stage. And, as Goddard has shown,[56] the *effect* on Iago is not completely concealed from the audience, even though his thoughts remain a secret.

When Desdemona goes out, Roderigo enters, and in the first part of what ensues we see Iago for the first time at his wit's end, unable to devise anything by way of answer to Roderigo's importunities. In his brief and stalling replies to his dupe's reiterated complaints Shakespeare is plainly registering the profound and disturbing effect that Desdemona – and incidentally Emilia – has just had on him. She has sapped his power.

In the scene with Desdemona Iago also gives stalling replies because her emotion confounds him, being utterly beyond his expectation and imaginative range (as indeed are all forms of love). For a while he flounders (to 'Do not weep, do not weep. Alas the day!', IV. 2. 125), then he sets his teeth and decides to brazen it out. But here, and in the next scene, the audience sees just enough of his secret confusion to be itself perplexed – and therefore, I think, it cannot respond quite as straightforwardly as Bradley suggested, with 'burning hatred and burning tears.'[57]

Secret motives have a special importance in the play's concluding scene. When Emilia exclaims 'My husband!' she reviews her marriage, and thereafter she all but visibly weighs her obligations to Iago against her feeling for Desdemona, 'the sweetest innocent/That e'er did lift up eye.' Othello, likewise, goes through a painful process of readjustment – more 'secretly' than Emilia, so that each of his three attempts to kill[58] comes as a surprise to the other characters and to the audience. We know even less of Iago's inner processes when, exposed in all his villainy, he stands before us at last a helpless prisoner. Yet, again and again, as one discovery follows another and the survivors express their horror, Shakespeare directs attention back to the fixed point on the stage around whom all else still revolves – and to the mystery of mysteries, his secret motives.

# 7
# Lear's Mind

The greatness of Lear is not in corporal dimension, but in intellectual: the explosions of his passion are terrible as a volcano: they are storms turning up and disclosing to the bottom that sea, his mind, with all its vast riches. It is his mind which is laid bare . . . while we read [the tragedy] we see not Lear, but we are Lear, – we are in his mind. (Charles Lamb)[1]

How shall we explain the irresistible power of *King Lear*, considered by many to be Shakespeare's greatest tragedy? If Lamb meant that we identify ourselves with the hero ('we see not Lear, but we are Lear'), this will be less true of our experience in the theatre than when we are readers, as Lamb acknowledged: 'to see an old man tottering about the stage with a walking-stick, turned out of doors by his daughters in a rainy night, has nothing in it but what is painful and disgusting.' It would be fair to add that in the theatre many of the characters arouse pain and disgust, not only the old king. From the very first scene they rage at one another, which cannot endear them to the audience, and soon advance from verbal to physical assaults, culminating in the most horrific stage-spectacle in Shakespeare's mature work, the blinding of Gloucester, and the most bewilderingly shocking death, Cordelia's. The tragedy's power depends significantly on its manifold alienation techniques, on its sheer unpleasantness, and many have thought it 'certainly the most terrible picture that Shakespeare painted of the world. In no other of his tragedies does humanity appear more pitiably infirm or more hopelessly bad'.[2] Keats, as is well known, paid less attention to the tragedy's 'disagreeables'. 'The excellence of every art is its intensity, capable of making all disagreeables evaporate, from their being in close relationship with Beauty and Truth. Examine 'King Lear', and you will find this exemplified throughout...'[3] Rather than ask whether Gloucester's blinding 'evaporates' as painlessly in the theatre as when we merely read the play, we may concede that in several of the other tragedies intensity and disagreeables also play their part, and that the special impact of *King Lear* requires a special explanation. As I shall argue, Lear differs from the other tragic heroes in various important ways: whether or not 'we are in his mind', as Lamb believed, his mind works very strangely, we have constantly to adjust to its vagaries, and this affects our response to the play as a whole.

(i) Watching a performance, a modern audience sometimes laughs in the wrong places.[4] The Jacobeans, who visited madhouses for entertainment, could well have reacted even more unfeelingly. Aware of the danger, Shakespeare tried to deflect them from a stock-response in Lear's maddest scenes: the mock trial lasts a mere thirty-five lines (III. 6. 20–55), then, just as the audience recovers from its first surprise, stage-commentators interrupt:

> Kent   O pity! Sir, where is the patience now
> That you so oft have boasted to retain?
> Edgar [Aside]   My tears begin to take his part so much
> They mar my counterfeiting.

In Lear's next scene, as soon as he enters 'fantastically dressed with weeds', Edgar guides the audience to the correct response: 'O thou side-piercing sight!' And at the end of the same episode, when Lear runs off-stage pursued by attendants, and the audience could easily have been pulled in the wrong direction, Shakespeare firmly checks it.

> Gent.   A sight most pitiful in the meanest wretch,
> Past speaking of in a king!

In no other mature tragedy has Shakespeare to contend with the problem of unwanted laughter on anything like the same scale.

(ii) Lear's age and social status also create unusual difficulties. Being so much older than the other tragic heroes, his relationships with secondary characters have to be different. He alone, of all the tragic heroes, never interests us as a husband or lover; he alone comes to life, emotionally speaking, through his children – from whom the play immediately separates him. Having occupied an almost god-like position in society he differs from the other tragic heroes in being unable to accept lesser mortals as his equals, clinging to 'the name and all th' addition of a king' (I. 1. 135) even when he gives up his kingdom. Age, family relationships and social position cut him off from human fellowship even more than his race isolates Othello, since Lear may not express any heart-warming, genuinely other-

directed emotions until half-way through the play. Though he calls
Cordelia 'our joy', and exhorts her to bid for 'a third more opulent
than your sisters', this is a self-centred love with more than a trace
of favouritism, an old man's folly, not an emotion that the audience
is expected to rejoice in. And when he begins to reach out less
spuriously to other human beings he still sees himself as king and
asks for no return of fellow-feeling.

> Poor fool and knave, I have one part in my heart
> That's sorry yet for thee. (III. 2. 72–3)

> Poor naked wretches, wheresoe'er you are,
> That bide the pelting of this pitiless storm,
> How shall your houseless heads and unfed sides,
> Your loop'd and window'd raggedness, defend you
> From seasons such as these? O, I have ta'en
> Too little care of this! (III. 4. 28ff.)

Naturally we give him credit for thinking of others. But only 'one
part' in his heart feels for the Fool, Lear being preoccupied with his
own troubles; and in his 'prayer' for poor naked wretches he speaks
to the winds, not face to face with human misery. Fellow-feeling, in
the full sense of the word, comes to him very slowly.

(iii)   Less attractive feelings come far too quickly, and make it difficult for the audience to admire him, or even to like him. Every hour
'he flashes into one gross crime or other' (I. 3. 5): though the words
are Goneril's they point to an important truth – that Lear cannot
check his own aggressiveness.

> Goneril   Did my father strike my gentleman for chiding of his
> fool?
> Oswald   Ay, madam.
> Goneril   By day and night he wrongs me . . .

We have no reason to disbelieve them for the whole play dwells on
Lear's propensity to *strike*, and closes with a character-revealing
tribute to his 'servant Caius'.

> Strike flat the thick rotundity o' th' world!

> And when I have stol'n upon these son-in-laws,
> Then kill, kill, kill, kill, kill, kill!

He's a good fellow, I can tell you that;
He'll strike, and quickly too.[5]

Lear's aggressiveness alienates the audience most of all, I think, in his face-to-face exchanges with individuals. 'Come not between the dragon and his wrath', he warns Kent, then the dragon in him quickly rouses, a monster of rage, to banish a truly well-meaning subject. Turning against Goneril in a speech that has always been 'considered crucial in winning or losing audience sympathy',[6] his terrible curse (I. 4. 275ff.) overtops all that she has so hatefully said: greatly provoked though he was, an audience must shudder at his implacable passion.

Even the love-test in Scene 1 partakes of Lear's alienating aggressiveness. Ever since Coleridge it has been customary to dismiss it as a gross improbability – either a ritual, a 'naked myth', in which 'all questions of motivation are bypassed', or an arbitrary nursery-tale device for starting the story and scarcely a part of it, from which attention is forced away 'the moment it has answered its purpose'.[7] If so, why did Shakespeare place thirty lines of natural, conversational prose before the love-test, the effect of which is to make Lear's behaviour even more grossly improbable? The love-test, being the first of Lear's many improbable tests,[8] expresses his character quite as perfectly as it starts the story, a nursery-tale idea appropriate for one who wishes to retire to a nursery (I. 1. 123), a waywardness (I. 1. 297) in keeping with his other follies. Unlike the plan to divide the kingdom, which was known before (I. 1. 1ff.), Lear's 'darker purpose' to test his daughters comes as an old man's nasty surprise, by no means softened by his round-about approach, almost a sadistic surprise in the final phrasing – 'Which of you *shall we say* doth love us most?' O, as Coleridge might have exclaimed, the infinite suggestiveness of that *shall we say!* He has them at his mercy, a rich old man making his will, the circus-animals have to perform, and it is not a pretty sight. He invites them to *say*, he may even repeat what they *say*, but hints that saying is not believing. (The *we* of *shall we say* could refer to himself as in the next line, or to the world at large.) Far from being an artistic embarrassment the love-test is a foretaste of all that follows, not least of Lear's darting aggressiveness.

(iv)  Lear's sadism becomes more marked as the play proceeds, and also distinguishes him from the other tragic heroes. Macbeth commits more murders, yet what we are chiefly conscious of is his horror of

murder, his struggle to maintain his humanity. Lear kills only one
man, perhaps justly (V. 3. 274), but in scene after scene luxuriates in
murderous fancies:

> You nimble lightnings, dart your blinding flames
> Into her scornful eyes!

> Now all the plagues that in the pendulous air
> Hang fated o'er men's faults light on thy daughters!

> To have a thousand with red burning spits
> Come hizzing in upon 'em![9]

Who is more guilty – Macbeth, straining away from murder and
never delighting in it, or the old king, whose mind never stops hunting after the most exquisite tortures? –

> I will have such revenges on you both
> That all the world shall – I will do such things –
> What they are yet I know not; but they shall be
> The terrors of the earth. (II. 4. 278ff.)

Macbeth's imagination pulls the audience towards him, Lear's too
often repels. And Lear's even includes the audience in its denunciations, wishing destruction upon the world, engulfing all mankind in
its hatred:

> And thou, all-shaking thunder,
> Strike flat the thick rotundity o' th' world;
> Crack nature's moulds, all germens spill at once
> That makes ingrateful man! (III. 2. 6–9)

Only Timon can compare with Lear in generalised hatred, and in
both plays Shakespeare pointed their hatred more or less directly at
the audience. The platform-stage would make such speeches particularly effective:

> Tremble, thou wretch,
> That hast within thee undivulged crimes!

> I pardon that man's life. What was thy cause?

> Behold yond simp'ring dame . . .[10]

(v) Shakespeare's use of the initial stage-response also distinguishes
*King Lear* from the other tragedies. Normally the stage-response first

magnifies the tragic hero, before it turns decisively against him in the second or third act. Macbeth is 'full of growing' until after the murder, *brave* and *noble* and *worthy* as seen from outside, and no one does more than Duncan to 'plant' him favourably with the audience: 'O valiant cousin! worthy gentleman!' Antony, though first described by a hostile speaker and thereafter ridiculed by Cleopatra, benefits from Octavius' grudging praise and Cleopatra's despondency in his absence (I. 4. 55ff., I. 5), surviving in magnificence until Actium. In Lear's case the stage-response works against him more consistently from the first scene: Cordelia cannot let her love speak out, and Kent's one well-disposed utterance is merely conciliatory:

> Royal Lear,
> Whom I have ever honour'd as my king
> Lov'd as my father, as my master follow'd,
> As my great patron thought on in my prayers . . .

And then Kent swings the response irresistibly against Lear, whose *folly* and *hideous rashness* in the love-test Shakespeare insists on driving home, not only in Goneril and Regan's dialogue at the end of Scene 1 but in the Fool's riddling and in Lear's self-reproaches:

> O Lear, Lear, Lear!
> Beat at this gate that let thy folly in . . . (I. 4. 270)

It would be wrong to pretend that the stage-response remains unaltered throughout the play. Shakespeare, however, depriving Lear of the praise that he lavished on other tragic heroes in Act I, set him on an unusual course, one that experienced producers have thought too difficult for an actor precisely because the audience's first response lingers on too long.

> The 'poor, infirm, weak and despis'd old man' has too much to answer for. It is here, I believe, that Shakespeare's unsparing treatment of Lear in the early scenes does him, and us, the greatest disservice. We, in the theater, cannot be brought to ignore the shortcomings of the stage illusions because we are not swept away by the man himself; we stand aloof from him . . .[11]

&ast; &ast; &ast;

From the start, then, Lear is at a disadvantage in his relations with the audience. I have left aside the greatest difficulty, however, the functioning of Lear's mind, which makes special demands upon the audience even before the 'mad' scenes begin. Ever since Lamb drew attention to the 'vast riches' of Lear's mind others have recognised that it presents a challenge – but few have gone treasure-hunting in that misty territory. One of the few, Henry James, reported that 'the agents in any drama are interesting only in proportion as they feel their respective situations.' There are degrees of feeling, he went on, the highest kind being 'the power to be finely aware and richly responsible'. 'It is those moved in this latter fashion who "get most" out of all that happens to them and who in doing so enable us, as readers . . . also to get most. Their being finely aware – as Hamlet and Lear, say, are finely aware . . . gives the maximum of sense to what befalls them.'[12] Hamlet and Lear! Two minds could scarcely be more unlike. And yet, though we may prefer to call Lear finely unaware and richly irresponsible, the comparison with Hamlet is illuminating: the old king's mind no longer functions smoothly but in its own way it rivals Hamlet's for range of feeling and thought, and it would not be too much to claim that the tragic hero's mind, as much as any other single factor, places *Hamlet* and *King Lear* at the pinnacle of Shakespeare's achievement.

As soon as we try to advance from Lamb's or James's generalities to the thing itself, Lear's unaccommodated mind proves as elusive as all buried treasure. Lear exists in a twilight world of acute perception and withdrawal, of poetry and gabble; whereas Hamlet's mind works as a wonderfully efficient instrument, a surgeon's knife probing the imposthumes of society, Lear wields an axe, he hacks at man's false pretensions, denouncing or cursing, then retreats one knows not whither, and mutters to himself in the soul's recesses. Quite apart from his madness in Acts III and IV, and his enfeebled condition in Act V, Lear seems from the first less completely present than the other characters. Kent, Gloucester and Edmund start the play with easy conversation but Lear orates, reporting on things determined elsewhere, and he appears to catch up with the here and now only when the fine phrases stop.

*Cordelia*   Nothing, my lord.
*Lear*   Nothing!
*Cordelia*   Nothing.
*Lear*   Nothing will come of nothing! Speak again.

We have the same sense of his awakening from an inner world when

Goneril complains of his insolent retinue. ('Are you our daughter?'
I. 4. 216), and when he discovers Kent in the stocks (II. 4. 14ff.); and
most of all in his scenes with the Fool, who tries to engage his mind
when it tugs in a contrary direction.

Lear is the most inaccessible of the tragic heroes, as far as the other
dramatic characters are concerned. They fail to 'get through' to him,
either because he cannot understand or because he will not listen or,
in the middle scenes, because his wits have turned. He not only
retires from cares of state, he withdraws more and more from human
contact: he rushes away from Goneril ('Away, away!' I. 4. 289),
retreats into the storm, escapes Cordelia (IV. 4. 1), runs away from the
Gentleman (IV. 6. 205), and finally looks forward to prison, where he
and Cordelia can withdraw for good: 'We two alone will sing like
birds i' th' cage' (V. 3. 9). And when things go badly for him he
retires into the inner self, where no one can follow – we hear him
talking to himself but feel shut out from his inwardness, a retreat
more impenetrable than Hamlet's or Othello's, because we hear only
a part of a continuing private dialogue, Lear answering himself:

> No, I will be the pattern of all patience;
> I will say nothing. (III. 2. 37–8)
> No, they cannot touch me for coining; I am the King himself
> (IV. 6. 83–4)

Torn open by grief and rage, pitifully exposed by madness, the
quintessential Lear shrinks into a secret place and wards off the pry-
ing world with his characteristic verbal gesture, negation, which is
psychologically necessary to him as he tries to maintain his identity.

> No, you unnatural hags,
> I will have such revenges on you both . . .

> You think I'll weep.
> No, I'll not weep.

> No, I will weep no more.

> No, no, no, no! Come, let's away to prison.[13]

He holds off the world – including the audience, which finds him the
most inaccessible and unknowable hero of all the central tragedies.

Lear, when on-stage, is present and not present, his mind operating
in its own distinctive way even before the storm unsettles his brain.

And after the storm has done its worst his mind still works in its own
way, though not quite as previously: comparing his mad speeches
with those of poor Tom, who rambles on in a style that sounds close
to authentic Bedlam ('Do, de, de, de. Sessa! Come, march to wakes
and fairs . . .') we observe that while Lear occasionally sinks to the
same level he also struggles so desperately to understand, in the
central 'mad' scenes, that we have to give him a different kind of
attention. Uttering 'reason in madness' Lear retains a precarious
contact with the world: his mind slips, surrendering to fixed ideas,
then steadies again and grapples with real problems (justice, ingrati-
tude, man's inhumanity to man); and, though his words may not
hang together as neatly as do those of less tormented speakers, we
marvel at his intermittent insights. Sane or mad, Lear therefore
participates in the life around him fitfully, switching himself on and
off, recognising only what suits him and otherwise retreating where
he cannot be followed – a mental habit often translated into visual
terms, most revealingly in I. 4. 288–310, where he chooses not to wait
for replies but switches himself off *physically* by twice rushing off-
stage.

His mental processes are also quite distinctive in what I shall call
(perhaps misleadingly) the 'Lear soliloquies'. Lest it be said that he
never soliloquises, I refer to the many occasions when, instead of
conversing with others, he talks to himself – a form of speech that
begins in I. 5, often indistinguishable from true soliloquy or aside in
that we believe him to be thinking aloud and cannot always tell
whether or not other stage-characters are supposed to hear him. As
far as the audience is concerned Lear's thoughts are 'externalised'
more and more as he approaches madness, and the internal and
external melt into one another. Closely related to the soliloquies,
Lear's curses and invocations also externalise the internal, not so
directly as Hamlet's introspective soliloquies but still as utterances
dragged forth from the inner man, soliloquy at one remove: we can
imagine Goneril, tight-lipped, looking away from her father as he
repudiates her,[14] Albany staring uncomprehendingly, and Lear's curse
turning him into a man talking to himself ('Hear, Nature, hear',
I. 4. 275). In many of these speeches Lear addresses imagined beings
that he appears to see, while the stage-characters recede from his
vision; they displace the world about him as they press into his
mind, poor naked wretches, a rascal beadle,[15] and sometimes his mind
can scarcely keep up with them.

Tremble, thou wretch,
That hast within thee undivulged crimes
Unwhipp'd of justice. Hide thee, thou bloody hand;
Thou perjur'd, and thou simular man of virtue
That art incestuous; caitiff, to pieces shake,
That under covert and convenient seeming
Hast practis'd on man's life . . . (III. 2. 51ff.)

Though often in the imperative mood and to all appearance outward-looking, Lear's 'soliloquies' and denunciations describe what
only he can see and thus disclose an interior landscape no less than
Hamlet's, whether he talks of Goneril's hypothetical child (I. 4. 275ff.)
or of Goneril herself as 'a disease that's in my flesh' (II. 4. 221ff.):

If she must teem,
Create her child of spleen, that it may live
And be a thwart disnatur'd torment to her.

thou art a boil,
A plague-sore, or embossed carbuncle
In my corrupted blood.

In the second passage Lear describes what he sees in imagination,
unlike some of Shakespeare's other name-callers, who toss around
their terms of abuse like so many interchangeable objects.

*Apemantus*  Beast!
*Timon*  Slave!
*Apemantus*  Toad!
*Timon*  Rogue, rogue, rogue! (*Timon* IV. 3. 369ff.)

Even when Lear addresses the storm he describes what he *imagines*,
his inward eye presenting cataracts and hurricanoes, drenched
steeples, submerged weathercocks; he thinks not only of a particular
storm but of a Deucalian catastrophe overwhelming all created
things, a return to Chaos. So, too, when he declaims against the evil
in man and woman ('Down from the waist they are centaurs . . .',
'Thou rascal beadle . . .', IV. 6. 124, 160ff.) he approaches a visionary
state: transfixed by the horror of what he sees he becomes a medium
reporting back from another world, and only re-awakens to his
surroundings when he comes out of his poetic trance. (He himself
notes the moment of awakening several times: 'My wits begin to

turn'; 'O, that way madness lies'; 'Fie, fie, fie! pah, pah! Give me an ounce of civet, good apothecary'.)[16]

Attempting Lear's most violent speeches an actor would do well to remember that they are essentially inward-looking and to heed Hamlet's words: in the very torrent, tempest and whirlwind of passion 'you must acquire and beget a temperance that may give it smoothness', and not 'tear a passion to tatters, to very rags'. This is particularly relevant to King Lear, Shakespeare's most tempestuous hero, because when most agitated he often freezes physically. Some actors make him too 'physical', especially in the storm scenes, where he ought to contrast with Poor Tom, traditionally played as a jittery creature with rolling head and slapping arms who starts violently, trembles, scratches himself, half man and half animal. Rather than compete with Poor Tom, Lear could remain fairly immobile, seated or standing, without over-indulging in physical jerks when reporting his 'visions'.

Elsewhere, of course, his physical behaviour may reflect his disjointed mental processes, and may even aid the audience to read his mind. He begins to perform his fantasies as he approaches madness, pretending not to know himself, kneeling to an imaginary daughter, and such 'new pranks' and 'unsightly tricks'[17] prepare the audience for later scenes where he acts out his fixed ideas. And Shakespeare took other precautions to make Lear's mad speeches intelligible. All of his 'mad' thinking refers back to what the audience has witnessed, or translates earlier events into a new but immediately recognisable idiom:

> The little dogs and all,
> Tray, Blanch and Sweetheart, see, they bark at me. (III. 6. 61)

The little dogs that he imagines turning against him, three in number, are females of course; as he has already addressed his daughters as 'she-foxes' (III. 6. 22) we can follow the general drift of his mind. We have been trained to follow him, in fact, by the Fool's somewhat similar addiction to mental jumps: an egg or a snail, whatever seeming irrelevance he picks upon, the Fool's riddling turns into a comment on Lear's folly – and Lear later twists all that enters his mind to point the same way, with similar gaps between the object and the thought, a kink that the audience quickly adapts to. The door opens, the tiger leaps – and Poor Tom turns into a robed man of justice, a joint-stool into Goneril (III. 6. 36, 52).

In addition Lear's own rapid changes of *mood* in the earlier scenes prepare for his later, equally sudden changes of *thought*. I refer not only to his volte-face in the encounters with Cordelia (I. 1) and Regan (II. 4. 131ff.) but also to much slighter fluctuations of mood that are made clearly visible. Notice, for example, the precision of his many expletives, at the farthest possible remove from the man who falls back on the same four-letter word for all occasions. Even the most commonplace *What* or *Ha* becomes meaningful, telling us exactly how far he is from his flash-point, and most of his expletives blend so naturally into their context, and are so subtly coloured by it, that one *O ho* can be worlds apart from another:

> But yet I call you servile ministers
> That will with two pernicious daughters join
> Your high-engender'd battles 'gainst a head
> So old and white as this. O, ho! 'tis foul. (III. 2. 21–4)

> O, ho, are you there with me? No eyes in your head. (IV. 6. 145)

The first is a howl of misery, the second an incipient chuckle. And what could be more expressive than the first warning notes to Cordelia, 'How, how, Cordelia! Mend your speech a little', catching the old man's startled uncertainty, so utterly different from his assured *How now!*[18] – and at the same time quite different from his other startled awakenings into resentment: 'Ha! say'st thou so?' 'Say, how is that?'[19] Notice, again, the give-away vocatives as he addresses Oswald and the Fool, each one of which registers a slight shift of mood as each series ripples meaningfully on:

> [To Oswald] You, you, sirrah, where's my daughter? . . . O, you sir, you! Come you hither, sir. Who am I, sir? . . . you whoreson dog! you slave! you cur! . . . Do you bandy looks with me, you rascal!

> [To the Fool] How now, my pretty knave! . . . Why, my boy? . . . Take heed, sirrah, the whip . . . Why, no, boy . . . No, lad . . . When were you wont to be so full of songs, sirrah? (I. 4. 44ff.)

When he speaks about others there can be the same rippling variation:

> [About Oswald] What says the fellow there? Call the clotpoll back . . . Where's that mongrel? . . . Why came not the slave back? (I. 4. 46ff.)

\*          \*          \*

Although there is precision in Lear's most trivial utterances, and we can read his moods from many signals, *King Lear* could also be regarded as Shakespeare's masterpiece of imprecision, a play that makes the audience grope through fogs and uncertainties. In many scenes we cannot know, when Lear speaks, whether his mind dwells in the present or the past, whether he generalises or thinks only of himself, whether he is mad or sane. Artful confusion starts much earlier than in the other tragedies: in the very first scene Lear's rage against Cordelia voices a fiercely possessive love, a 'mixed' emotion that blazes forth with the absolute minimum of preparation. Later, Lear's butterfly thoughts cannot be pinned down and neatly labelled – though editors will go on trying. It has been said, for example, that he 'doesn't yet recognise' Gloucester when he denounces 'Gloucester's bastard son' (IV. 6. 114) in the blind earl's presence.[20] Can we really tell? This is one of the play's many blurred effects, where clarification seems unwarranted. True, Lear only identifies Gloucester in so many words towards the end of the episode ('I know thee well enough; thy name is Gloucester'), and had earlier addressed him as if he thought him 'Goneril . . . with a white beard'. But what of that? Pretending not to recognise others had been one of Lear's unpleasant little games even before his wits were unsettled,[21] and the cruelty of his remarks to Gloucester could be an overflow from his fury against the world at large. We simply cannot know whether he recognises Gloucester, as his madness comes and goes and he has intervals of acute perception. There are times, indeed, when he seems to *act* madness, not like Hamlet, defensively 'putting on' an antic disposition, but simply to please his wayward humour, resorting to the 'pranks' and 'unsightly tricks' that had irritated Goneril and Regan – particularly in IV. 6, where an extraordinary playfulness alternates with deadly seriousness and he seems neither completely mad nor sane.

Artful blending can take various forms. Consider the emotions when Lear is reunited with Cordelia:

For, as I am a man, I think this lady
To be my child Cordelia. *Cordelia*   And so I am, I am.
*Lear*   Be your tears wet? Yes, faith. I pray, weep not;
If you have poison for me, I will drink it.
I know you do not love me; for your sisters
Have, as I do remember, done me wrong:
You have some cause, they have not. *Cordelia*   No cause, no cause.
(*King Lear* IV. 7. 69ff.)

Surprise, infinite tenderness, curiosity, compassion, humility: such rough-and-ready equivalents may describe the emotions of the foreground, behind which we are conscious of Lear's wide-eyed wonder as he very gradually comes to (a process that continues throughout the scene, matched by Cordelia's breathless expectancy); and at the same time we also dimly perceive the emotion of the opening scene, muted now but still recognisably the same cry for love ('I know you do not love me' meaning 'Say you love me!'). Here, at the still centre of the tragic experience, in a scene that appears to go into slow motion and, at times, to come to a pause between two worlds, things dying and things new-born, we may at first think that the emotions are clear-cut and almost frozen, as in a painting. But not so: here, as in Shakespeare's more explosive scenes, we find a blend of the distinct and indistinct, for in his handling of emotion as in so many other respects he was a master of chiaroscuro.

The play's most interesting technical innovation, the blurred vision of the middle acts, depends largely on its three 'madmen', the Fool, Poor Tom, the king, each of whom utters 'matter and impertinency mix'd', each in his own idiom. The Fool and Poor Tom twist and scramble their thoughts in repeating patterns. Lear's mind works more complexly, in ever-changing thought patterns, and, blurring the seen and unseen, becomes the play's central thoroughfare, where past, present and future meet, wishful thinking and random recollection, odds and ends of experience that could not otherwise have mixed – so that an exceptional range of words and images passes through this, the most inclusive of all Shakespeare's plays.

Lear's violent past in particular blurs into and confuses the present, and suggests a tragic nexus between his former life and the fate that overtakes him. As the play moves forward to IV. 6 the past seems to become more and more real – resurfacing in allusions to Lear's love of hunting and hawking, his horses and dogs, and above all his partiality for *the whip* and similar instruments of civilisation.

Take heed, sirrah – the whip (I. 4. 109)

> Tremble, thou wretch,
> That hast within thee undivulged crimes
> Unwhipp'd of justice (III. 2. 51–3)

Thou rascal beadle, hold thy bloody hand.
Why dost thou lash that whore? Strip thy own back . . .

> (IV. 6. 160–1)

I have seen the day, with my good biting falchion,
I would have made them skip ... (V. 3. 276–7)

Although the past mostly returns in shivered fragments, there are also some longer speeches that hang together, more or less, and that could be mistaken for mental flashbacks.

When I do stare, see how the subject quakes.
I pardon that man's life. What was thy cause?
Adultery?
Thou shalt not die. Die for adultery? No ... (IV. 6. 107ff.)

But in this speech, where Lear's sadistic satisfaction in his own power points forward (and back) to Goneril and Regan, the 'subject' of the flashback is assimilated into the adulterer Gloucester, to whom Lear addresses his words, and we quickly realise that the present overlays the past and distorts it. The play gives us several half-glimpses of royal Lear as a dispenser of justice[22] all of which are blurred by the emotions of the moment.

*   *   *

*King Lear* also blurs the inner and the outer world, as they present themselves to Lear and to the audience. The secondary characters fall into two groups in each of which, as Bradley observed, 'there is a quality common to all the members', devoted love and hard self-seeking, the common quality being exhibited by each person in an extreme form; and, Bradley added, 'this tendency to extremes is found again in the characters of Lear and Gloucester'.[23] Many other tendencies of the outer world are in fact 'found again in the character of Lear' (and, to a lesser extent, of Gloucester). In his 'little world of man' (III. 1. 10) Lear experiences a storm that coincides mysteriously with the elemental storm, and indeed appears to energise it, since Lear (who swears by Jupiter, the Thunderer, at two early climactic moments)[24] calls down thunder and lightning on his detested daughters before the storm begins:

You nimble lightnings, dart your blinding flames
Into her scornful eyes! ...

O heavens ... send down and take my part! (II. 4. 163–91)

However we choose to explain it we cannot ignore this interaction of microcosm and macrocosm, Lear himself relating 'this contentious storm' and 'this tempest in my mind' (III. 4. 6, 12).[25] And the play suggests a similar correspondence between Lear and his three daughters, negatively in Kent's speech –

> It is the stars,
> The stars above us, govern our conditions;
> Else one self mate and make could not beget
> Such different issues. (IV. 3. 32ff.)

– but positively when Lear matches Goneril and Regan's hardness with his curses (I. 4, II. 4) and Cordelia's tears with his own (IV. 7). We see the daughters as extensions of Lear's own personality. And, partly because the play's symbolic action divides the principal characters into two groups, each with its own elective affinities, Lear seems to have a genetic relationship with almost everyone else, the other characters serving as extensions of his daughters. Thus Cordelia, Kent and the Fool sympathise and obscurely communicate with one another, and in a sense melt into one another: Kent not only talks of Lear as one whom he has 'lov'd as my father' (I. 1. 140), as the Fool calls him 'nuncle', but we hear that since Cordelia's going into France 'the Fool hath much pined away' (I. 4. 72), that Kent and Cordelia are secretly in touch and admire each other,[26] and finally that Cordelia and the Fool have become one in Lear's mind (V. 3. 305: 'And my poor Fool is hang'd'). All three, Cordelia, Kent and the Fool, exist separately and yet partake of one another's identity, and all three are refracted images of Lear, or of his better nature.

Before I proceed to the second group I must comment on what Bradley called the 'unselfish and devoted love' of the first. Standing back from the play we have to agree that Bradley gave Cordelia and Kent (and perhaps the Fool) no more than their due. During a performance, however, the champions of love impress us differently, until we reach the storm-scenes, each one of them inflicting pain on Lear, which we must ascribe to his or her character rather than to selfless devotion. The Fool, whose 'efforts to outjest his master's injuries' struck Bradley as heroic, laughs when he finds Kent in the stocks ('Ha, ha! he wears cruel garters!'), and a similar *Schadenfreude* tinges much of what he says to Lear. Bradley sentimentalised him as 'a timid, delicate and frail being', one 'to whom a responsible and consistent course of action, nay even a responsible use of language, is at the best of times difficult',[27] but, whether or not we regard him as completely responsible, there is no mistaking his embryonic satisfaction as he twists the knife in nuncle's wound: 'I am better than thou art now: I am a fool, thou art nothing' (I. 4. 192). Kent's truth-telling, though not sadistic, affects Lear like hammer-blows, most noticeably when he insists five times that Regan and Cornwall set him in the stocks: as he contradicts the old king, who staggers back incredulously, he sounds more like a relentless persecutor than a devoted friend (II. 4. 11ff.). And a similar relentless-ness marks Cordelia's behaviour in the first scene – admirable in its long-range intentions, but wounding in the immediate context, especially for Lear, who receives no private notice from her asides (as does the audience) and cannot suspect that the flow of rhetoric, so carefully arranged, will suddenly be halted by 'Nothing, my lord.' True, it has been urged that rather than accuse Cordelia, with Coleridge, of 'some little faulty admixture of pride and sullenness', we should consider the 'muteness of Cordelia' as the embodiment of an idea – from which it could comfortably follow that 'no faintest stain of guilt or responsibility attaches to her'.[28] Who would not wish to agree, for such a reward? But although we may willingly label some later episodes 'symbolic action', the first scene is more compli-cated. After the exceptionally 'natural' opening dialogues, counter-pointed by Lear's more formal exchanges with Goneril and Regan, Cordelia reverts to a natural style, very close to prose: 'Unhappy that I am, I cannot heave my heart into my mouth. I love your majesty according to my bond, no more nor less.' At this stage we must not make too much of the symbolic and folk-tale overtones, for the dialogue requires us to respond to Cordelia primarily as a person, not as an idea.

The idea, the symbolic action, grows with the play. At the end 'love' appears to expel the evil of the *Lear* universe – and yet the play is so arranged that the voice of love, soft, gentle and low, has scarcely been heard. Taking Cordelia, Kent and the Fool together we are struck by their common determination that Lear shall conform to *their* image of him, by their toughness in imposing their will. Only when Cordelia returns, in Act IV, can love at last speak softly, fully accepting the loved one for what he is, instead of dictating to him what he should be. Then, admittedly, love transcends all other experiences in the play, lifting Lear and Cordelia above the dross of the world in a scene unparalleled in Shakespeare for tenderness, one of his supreme achievements. But that scene, or rather the central episode of the father's reunion with his daughter, is only forty lines long.

Shakespeare reduced the portrayal of tender love and feminine softness to the absolute minimum. He kept Cordelia off-stage for long periods or placed her in difficult situations in which her kind of moral beauty cannot help flashing dangerously, in which a diamond is all cutting edge (I. 1, and again, V. 3: 'Shall we not see these daughters and these sisters?'). Kent, disguised, has to conceal his deeper feelings, is too clumsy to express them soothingly, and is handicapped by a harsh voice, one that bellows and clamours.[29] The Fool's love, if we may call it that, lacks all the softer graces.

The champions of love speak clumsily and woundingly at first because Lear himself, the play's central generator, for a while only transmits that kind of energy. Unlike the divine Desdemona, who lies about the handkerchief and about her own imminent death to spare Othello pain, quick-eyed love in *King Lear* cannot be deflected from the truth and feels an absolute commitment to it: 'So young, my lord, *and true*' (Cordelia, I. 1. 106); 'they'll have me whipped *for speaking true*' (the Fool, I. 4. 180); Kent being rebuked by Cornwall as one of those blunt knaves who '*must speak truth*' (II. 2. 94). Truth-seekers all, they nevertheless distort what they see, again exactly like Lear: we no more believe Cordelia's 'Nothing' or the Fool's witty inversions than we agreed with Lear that

> Down from the waist they are centaurs,
> Though women all above. (IV. 6. 124–5)

Related as they are to Lear, they only see and report on unpleasant truths – until Act IV, when the storm-clouds disperse, Cordelia returns, Lear's great rage 'is killed in him', and a new radiance briefly enters the play.

And they repeat Lear in other ways. If Kent is muzzled in disguise, unable to express his love directly, Lear's love is also muzzled at the outset, and cannot communicate with the loved one. To insist on a demonstrable causal connection between Lear's inarticulateness and Kent's would go too far, but we may say that in *King Lear* the interior and the outer landscape blend one into another, and are sometimes almost indistinguishable. This is particularly true of Lear and the Fool, since the Fool often appears to speak from inside his master's mind, uttering what Lear has dimly perceived but dare not acknowledge. The extraordinary oneness of the two continues after the Fool has dropped out of the play, for in IV. 6 Lear echoes the Fool's voice and personality, continuing his riddling (e.g. 'your eyes are in a heavy case, your purse in a light'), his *Schadenfreude*, his sex-obsession and, probably, his 'fantastic' general demeanour.

Lear's relationship with the second group of characters is, if anything, even closer, being reaffirmed in scene after scene. The present grows out of the past, his violence begot theirs: he had given the example, as king, and Goneril and Regan inherit his imperious appetites. If they reject him had he not taught them how, by disowning Cordelia and banishing Kent? Harsh, wilful, vindictive, self-enclosed – Lear too rashly assumes that he may have to divorce himself from his queen's tomb (II. 4. 129) when he himself could have passed on the genes that make Cordelia's sisters what they are. He would like to think them corruptions of his blood (II. 4. 220ff.), but the play suggests that his blood itself is corrupt.

In *King Lear* we witness a contest between two 'sides', devoted love and hard self-seeking, one of which attempts to injure the king, the other to protect him; and the same two sides battle within Lear himself. Love learns to contain the challenge politically, in the outer world, and simultaneously reasserts itself in the inner world, the personality of Lear. After the initial love-test the king moves away from Goneril and Regan towards Cordelia, without, however, entirely shedding his wilfulness and violence (they seem to disappear in IV. 7, but return in V. 3): a slow journey, one that lacks a clear sense of direction, being a journey in two worlds at once, the physical and the spiritual.

*        *        *

Many have testified to the extraordinary impact of the play's concluding scene, and many have tried to explain it. 'The most pathetic speech ever written', said Bradley of Lear's last words; and Johnson confessed 'I know not whether I ever endured to read again the last scenes of the play till I undertook to revise them as an editor'.[30] Yet despite the final scene's undeniable power, or perhaps because of it, we can neither describe what happens in Lear's mind nor how we respond, except in very general terms. To take the most striking example, Bradley thought that 'the agony in which [Lear] actually dies is one not of pain but of ecstasy' and that the actor must express, in Lear's last gestures and look, 'an unbearable joy' – an interpretation that was once widely supported but that has now been questioned. Lear dies, according to a more modern view 'torn apart by a thunderclap of simultaneous joy and grief. . . . between extremes of illusion and truth, ecstasy and the blackest despair'[31] (note the 'mixed response'). Whether or not an actor can suggest quite so much, Lear's last speeches are certainly effective because, though couched in the simplest language, they are to an unusual degree suggestive.

Lear's last speeches are more richly suggestive than those of the other tragic heroes, I think, since they reactivate even more memories of what has gone before. In the last seventy lines Lear and his three daughters are together again, for the first time since the play began, and Kent once more attempts to interrupt his master; while the daughters lie dead on the stage, shut off from their father as before, Kent again fails to make himself understood. Within this frame, so like that of the opening scene and yet so far removed, we are stirred by many poignant repetitions. 'Lend me a looking-glass', 'This feather stirs': Lear still believes in simple physical tests, as if they can speak more truly than the human heart, as he once believed in the love-test and in the simple proposition that Goneril's

> fifty yet doth double five and twenty
> And thou art twice her love.[32]

Lear can still explode into rage, and can still retreat into illusion:

> A plague upon you, murderers, traitors all!
> I might have sav'd her; now she's gone for ever.
> Cordelia, Cordelia! stay a little. Ha!
> What is't thou say'st?

We also glimpse his former sadism and his indifference to the feelings of others,[33] and then come the seven lines that crown the play.

> And my poor fool is hang'd! No, no, no life!
> Why should a dog, a horse, a rat have life,
> And thou no breath at all? Thou'lt come no more,
> Never, never, never, never, never.
> Pray you, undo this button. Thank you, sir.
> Do you see this? Look on her. Look, her lips.
> Look there, look there!

In 'my poor fool', it seems most likely, he thinks of the Fool and Cordelia as one, a suggestive confusion.[34] In the fifth line theme and image hunters note another 'stripping gesture', but the words before

and after 'undo this button' are even more significant. How often
has Lear said 'Pray you'? Three times, but only when addressing
Cordelia.[35] How often had he thanked another? Or called another
'sir'?[36] We cannot pause for statistics in the theatre but we have
time enough to observe a change of tone. The most suggestive line of
all, however, is the fourth. 'Lear's five-times repeated "Never", in
which the simplest and most unanswerable cry of anguish rises note
by note till the heart breaks, is romantic in its naturalism.' So
Bradley,[37] and he may be right. But other suggestions are equally
possible, if the actor's voice is not made to rise note by note (which
I think the most difficult way to speak the play's most difficult line).
'The repeated cries of "Never!" are the steady hammering of truth
on a mind unable to endure it.'[38] Yes? Perhaps. And the line can be
just as powerful if, instead of a rising intonation or a steady hammering, it simply trails away, like the anger that flashed in 'A plague
upon you!' (v. 3. 269), a last distant rumble of the Lear thunder.

   In the concluding seventy lines Lear repeats some of his most
characteristic gestures, pathetic reminders of all that he has been. In
the other tragedies the hero's former glories are often recapitulated at
this point, and past and present are firmly juxtaposed. Lear's past,
however, being merely suggested or glancingly referred to ('Your
servant Kent. Where is your servant Caius?'), never competes with
the present, it only enriches it: far from pausing to look back the play
presses steadily forward. Notice, too, that Lear alone of all the tragic
heroes lacks a sense of foreboding at the end, and in Act v never
indulges in self-explanation. Instead of the usual rhetorical flow,
Lear's mind zigzags on in its established way, from one arresting
image to another, and compels the audience to zigzag after him.
When Lear and Othello both state, just before their own deaths and
quite unexpectedly, that they have committed a murder, the effect is
consequently very different.

> And say besides that in Aleppo once,
> Where a malignant and a turban'd Turk
> Beat a Venetian and traduc'd the state,
> I took by th' throat the circumcis'd dog
> And smote him – thus. (Othello v. 2. 355ff.)

> What is't thou say'st? Her voice was ever soft,
> Gentle, and low – an excellent thing in woman.
> I kill'd the slave that was a-hanging thee. (King Lear v. 3. 272ff.)

Othello's image seems to be swept into his mind by a mounting emotion; the last of his self-accusations, it fits into place like the last piece of a jig-saw puzzle. Lear's 'I kill'd the slave', on the other hand, abruptly switches to a different emotion: here, as in many other scenes, the audience struggles to keep up with Lear's mind.

I shall not discuss the scene's philosophical implications, important though they are, except to say that its pessimism is matched by an appropriate stage-response. Lear exclaims against a final injustice –

> Why should a dog, a horse, a rat have life,
> And thou no breath at all?

– and his mood engulfs everyone else. Whereas in the other tragedies it is clearly understood that the survivors take the road back to order, there is no obvious road in *King Lear*: no one wants to rule (v. 3. 297, 320–1), there is little sense of purpose or hopefulness. Indeed, the play ends without the usual public statement from the senior survivors, who wish only to 'speak what we feel, not what we ought to say.' In the closing moments of Shakespeare's bleakest tragedy the stage-response remains, fittingly enough, more 'cheerless, dark and deadly' than in any other.

*  *  *

As there are said to be two 'sides' in *King Lear*, each with its own distinctive philosophical outlook, it is worth asking how we respond to the play's ideas. Do we align ourselves with 'the benignant Nature of Bacon, Hooker and Lear' against 'the malignant Nature of Hobbes, Edmund, and the Wicked Sisters'?[39] Theodore Spencer, commenting on Gloucester's conversation with Edmund in I. 2, gave a straight answer.

> Gloucester sees everything as conditioned by the heavens, and all the right thinking people in Shakespeare's audience would have agreed with him. But when he leaves the stage, Edmund illustrates the villainy of his own nature, his cynical disregard of correspondences and inter-relations, by taking the opposite point of view from that of his father.[40]

Did the right thinking ever feel so certain about correspondences and interrelations, and ideas in general? Only if the right thinking were the entirely unthinking – and *King Lear*, it seems safe to say, was not written for a mindless audience. A very different answer was given by Margaret Webster.

Edmund, in *King Lear*, is the play's chief soliloquizer. The dash and daring of his first outburst, his hand against all the smug conventions of society, his analysis of them so brilliantly specious, will carry us most unmorally with him throughout the play . . . We may more readily identify Shakespeare with Edmund than with Gloucester . . .[41]

If Spencer attached too much importance to the play's ideas and Miss Webster too little, J. F. Danby proposed a useful compromise. Lear identifies himself in the earlier scenes[42] with what has been called the 'orthodox' medieval and Elizabethan outlook, yet, as Danby has shown, the sentiments expressed by Edmund ('Thou, Nature, art my goddess', I. 2. 1ff.) must also have been 'fairly widespread in Shakespeare's society.'

Edmund belongs to the new age of scientific inquiry and industrial development, of bureaucratic organization and social regimentation, the age of mining and merchant-venturing, of monopoly and Empire-making, the age of the sixteenth century and after: an age of competition . . . Hobbes is Edmund's philosopher. Hobbes's world of the 1640's is only different from the world of the 1600's in being a slightly more developed form of the same thing.[43]

Because there was 'a current of doubt in Shakespeare's time as to what Nature really was like' Edmund could have impressed the Jacobeans very much as Danby suggested – as 'a normal, sensible, reasonable fellow: but emancipated.' And Edmund's philosophy, sugared over with humour, need not have repelled any but the most blinkered traditionalists, expressing, after all, an opportunism not very different from that of Bacon's popular *Essays*. Bacon, be it noted, offering advice on how to make friends and influence people, described the very stratagem employed by Edmund to dupe his father (I. 2. 26ff.), one of a number of low tricks that evidently pleased him. 'Some procure themselves, to be surprised, at such times, as it is like, the party that they work upon, will suddenly come upon them: and to be found with a letter in their hand . . . to the end, they may be apposed [questioned] of those things, which of themselves they are desirous to utter.'[44]
Edmund's philosophy will hardly have repelled Shakespeare's audience, though it challenged a more traditional one, now known as 'the Elizabethan World Picture'. We need not choose between the

two, since Shakespeare (unlike Ibsen) did not steer his audience towards a conversion in the last act: he used ideas to point towards complexity, not simplicity. The familiar simplicities are usually placed before the audience in the opening scenes,[45] then words change their meanings, the play moves away into uncharted regions and the audience is left to its own devices – 'out went the candle, and we were left darkling.' The stark initial contrast between Edmund's *Nature* and Lear's can consequently be quite misleading, if it traps us into thinking of two 'sides', each with a fixed outlook.

> With varying emphases, critics have repeatedly noted basic similarities in the characters of Goneril, Regan and Edmund. While all three share certain traits, they are most closely related by a common philosophical outlook: representatives of a new world, they hold values radically different from Lear's. Their world is one in which nature is not fundamentally good . . .[46]

Lear himself, violently as he reacts against his older daughters, comes to express 'values' that are not so radically different from theirs. The appeal to Nature is followed by the appeal to Thunder ('*Crack nature's moulds, all germens spill at once*', III. 2. 8), and then Lear voices doubts about the traditionalists' world-picture that are as cynical as Edmund's: 'a dog's obey'd in office' (IV. 6. 159) repeats the Bastard's joke against legitimacy (I. 2. 1ff.), while Lear's thoughts about justice, authority and sex all question the rightness of an established order. Shakespeare may seem to dissociate himself from this cynicism by ascribing it to one whose wits have turned, just as Marlowe insures against Faustus' questioning by assigning it to one who has renounced heaven, but there can be no doubt that the whole play hurls itself towards Lear's terrible denunciations, that only Lear has the power to make ideas burst like bombs upon the audience.

Rather than think of the play's ideas as belonging to one of two 'sides' we should consider another possibility – that its attention-catching ideas move steadily in one direction. Edmund's amused cynicisms are placed at the start, to manipulate the audience into a proper receptiveness of mind (I. 2. 1ff., I. 2. 110ff.: 'This is the excellent foppery of the world . . .'). Thereafter the Fool's riddling returns more sharply to the admirable evasions of whoremaster man ('May not an ass know when the cart draws the horse?' I. 4. 223), and Goneril and Regan advise Lear to shed his illusions.

O, sir, you are old;
Nature in you stands on the very verge
Of her confine. You should be rul'd and led ...
I pray you, father, being weak, seem so. (II. 4. 144–200)

In the storm-scenes Lear himself begins to question the comfortable
illusions of man. Aided and abetted by the Fool and by a 'noble
philosopher' (Edgar disguised as Poor Tom) he first discovers that
'unaccommodated man is no more but such a poor, bare, forked
animal' as the wandering madman (III. 4. 105), and soon proceeds to
particular cases, always searching for the hidden reality.

Let them anatomize Regan; see what breeds about her heart ...
(III. 6. 75)

They told me I was everything; 'tis a lie – I am not ague-proof ...
(IV. 6. 103)

Through tatter'd clothes small vices do appear;
Robes and furr'd gowns hide all. (IV. 6. 164–5)

All is not for the best in the best of all possible worlds. The
verbalised attack on man's illusions more or less ceases after IV. 6,
however, being succeeded by Cordelia's reunion with her father,
where another view is not argued but certainly presented. Yet the
play's bleak cynicism, uttered by representatives of both 'sides', leads
on to the rending of a final illusion – that 'the gods are just' (V. 3.
170). Edmund, panting for life, tries to save Cordelia, and describes
the danger she is in. 'The gods defend her!' exclaims Albany, and
immediately Lear arrives with the body of Cordelia in his arms – so
that the audience is nudged to the conclusion that the gods, about
whom the *dramatis personae* have talked so confidently, do not exist.
Here, however, the ideas have gone underground, as it were: we are
asked not so much to think as to feel.

Although ideas play an important part in some scenes, *King Lear*
comes to no clear-cut conclusions. The survivors may wish to re-
establish something like the old 'order' politically, but this by no
means invalidates Lear's general thinking about man's animal nature
and abuse of power. The traditionalists have the last word, but those
who question traditional thinking have the most disquieting poetry.

# 8

## *Macbeth*: the Murderer as Victim

Let us begin with an early attempt to analyse audience-response in some detail, Thomas De Quincey's 'On the Knocking at the Gate in *Macbeth*', first published in 1823 and still regarded as an anthology-piece. Important for its recognition of a major critical task, De Quincey's essay fails, I think, as an explanation of the effect of one of Shakespeare's greatest scenes – yet, right or wrong, it raises questions about response that are still worth asking today.

De Quincey held that normally, when we contemplate a murder, 'the sympathy is wholly directed to the case of the murdered person', Shakespeare's problem in *Macbeth* being therefore that 'he must throw the interest on the murderer.' To succeed, said De Quincey, Shakespeare made us feel in the murder-scene that

> human nature, i.e. the divine nature of love and mercy, spread through the hearts of all creatures, and seldom utterly withdrawn from man – was gone, vanished, extinct, and that the fiendish nature had taken its place . . . Another world has stepped in; and the murderers are taken out of the region of human things, human purposes, human desires. They are transfigured: Lady Macbeth is 'unsexed'; Macbeth has forgot that he was born of woman; both are conformed to the image of devils; and the world of devils is suddenly revealed. But how shall this be conveyed and made palpable? In order that a new world may step in, this world must for a time disappear. The murderers and the murder must be insulated – cut off by an immeasurable gulf from the ordinary tide and succession of human affairs – locked up and sequestered in some deep recess; we must be made sensible that the world of ordinary life is suddenly arrested – laid asleep – tranced – racked into a dread armistice; time must be annihilated; relation to things without abolished; and all must pass self-withdrawn into a deep syncope and suspension of earthly passion . . . [Then] the knocking at the gate is heard; and it makes known audibly that the reaction has commenced; the human has made its reflux upon the fiendish.[1]

This is fine Romantic prose – but is it true? With the general argument, that Shakespeare had to throw our interest on the murderers, one cannot disagree. But do we really feel that Macbeth and Lady Macbeth are transfigured by the murder and 'conformed to the image of devils'? Lady Macbeth speaks for a time like one possessed, or exalted; but not her husband. His first line, after he has murdered Duncan, expresses an absolutely human fear – 'I have done the deed. Didst thou not hear a noise?', which gives way, almost at once, to a most human regret as he looks at his gory hands – 'This is a sorry sight.' To suppose that he thinks only of himself at this moment is to overlook that in the simplest sentences uttered in moments of crisis Shakespeare's tragic heroes imply much more than they state. But whatever we make of these opening remarks – and I admit that they might be seen as purely self-centred, therefore fiendish – there is no disputing that throughout the rest of the scene, until the knocking, Lady Macbeth has to guide, protect and mother her husband, whose voice sounds pitifully human, and almost child-like, as he wonders aloud

> But wherefore could not I pronounce 'Amen'?
> I had most need of blessing, and 'Amen'
> Stuck in my throat . . .
> I am afraid to think what I have done,
> Look on't again I dare not.

To describe Macbeth, as he comes from the murder, as a devil, a fiend, seems utterly wrong. And De Quincey also erred when he claimed that the knocking at the gate 'makes known audibly that the reaction has commenced; the human has made its reflux upon the fiendish.' For it is an odd fact that the knocking is only the last of a series of noises all of which terrify Macbeth and therefore humanise him:

> I have done the deed. Did'st thou not hear a noise? . . .
> There's one did laugh in's sleep, and one cried 'Murder!' . . .
> One cried 'God bless us', and 'Amen' the other . . .
> Methought I heard a voice cry 'Sleep no more . . .'

Though these noises and voices are only heard in Macbeth's imagination, the audience relives his experience with him and, as he speaks, believes or half-believes in them. The knocking at the gate by no means commences a reflux: it is the crest of a wave that has gathered

momentum throughout the scene. Indeed, dreadful sounds continue
throughout the play to assail Macbeth: unconsciously we come to
accept this as meaningful, and so, when the Second Apparition
screams 'Macbeth! Macbeth! Macbeth!' we do not respond at the
purely literal level and laugh at the reply – 'Had I three ears I'd hear
thee!' (IV. 1. 78)

I see Macbeth, when he reappears after the murder, not as a devil,
a fiend, but as a man who has done himself a terrible injury – so
terrible that he cannot even locate his pain. He is in a state of shock,
like someone who has escaped from a badly smashed car. Not a fiend,
but a mutilated human being. For this is Macbeth's sleep-walking
scene: he sees the blood on his hands, and he scarcely knows whether
it is Duncan's blood or his own, just as he seems confused as to
whether he has murdered Duncan, or Sleep, or himself. With a
wonderful instinct Shakespeare makes his hero refer to himself by his
three titles –

> Glamis hath murder'd sleep, and therefore Cawdor
> Shall sleep no more – Macbeth shall sleep no more! (II. 2. 42–3)

– which suggests a sense of dispersed identity, as when a man in a
state of shock cannot collect himself. The difference between a fiend,
who has an implacable sense of purpose, as revealed by the Weird
Sisters in their incantations and, at times, by Lady Macbeth, and a
shattered personality like Macbeth's after the murder, is, I need
hardly add, a considerable one.

The difference between Macbeth's and Lady Macbeth's state of mind is
important when they are together, especially in the murder-scene. *He*
attempts to define what he sees or feels – the two are almost one – by
resorting to extraordinary abstractions (pity like a naked new-born
babe striding the blast, tomorrow and tomorrow and tomorrow), or
he indicates uncertainty by asking questions (Is this a dagger? What
hands are here? What noise is that?) *She* scarcely ever doubts that
she sees the object as it really is; her unimaginative literalness being
most terrifyingly non-human in her sleep-walking scene: 'Wash
your hands, put on your nightgown, look not so pale. I tell you yet
again, Banquo's buried; he cannot come out on's grave.' (V. 1. 60ff.)
There are a few moments, true, when her mind rises above itself –
'had he not resembled/My father as he slept, I had done't', 'all the
perfumes of Arabia will not sweeten this little hand.'[2] But character-
istically her mind grasps only surface facts and not the mystery

beneath, and this essential difference from her husband is brought home to us in the murder-scene.

> *Macbeth*    This is a sorry sight.
> *Lady Macbeth*    A foolish thought to say a sorry sight.
> *Macbeth*    There's one did laugh in's sleep, and one cried 'Murder!'
> That they did wake each other. I stood and heard them;
> But they did say their prayers, and address'd them
> Again to sleep. *Lady Macbeth*    There are two lodg'd together.

Shakespeare took a risk, I think, with that last line. Lady Macbeth's calm assumption that she knows what is going on ('There are two lodg'd together'), when her husband's mind manifestly operates at a level of insight quite beyond hers, is so inept as to verge on the ridiculous. But Shakespeare knew what he was doing: the generalised tension neutralises the line's comic potential, and the sudden descent, from Macbeth's tortured insight to Lady Macbeth's flat statement, merely points to the gulf between them – an all-important fact overlooked by De Quincey.

The murderers were seen by De Quincey as 'insulated – cut off by an immeasurable gulf from the ordinary tide and succession of human affairs – locked up and sequestered in some deep recess.' Physically, I would admit, they may be in the same place; yet Macbeth's mind is transfixed and held prisoner elsewhere, and functions in its uniquely self-determined way, so much so that he scarcely hears his wife's voice. Husband and wife are so far from being locked up in a deep recess that I would rather describe him as locked away from her, insulated in a deep recess of his own. De Quincey stressed their togetherness; I feel much more conscious of their separation – as did Henry Irving when he wrote in his copy of the play, just before Macbeth talks of the mutterings of the sleepers, 'Don't look at each other.'[3]

\*          \*          \*

A victim or a villain? Macbeth seems to be both in the murder-scene and, though the mixture differs from moment to moment, throughout the first two acts. This impression partly depends upon the flow of information, which the dramatist can regulate as he chooses. The less an audience understands the more inclined it will be to reserve judgement: in *Macbeth* the opening scenes are so arranged that we never know quite enough about the hero's guilt, and he captures our sympathetic attention as it were under cover of darkness.

Commentators who translate surmise into certainty consequently distort the spectator's relationship with the dramatic character: clarifying what the dramatist deliberately left obscure they give us either a villain or a victim, and falsify the very nature of their experience.

A 'criminal' hero in particular can benefit from the audience's uncertainties. In the opening scenes of *Macbeth* we are made to wonder about the Weird Sisters, their powers, their connection with Macbeth and Lady Macbeth, and Shakespeare artfully withholds the answers. But not the commentators:

> The Witches . . . are not goddesses, or fates, or, in any way whatever, supernatural beings. They are old women, poor and ragged, skinny and hideous, full of vulgar spite . . . There is not a syllable in *Macbeth* to imply that they are anything but women. But . . . they have received from evil spirits certain supernatural powers.[4]

If we dissect the play at our leisure all this may well seem true. In the theatre, however, we can only interpret our impressions as they come to us, in a fixed order, and, I venture to say, we never share Bradley's certainty that the Weird Sisters are not 'in any way whatever, supernatural beings.' When the play begins Macbeth and Banquo can make nothing of them ('What are these?', 'What are you?'), except that they 'look not like th' inhabitants o' the earth.' Shakespeare's audience must have been just as puzzled, for the 'Weird Sisters' were foreign to English mythology, so much so that Holinshed (from whose chronicles Shakespeare borrowed the name) felt obliged to give help: 'the weird sisters, that is (as ye would say) ye Goddesses of destinie.' As the play progresses we learn that Banquo thinks them 'the instruments of darkness' (I. 3. 124), and that they acknowledge spirits as their 'masters' (IV. 1. 63). But their exact status remains undefined, except that they are closely associated with an 'unknown power' (IV. 1. 69). They may be witches, but we cannot take even this for granted:[5] and at the beginning of the play, when we feel our way into Macbeth's mind, a spectator uncontaminated by criticism must think of them as *sui generis*, a mystery.

The mystery extends to their relationship with Macbeth. Dover Wilson assures us that 'Macbeth exercises complete freedom of will from first to last'.[6] Another critic wrote, more cautiously, that 'Macbeth makes no bargain with the emissaries of the powers of darkness; nor are they bargainable. The knowledge offers itself to him: it is, indeed, as he says, "a supernatural soliciting". But he is not solicited to the treachery and murder which he commits.'[7]

True, as long as we can be certain that there is no connection between the Weird Sisters and Lady Macbeth. But if Moelwyn Merchant was correct in saying that 'it is surely unnecessary to argue today that Lady Macbeth's invocation of "the spirits that tend on mortal thoughts" . . . is a formal stage in demonic possession',[8] then Lady Macbeth solicits her husband on behalf of the Weird Sisters. She does so, it should be observed, by hailing him by his three titles, just like the Sisters –

> Great Glamis! Worthy Cawdor!
> Greater than both, by the all-hail hereafter!

She continues where they left off. The Weird Sisters strike first, then Lady Macbeth assaults him in his imagination, blow after blow, and her words have an even more fearful effect – so that theirs seems a joint attack, master-minded from afar. And even if not formally 'possessed', Lady Macbeth appears to be somehow in league with evil and Macbeth its victim, a fly in the spider's web who struggles mightily but cannot escape.

'Somehow' in league may sound vague, but we must beware of asserting more than we can prove where the Weird Sisters are concerned. Somehow they make contact with Macbeth's mind, even before he sees them: his very first words, 'So foul and fair a day I have not seen', suggest their influence, since he unconsciously echoes their earlier chant. And as they somehow give Banquo 'cursed thoughts' in his dreams (II. 1. 8), and can invade the sleeping mind, what are we to make of the dagger that seems to marshal Macbeth to Duncan's chamber a mere thirteen lines later? Another cursed thought, planted in Macbeth's mind to draw him to the murder? All of these impressions work together, suggesting that the Weird Sisters have access to the human mind (Lady Macbeth, Banquo, Macbeth), and can attack Macbeth's directly and indirectly.

Yet these impressions never harden into certitude. Neither the very first scene, which was dropped by Tyrone Guthrie because he mistakenly thought it assigned a 'governing influence'[9] to the Weird Sisters, nor any other scene proves beyond doubt that Macbeth is just a victim. The dramatic perspective merely inclines us to fear for him. Shakespeare stimulates an anxiety for the hero, before the murder. similar to the audience's protective anxiety for Othello, even though Macbeth's intentions are more straightforwardly criminal than the Moor's. A single passage may illustrate the dramatic advantages – Lady Macbeth's allusion to an earlier meeting when her husband broke 'this enterprise to me' (I. 7. 47ff.). On the strength of this passage some editors have postulated lost scenes or an earlier version of the play.[10] Had the audience actually witnessed a scene where 'the husband and wife had explicitly discussed the idea of murdering Duncan at some favourable opportunity',[11] we must reply, Shakespeare would not have been able to arouse the required response, the sense that Lady Macbeth exaggerates her husband's guilt. Such a discussion would have left no room for doubt, whereas Lady Macbeth's oblique reference to a previous meeting, in a speech that begins so oddly, exists only to beget doubt.

> What *beast* was't then
> That made you break this enterprise to me?
> When you durst do it, *then you were a man* . . .

The tendency to overstatement and emotionalism is as marked as, after the murder, her understatement and emotional deadness. Accordingly, though we believe in a previous meeting, we cannot trust her account of it. She *says* that he broke the enterprise to her and swore to carry out the murder, but we have seen how she puts her ideas into his mind ('Hie thee hither/That I may pour my spirits in thine ear'[12]) and, though Macbeth lets her words pass unchallenged, we distrust all that she asserts. Her speech, in effect, makes Macbeth not more but less guilty; we hear her say that he proposed the murder but, not knowing what really happened, we overreact to her emotionalism and think him the more likely to be innocent.

Much depends on the actor's intonation and by-play. He can slant his performance to make Macbeth more or less a victim (or villain), and, as theatrical records amply demonstrate, great actors often chose to clarify these uncertainties. Irving stressed Macbeth's guilt from the beginning, as we see from his note beside 'Stay, you imperfect speakers . . .' (I. 3. 70): 'Burning in desire'.[13] One crucial line lent itself to three very different interpretations:

To Lady Macbeth's question, 'When does Duncan go hence?', Mr Kemble replies indifferently, 'Tomorrow as he purposes'. With Mr Kean it assumes a very different aspect. In an emphatic tone, and with a hesitating look . . . he half divulges the secret of his

breast – 'To-morrow as he . . . purposes!' . . . [Kean] gave the
impression that the idea of murdering Duncan at Dunsinane had
already occurred to him. From then on he appeared not the pawn
of his wife's ambition but the master of his own destiny.[14]

James Rees suggested a third possibility to Edwin Forrest, who
adopted it in performance. Macbeth says 'Tomorrow' and

at that moment he meets the eye of his wife – like an electric
shock, the infernal spark acts upon his already overcharged brain –
he starts, gazes as if upon the fabled basilisk, and mutters in fear
and dread, as if in the presence of a supernatural being, "As he
purposes." Here it is they fully understand each other.[15]

All three are perfectly legitimate readings at this point. But, although
there are signs in the text that the idea of murdering Duncan
presents itself first to Macbeth,[16] Lady Macbeth later so completely
overawes her husband that the first impression is supplanted by a
much stronger one. The more she presses him the more reluctant he
becomes: and when he finally goes to kill Duncan her hypnotic
influence, the vision of the dagger and his 'heat-oppressed brain'
make him move like a ghost (II. 1. 56) – a mere ghost of himself, far
from exercising complete freedom of will.

Just before the murder of Duncan and immediately afterwards
Macbeth impresses us as a victim rather than a villain. The deed is
done in horror and, as Bradley has finely said, 'as if it were an appalling duty'.[17] This is not to claim that Macbeth is simply a victim,
only that he seems to be so when it matters most, at the cross-roads
of the play, when he feels most intensely, speaks his most moving
lines and is most fully himself. And we are given the same sense that
he is a victim, it should be noted, by his general way of thinking and
imagining. Unlike Hamlet, who tries to master his thought in his
soliloquies, who even interrupts its headlong rush from the outside,
as it were ('Why, what an ass am I!', 'About, my brains!'[18]) Macbeth
gets carried away by his thought, thought turns into vision, and he
himself impresses us as a helpless, horrified onlooker. Just as the
sorcerer's apprentice cannot stop the show of kings ('What, will the
line stretch out to th' crack of doom?', IV. 1. 117) so he cannot halt
his imagination once it begins to conjure forth tomorrow and tomorrow and tomorrow, or hounds and greyhounds, mongrels,
spaniels, curs, shoughs, water-rugs and demi-wolves.[19] The broken

syntax of 'If it were done when 'tis done' (I. 7. 1–12) also suggests Macbeth's helplessness, a mind bombarded by thoughts that it cannot hold back and yet, in this instance, dare not finish. And his hallucinations have a similar effect. Not only the ghost of Banquo, the dagger, the voices in the murder-scene, the hands that pluck at his eyes, the stones that prate of his 'where-about': throughout the play mysterious objects and noises float towards him out of the unknown, across the normal boundaries of space and time, always threateningly, so that his characteristic mode of perception also presents him to the audience as a victim, a sufferer who demands the audience's sympathetic response.

\*     \*     \*

After De Quincey, attempts to explain this response continued, often in brief asides or assertions that achieved very little. I have already quoted Johnson and Hazlitt on Macbeth and Lady Macbeth. Having dared to disagree with them[20] I must mention that they have not lacked supporters: J. H. Barnes urged in 1914, as did Francis Gentleman in the eighteenth century, that there is not a moment in the play 'when the audience is not antagonistic' to the hero.[21] E. E. Stoll claimed the opposite, that Macbeth engages and secures our sympathy, benefiting from various devices of mediation and conciliation, not least 'an all-encompassing cloud of poetry'.[22] At last, however, there appeared an essay in which Shakespeare's technical problems and some of his solutions were clearly expounded, an essay that deserves to be widely read and one that it will be useful to summarise.

Wayne Booth[23] assumed at the outset that Shakespeare wished to make Macbeth 'a tragic hero with full stature, commanding our sympathy to the end.' How then, he asked, was Macbeth's moral degeneration to be portrayed 'without muddling the audience's responses? Shakespeare, he answered, first persuades us that Macbeth is not naturally evil but rather an admirable man, a man who matters. Everyone thinks of him as a 'worthy gentleman', even Lady Macbeth, who thus provides 'the unimpeachable testimony of a wicked character deploring goodness', the best evidence of his 'essential goodness' being his vacillation before the murder. Having established Macbeth's general character, Shakespeare 'has the task of trying to keep two contradictory streams moving simultaneously: the events showing Macbeth's growing wickedness and the tide of our mounting sympathy.' The first sure sign that Shakespeare recognised a response-problem 'is his care in avoiding any representation of the murder of Duncan.' And the very general portrayal of Duncan before the murder must also have been deliberate, since it prevents the audience from taking a personal interest in him: 'there is little for us to love or attach our imaginations to.' Banquo, the second victim, is more of an individual. 'We have heard him in soliloquy, that infallible guide to inner quality.' We sympathise with him more than with Duncan, and 'his murder is shown on the stage' – so that 'we are led to the proper, though illogical, inference: it is more wicked to kill Banquo than to have killed Duncan.' To preserve sympathy for the criminal hero, Shakespeare has this murder done by accomplices. The murder of Lady Macduff and her children, the last atrocity 'explicitly shown in the play', seems even more reprehensible, yet Shakespeare again shields Macbeth. Lady Macduff 'is more vividly portrayed even than Banquo', and the murder of women and children 'is wicked indeed': for the first time 'pity for Macbeth's victims really wars with pity for him, and our desire for his downfall threatens to turn the play into what some critics have claimed it to be: a punitive tragedy.' Yet here again Macbeth himself is not shown in an act of violence, and he seems even further removed from his victims than before: 'as far as we know, he has never seen them'. More important, immediately after Macduff's tears 'we shift to Lady Macbeth's scene, one effect of which is to "prove" once again that the suffering of these criminals is worse than their crimes.' All three murders, Wayne Booth concluded, 'are followed immediately by scenes of suffering and self-torture', almost as if Shakespeare had decided that each step in the hero's degeneration should be 'counteracted by mounting pity'.

An essay as closely argued as Booth's cannot be summarised without loss. I hope that I have accurately indicated its general drift, if not its incidental subtleties, as there are many points in it that ought to be pondered, and perhaps challenged. The most important is Booth's insistence on 'mounting sympathy' and 'mounting pity', which I think makes the play much tidier than Shakespeare left it. Only by concentrating on the three murder scenes, and by neglecting equally relevant factors, can Booth describe the play as he does, for it could be argued that sympathy and pity for the tragic hero depend more on scenes where he is present than on those, however powerful, where he is absent. Macbeth never appears in the second and third murder-scenes, but we see him planning them – we observe a steady decline as he becomes hardened to murder, and here I respond to him less and less 'sympathetically'. He struggles desperately against the killing of Duncan; he proceeds to the murder of Banquo without the same agonising preliminaries, less directly impelled by the Weird Sisters, unprompted by Lady Macbeth; yet he still looks forward to Banquo's death regretfully, as a political necessity, admires the victim and his 'royalty of nature' (III. 1. 47ff.), whereas Macduff's death means nothing at all to him, he decides on it as an afterthought, unconvinced of its necessity:

> Then live, Macduff; what need I fear of thee?
> But yet I'll make assurance double sure ... (IV. 1. 82–3)

And he decides to massacre Macduff's family after even less preliminary hesitation, as a mere act of revenge (IV. 1. 144ff.).

On the evidence of this growing indifference to murder we might wish to argue, against Booth, that we respond to Macbeth with diminishing rather than 'mounting' sympathy. Yet, although I believe that the audience's sympathy and pity for Macbeth never again rise to the intensity of II. 2 (the scene that follows Duncan's murder), I would not care to suggest another 'tidy' line of response, such as 'mounting antipathy'. Booth correctly described the play's response-problems and some of the measures taken by Shakespeare to solve them, but erred in looking for a tidy, a too schematic design. Shakespeare was often untidy, and in his best work the response may pull simultaneously in different directions. Thus the steady coarsening of Macbeth's moral nature is bound to affect the audience adversely, yet Shakespeare also took steps to protect his tragic hero, and perhaps did so even more successfully than Booth imagined. Booth called the murder of Lady Macduff and her children 'the third and last atrocity explicitly shown in the play', and thought that 'for the first time, pity for Macbeth's victims really wars with pity for him'. The question arises whether Shakespeare in fact wished to take such a risk. Glen Byam Shaw's Stratford production of 1955 demonstrated how the murder, explicitly shown, can antagonise the audience.

> The murderers entered to a startled hush; they paused, and then the boy made his ungainly run across the stage, a puny, unplanned, forlorn attempt at defence. A blow with the hilts, a thrust. The murderer hung back, as if himself aghast at what he had done,

leaving the boy standing isolated in mid stage, with both hands huddled over his wound. For a long moment he hung, wavering, then crumpled slowly to the ground. There was still silence, a long, shocked silence, before the first animal scream broke from his mother.

This was hitting below the belt, but that is precisely what Shakespeare intended to do. It is not until this moment that the full horror of Macbeth's action bursts upon the audience.[24]

A splendid stage-effect, and splendidly reported. But is it really 'what Shakespeare intended to do'? Compare the scene-ending in the Folio and in a modern edition.

*Son*   He ha's kill'd me Mother,
Run away I pray you. *Exit crying Murther.*   (Folio)

*Son*   He has kill'd me, mother:
Run away, I pray you!                               [*Dies*
   [*Exit Lady Macduff, crying 'Murther!' and
   pursued by the Murderers.*                 (New Arden ed.)

Theobald first took the Folio's 'Exit crying Murther' to refer to Lady Macduff, in the year 1733, when editors treated stage-directions with little respect; and his emendation survived from text to text, as bad emendations often do, sanctified by time and editorial inertia. Presumably Theobald thought that someone who says 'He has killed me' had better die quickly. And yet, as the words are in any event proleptic, like Hamlet's 'I am dead, Horatio' (V. 2. 325), it matters little whether the son expires after he stops speaking or runs off-stage to die. But it matters to the audience-response whether or not a horrific child-murder is to be 'explicitly shown', and the natural interpretation of the Folio is surely that the boy escapes, and dies out of sight.[25] Indeed, Shakespeare seems to have wished to protect his criminal hero by hiding all the principal deaths from the audience. 'Dead' Banquo probably leaves the stage *via* the trap-door between III. 3. 16 and 22, since his body was left 'safe in a ditch' (III. 4. 26); his exit would thus have to be screened from the audience by the murderers' cloaks, and his 'killing' could not be too explicitly shown. If Macduff's wounded son runs off-stage, Lady Macduff can do the same. In short, though we must agree with Bradley that 'it is as if the poet saw the whole story through an ensanguined mist',[26] Shakespeare protected the hero of the bloodiest of all his mature tragedies by not allowing the audience to see a single death until v. 7. 11 (young Siward). The others all seem to be reported deaths, presumably because the dramatist thought it important that pity for the victims should *not* compete too directly with the response to Macbeth.

*          *          *

After glancing at two very different simplifications – Macbeth as a 'fiend' in the murder-scene (De Quincey), and the theory of 'mounting sympathy' (Wayne Booth) – we must ask how Shakespeare adjusts the response as he goes along, both for and against his hero, and how completely he changes it in the fourth act.

Most of the play's defensive manœuvres have been noticed before. Macbeth benefits from an unusual perspective: he speaks all the best verse, he alone engages the audience repeatedly in soliloquy, and in his inward-looking honesty, if not in his speech addressed to others, he represent's the play's most sympathetic human value. He appeals to us as his own accuser, so that we can participate simultaneously with his moral and his criminal nature (when the poetry and perspective demand it, in the first two acts). In addition he benefits from minor dramatic stratagems that are less obvious – for instance, the silence of Banquo's ghost (III. 4). Instead of calling for revenge, in the traditional manner, the ghost never competes with Macbeth verbally, which allows Macbeth's point of view to dominate the scene – and to prevail with the audience.

On the other hand, Shakespeare departed from his source, Holinshed's *Chronicles*, in order to 'heighten Macbeth's guilt and deliberately take away, it would seem, characteristics which might attract an audience's sympathy':[27] Holinshed's Duncan is a man of many faults, his Macbeth has grievances against Duncan that Shakespeare dropped, and, after seizing the throne, his Macbeth ruled virtuously for ten years. Though the theatre-audience could not know of these changes we may say that, far from consistently enforcing sympathy for his hero, Shakespeare took the opposite course as well.

In *Macbeth* the line of response zigzags on, at least in the first three acts, very much as in the other tragedies, except that different technical tricks are used. Consider, for example, the Christian imagery and its effect. Macbeth differs from almost all other Shakespearian villains in expressing deeply religious convictions, not once but many times, endorsed by the full force of some of Shakespeare's best poetry. He believes in 'mine eternal jewel', he feels 'the deep damnation of his taking-off', and, at the extremest push, his whole being aches for Christian comfort:

> But wherefore could not I pronounce 'Amen'?
> I had most need of blessing, and 'Amen'
> Stuck in my throat.[28]

Paradoxically, these very passages define Macbeth's guilt and at the same time enforce the audience's sympathetic response. Intense Christian feeling fills the imaginative foreground and, while it lasts, crowds out all awareness of Macbeth's guilt. But of course it cannot last, and the line of response soon resumes its zigzag course, until it reaches Act IV.

\*          \*          \*

That the play sags in Act IV is generally admitted. Malcolm's long interview with Macduff (IV. 3) is usually blamed, yet Macbeth's scene with the Weird Sisters may be just as great a weakness. Magnificently theatrical with its cauldron, its chanting hags, its screaming and silent apparitions, the scene presents a tragic hero dwarfed by gadgetry who, chameleon-like, seems to take on the local colour, becoming something of an automaton himself. And Macbeth also affects us as a mere shadow of himself for another reason. He can still soliloquise, yet his feelings now seem to lie at the verbal surface: he talks about them, but we are no longer deeply moved. He has lost his magic.[29] As R. B. Heilman has said, 'we expect the tragic protagonist to be an expanding character, one who grows in aware- ness and spiritual largeness; yet Macbeth is to all intents a contract- ing character, who seems to discard large areas of consciousness as he goes'.[30] Nowhere else in the play is Macbeth made to shrink as suddenly as in IV. 1. Distracted by the gadgetry we may not immedi- ately notice it: the scene nevertheless damages our 'sympathetic' relationship with the hero, and the play's suspense henceforth hangs on a much weaker thread – our detached interest in the second set of prophecies.

In IV. 1 Macbeth not only contracts as a person, he also shrinks in the play's perspective. Face to face with the Weird Sisters in I. 3 he could hold his own. Now, as the Weird Sisters' 'masters' (IV. 1. 63) rise out of darkness, their 'unknown power' scales him down: he thinks himself a free agent, he believes that he can conjure and compel them to answer him, but his words are mere bluster, the

unknown powers only show what they want to show, and in the end
they cruelly expose his helplessness.

> Another yet? A seventh? *I'll see no more!*
> And yet the eighth appears, who bears a glass
> Which shows me many more; and some I see
> That twofold balls and treble sceptres carry.
> *Horrible sight!* (IV. 1. 118ff.)

His first meeting with the Weird Sisters made Macbeth seem important to the audience; the second, in IV. 1, has the opposite effect,
making him unimportant, a point obliquely enforced by his frustrated rage.[31]

The play's perspective continues to work against him in the next
two scenes (IV. 2, 3), where his enemies talk about him and he cannot
defend himself. Nevertheless we should notice that Shakespeare
protects Macbeth, as far as he can: though the two scenes help to
turn the audience against the tragic hero, how gently and circuitously
Shakespeare goes about his business! Lady Macduff's prattle with her
young son reduces the seriousness of what might have been said,
Macbeth's name is never mentioned, and, if I am correct in thinking
that no deaths are shown, the audience has to wait till IV. 3. 204
before it knows the worst. Malcolm's extravagant self-accusations in
the next scene also help to shield Macbeth from the audience's
hostility, blunting its edge by first directing it upon a false target.
In addition Malcolm himself shoots beside the mark in at least one
particular.

> I grant him bloody,
> Luxurious, avaricious, false, deceitful,
> Sudden, malicious, smacking of every sin
> That has a name; but there's no bottom, none,
> In my voluptuousness. Your wives, your daughters,
> Your matrons, and your maids, could not fill up
> The cistern of my lust . . . (IV. 3. 57ff.)

We have seen no sign of a *luxurious* (or lascivious) Macbeth, the idea
contradicts our impression of his character, and when Malcolm
obliquely insists upon the point, by talking of his own voluptuous-
ness, we react uneasily to his testimony. What, after all, can he
know of Macbeth except from hearsay? Malcolm and Macduff only
see 'black Macbeth' from the outside, whereas the audience knows

him from his soliloquies and hesitates to accept the external image. Shakespeare, moreover, prevents the audience from giving its full confidence to Malcolm and Macduff by endowing them, initially, with a self-conscious eloquence that comes close to attitudinising.

> Let us seek out some desolate shade, and there
> Weep our sad bosoms empty.
> 　　　　　　. . . new sorrows
> Strike heaven on the face, that it resounds
> As if it felt with Scotland and yell'd out
> Like syllable of dolour. (IV. 3. 1–8)

At this point they have a reason for speaking so strangely. Yet their speech remains vaguely unconvincing: though they understand the world and its ways a little better than Lady Macduff and her son, Malcolm and Macduff still prattle like innocents when compared with Macbeth, who has looked into the abyss. They speak of things beyond their ken, until Ross brings the news about Macduff's family: and then, significantly, Macduff's rage turns swiftly from Macbeth to himself, which partly deflects the audience as well.

> 　　　　　　Sinful Macduff,
> They were all struck for thee – nought that I am;
> Not for their own demerits, but for mine,
> Fell slaughter on their souls. Heaven rest them now! (IV. 3. 224ff.)

In these three transition-scenes (IV. 1–3) the audience-response to Macbeth changes decisively. Shakespeare nevertheless ensures that antipathy will not go too far: the third one urges the case against 'devilish Macbeth' most explicitly, without permitting Malcolm and Macduff to win the audience's whole-hearted assent. And this much-maligned scene marks another important transition: the longest and slowest scene in the play, it introduces a new tempo, arresting the play's onward-rushing momentum just before Lady Macbeth's sleep-walking, where time stands still.

\*　　　　　　\*　　　　　　\*

Although the fifth act continues the process of spiritual 'contraction' we also see some signs of the earlier Macbeth, which help to complicate our response to his death. The honesty of his two stock-taking meditations reminds us of his great soliloquies, his habit of stating the case against himself.

> My way of life
> Is fall'n into the sear, the yellow leaf;
> And that which should accompany old age,
> As honour, love, obedience, troops of friends,
> I must not look to have; but, in their stead,
> Curses not loud but deep, mouth-honour, breath,
> Which the poor heart would fain deny, and dare not. (v. 3. 22ff.)

These lines ask not so much for our *pity* as for our *respect*. And the same is true of his speech when he hears of the queen's death: whatever the precise meaning of 'She should have died hereafter', we cannot accuse him of *bovarysme*, of endeavouring to escape reality.[32] Unlike the other tragic heroes, who had reacted so powerfully to the deaths of Portia, Ophelia, Desdemona and Cordelia, Macbeth feels very little, makes no pretence that it is otherwise, and, thinking of his own death as well, faces the facts. 'Out, out, brief candle!' His honesty extorts our respect – unless the actor insists on pity instead, as did J. P. Kemble, a possible but I think undesirable alternative.

> When the news was brought, 'The queen, my lord, is dead', he seemed struck to the heart; gradually collecting himself he sighed out, 'She should have died hereafter'. Then, as if with the inspiration of despair he hurried out distinctly and pathetically the lines 'To-morrow, and to-morrow, and to-morrow' . . . rising to a climax of desperation that brought down the enthusiastic cheers of the closely packed theatre.[33]

As Macbeth proceeds from one murder to the next his capacity to feel contracts, and his feeling for Lady Macbeth withers away as well. How deeply he loved his 'dearest partner of greatness' (I. 5. 10) before the murder of Duncan we cannot really tell, but after it she ceases to matter to him. He plans the murder of Banquo alone, and in the banquet scene she reveals that they are slipping apart. Informed that Macduff 'denies his person', she replies 'Did you send to him, *sir*?' – to the husband she had once taunted as 'the poor cat i' th' adage'.[34] A history of the marriage in a monosyllable! The other tragic heroes continue to radiate life-affirming emotions in the fourth and fifth acts, giving or begging for forgiveness, freely expressing love or admiration – emotions that the audience responds to and reflects back upon them. Not so Macbeth: when his wife dies he loses his last human link with the past, the only person left who might have lifted him to emotional heights, and he expresses little more than defeat and weariness. 'She should have died hereafter . . .'

In the fifth act Shakespeare denies Macbeth some of the emotions that appear to be indispensable in the other tragedies. No love, no fellow-feeling. Not even tears from the depths of some divine despair: only dry-eyed regrets and sudden bouts of desperation. Macbeth contracts within himself, and his relationships with others shrink and lose their humanity as well. We see him in the company of servants, messengers, a doctor, Seyton[35] – unwilling hangers-on, rats that would leave the sinking ship (even Seyton's slowness in answering Macbeth's call, v. 3. 19ff., adds to this impression). And yet, although the play's imagery points to Macbeth's shrinking –

> Now does he feel his title
> Hang loose about him, like a giant's robe
> Upon a dwarfish thief. (v. 2. 20–2) –

we must not make too much of this process. For what is the logical conclusion?

> Though the death of Macbeth brings the play to a close, that death, we are made to feel, is no loss. 'The time is free' (v. 8. 55) cries Macduff, displaying the 'usurper's cursed head.' And Malcolm speaks of 'this dead butcher and his fiend-like queen' (v. 8. 69). The fall of the protagonist brings no tragic release, no feeling of woe or wonder, for Shakespeare mutes such feelings by transferring interest from Macbeth's personal plight to society's salvation . . .[36]

If there is any significance in the Folio's title, *The Tragedie of Macbeth*, the protagonist's death should certainly bring tragic release. Shakespeare, I believe, steers towards such a response by stressing the external image of the hero, Macbeth as seen by others, and in particular by repeating one word, *tyrant*, which is used by both Siwards, Macduff and Malcolm: 'Thou liest, abhorred tyrant!' 'Tyrant, show thy face!' 'The tyrant's people on both sides do fight.'[37] True as it may be, the external view fails to give the whole truth; and the more Macbeth's enemies insist upon it, the more we are inclined to resist it. Hearing him described as *tyrant*, *usurper*, *butcher* and so on, an audience that has thrilled to a competent actor's rendering of the terrible soliloquies cannot but feel that a man's outer life is a tale told by an idiot, full of sound and fury, signifying very little, and that the inner life is all in all.

The responsibility for drawing such a conclusion is left with the audience. Shakespeare, however, took his precautions – not only by using words like *tyrant* that are meant to leave us dissatisfied, but also by preparing in two other ways for our final response to his hero's death. '*Enter Macduffe; with Macbeths head*' we read in the Folio. No other hero or villain in Shakespeare's mature work suffers an end so gruesome, though Iago and others are at least as guilty. Why should we be subjected to this horror?

The shocking climax with Macbeth's head follows another death, the whole point of which is to focus attention upon *response*. Siward hears that his son died in battle. Unlike Macduff, who was struck speechless by similar news, Siward reacts with what can only be called heartiness.

> *Siward*  Had he his hurts before?
> *Ross*   Ay, on the front. *Siward*  Why, then, God's soldier be he!
> Had I as many sons as I have hairs
> I would not wish them to a fairer death.
> And so – his knell is knoll'd.

Shakespeare meant us to wonder at such a phlegmatic grief, and makes Malcolm speak for us.

>               He's worth more sorrow,
> And that I'll spend for him.

But Siward persists:

>               He's worth no more.
> They say he parted well and paid his score;
> And so, God be with him!

Here, manifestly, Shakespeare raises the question of appropriate response – and then at once '*Enter Macduffe; with Macbeths head*'. How carefully it was all planned!

Why had the severed head to be brought back?[38] Precisely because it too focuses our response: we no sooner see it than we decide, if only unconsciously, that *this* is not Macbeth. The head, from which life has fled, represents the tyrant, the outer man; it serves as a ghastly reminder that there was an inner man. No one, of the survivors, can speak for the Macbeth of the soliloquies: we, the audience, have to do so for ourselves, and the play's tragic effect depends on our accepting this challenge.

*      *      *

The response to Lady Macbeth was once highly emotional. 'Lady Macbeth is merely detested'; 'she is a great bad woman, whom we hate, but whom we fear more than we hate'.[39] Detested, hated, feared: no golden opinions for the fiend-like queen. Some actresses, however, aimed at a very different response. Mrs Siddons made Lady Macbeth human, and gave her 'the graces of personal beauty', while Ellen Terry's performance was 'pungent with the *odeur de femme* . . . She rushed into her husband's arms, clinging, kissing, coaxing, flattering.'[40] Bradley, at last, in a few truly indispensable pages, compounded the two responses, showing that they interpenetrate one another even when one seems predominant. In the opening act he thought Lady Macbeth 'the most commanding and perhaps the most awe-inspiring figure' ever drawn by Shakespeare. 'However appalling she may be, she is sublime.' Her courage and force of will move our admiration:

> Yet if the Lady Macbeth of these scenes were really utterly in-human, or a 'fiend-like queen', as Malcolm calls her, the Lady Macbeth of the sleep-walking scene would be an impossibility. The one woman could never become the other. And in fact, if we look below the surface, there is evidence enough in the earlier scenes of preparation for the later.[41]

Evidence, that is, of feminine weakness and human feeling, some of it so overlaid by contrary impressions that only a great critic would understand its 'secret' effect. Others observe, in her invocation to the spirits of evil (I. 5. 37ff.), a relentless inhumanity; Bradley added that the same speech also reveals a 'determination to crush the inward protest'. It prepares for the sleep-walking scene, where Bradley found Lady Macbeth the same woman as before, despite the sinking of her nature in the middle acts, one whose misery and piteousness by no means crowd out other responses.

> The sleep-walking scene . . . inspires pity, but its main effect is one of awe. There is great horror in the references to blood, but it cannot be said that there is more than horror; and Campbell was surely right when . . . he insisted that in Lady Macbeth's misery there is no trace of contrition.[42]

The sleep-walking scene, the one scene in Acts IV and V that can compare with the best in Acts I to III, deserves closer attention. Notice that the stage-response includes horror and pity, but points elsewhere as well. The Doctor and Gentlewoman guess the cause of Lady Macbeth's 'perturbation', and yet neither dares to put thoughts into words. The Gentlewoman resolutely refuses to repeat what Lady Macbeth has said: the doctor also shies away, then excuses himself. Their homely, troubled exclamations cannot disguise the fact that they are deeply *afraid*, a feeling that flows from them into the audience. They fear for themselves, because a king's secrets can be dangerous, but more especially because they have spied upon a terrifying, unknown power, perhaps the Prince of Darkness.

> More needs she the divine than the physician.
> God, God forgive us all. Look after her . . .
> My mind she has mated, and amaz'd my sight.
> I think, but dare not speak. (V. 1. 72–7)

The sleep-walking scene's extraordinary impact depends less on our feeling for Lady Macbeth than on our apprehension of non-human powers invisibly locked in battle. From the very first we have sensed that evil spirits hovered in Macbeth's vicinity, brooding and hatching evil thoughts and deeds, an impression planted by the Weird Sisters in the exit lines of their opening scene, where they seem to lay a charm upon the entire world of the play:

> Fair is foul, and foul is fair:
> *Hover* through the fog and filthy air.

Lady Macbeth believes that the evil spirits that tend on mortal thoughts can hear her when she invokes them,[43] and Macbeth himself flings some of his enraged thoughts into the air as if he expects to be heard by the hoverers.

> And be these juggling fiends no more believ'd
> That palter with us in a double sense,
> That keep the word of promise to our ear,
> And break it to our hope! (V. 8. 19–22)

Lady Macbeth also knows of another supernatural power called *heaven*, which may peep through the blanket of the dark to cry 'Hold, hold' (I. 5. 50–1), but the play never presents angels or the like as counterparts to the Weird Sisters and apparitions, and so for a while heaven seems to be less actively concerned. There are signs, however, that heaven can intervene – when Macbeth thinks he hears a voice cry 'Sleep no more', or when a doctor describes the English king's miraculous cure of a disease called 'the evil':[44]

> at his touch,
> Such sanctity hath heaven given his hand,
> They presently amend.

In the sleep-walking scene we are made to feel that the two super-natural sides, which have so far avoided one another, are at last in close proximity – even though neither party puts in a personal appearance. Dickens attempted something similar in *Oliver Twist*, which may help to explain what I mean. The secret of Oliver's parentage is preserved by a series of coincidences: his mother charged Old Sally, who nursed her when Oliver was born in the workhouse, to keep safe a gold locket and ring, and immediately died; Old Sally begins to confess to the future Mrs Bumble that she pawned the gold, and dies before she can finish; Mrs Bumble tells Monks that she redeemed the pawned locket and ring, Monks buys them from her and tosses them into a river, in order to destroy the last clue that Oliver is his half-brother; Monks later tells Fagin all he knows, Nancy eavesdrops on them, informs Rose Maylie, Rose tells old Mr Brownlow, who finally confronts Monks. '"Every word," cried the old gentleman, "every word that has passed between you and this detested villain is known to me! Shadows on the wall have caught your whispers, and brought them to my ear; the sight of the perse-cuted child has turned vice itself, and given it the courage and almost the attributes of virtue!"' (ch. 49) Providence intervenes every time, just before the vital clue disappears, and in the end Oliver's identity can be established. Providence observes every move, and works its will through whatever instrument lies at hand, trans-forming vice itself and making it part of a human net to catch and hold the truth.

We only begin to understand the providential design towards the end of *Oliver Twist*. In *Macbeth* the sleep-walking scene makes a similar point, that 'someone is watching'. By a stroke of dramatic irony Lady Macbeth's own conscience-recorded words switch on to tell us this. 'What need we fear who knows it, when none can call our power to account?' (v. 1. 35) She reminds us that heaven calls all men to account;[45] and, as in *Oliver Twist*, heaven makes use of vice itself, in the person of Lady Macbeth, whose inner self spied on her when she pushed her husband into crime, whose inward protest now betrays her to 'shadows on the wall'. Though the 'unknown power' of evil (IV. 1. 69) seems to hover nearby as Lady Macbeth re-enacts her crimes, others too are watching and together catch and hold the truth. Lady Macbeth watched herself, the doctor and gentlewoman watch her, the theatre-audience watches the three of them, heaven watches over all. The audience's self-awareness, it should be noted, binds the scene together: knowing itself to be invisible to the doctor and gentlewoman, as they are invisible to Lady Macbeth, the audience can the more readily believe in the invisible presence of supernatural powers – and this helps to give the scene its extraordinary effect.

\*        \*        \*

A word, finally, about the Porter scene (III. 3), perhaps the best known example of 'response engineering' in Shakespeare. Comic relief? That used to be the explanation, although Bradley declared that 'the Porter does not make me smile: the moment is too terrific'.[46] The Porter certainly angles for laughter, and succeeds in the theatre if not in the study; yet Bradley rightly observed that Shakespeare 'could have written without the least difficulty speeches five times as humorous', from which we must conclude that the scene has other assets apart from weak jokes about drink.

The most valuable is the Porter's tipsy contentment. Having caroused till the second cock he is on excellent terms with himself, and at peace with the world. Nothing can shake him out of this state of physical wellbeing: the knocking that goes like a knife through Macbeth has no urgency for him, and only just penetrates through the pleasing patter of his own voice. Knock, knock, knock! 'Don't hurry me', he seems to say, 'I have important thoughts to think, I'll attend to you by and by.' He contrasts in several other ways with Macbeth, but chiefly in being so very comfortable within himself – a man who takes life as it comes, and who cheerfully welcomes all sinners as his fellows. 'Knock, knock! Who's there, i' th' other devil's name? Faith, here's an equivocator that could swear in both the scales against either scale; who committed treason enough for God's sake, yet could not equivocate to heaven. O, come in equivocator!'

'Comic relief' fails to indicate the Porter's other functions. He is introduced to transform the mood and pace of the play. His humour helps, but his very brief scene leaves an indelible impression because he brings to it so much more – a pagan tolerance and comfortableness, expansiveness, a glimpse of a man who remains immovably himself.

# 9
# Antony versus Cleopatra

Majesty, affability, benevolence, liberality, placability, amity,
justice, fortitude, patience in sustaining wrong; all and more are
Antony's . . . in a word, Antony, not Julius Caesar, as some vainly
suppose, is [Shakespeare's] portrait of true greatness.

(J. Dover Wilson)[1]

Once we have the idea in our heads that amusement is a permissible (and indeed essential) response to large tracts of this play,
Antony's fury after Actium, his treatment of Thidias [Thyreus],
and his row with Cleopatra, come into sharper focus.

(A. L. French)[2]

Heroic tragedy or comical tragedy? Our uneasiness in defining the
response to Antony mirrors our difficulty in describing the whole
play's genre and tones. Whether or not we accept either of the views
quoted above, we cannot deny that Antony, first served to the
audience in a piquant sauce of Cleopatra's humour, elicits a response
that sets him apart from all the other tragic heroes. Smarting in
lingering pickle he loses tragic stature, at least in the opening scenes.
Approaching the play through our response to the hero I am
struck by the fact that it differs greatly from its source, Plutarch's
Life of Marcus Antonius, in its humour. For Antonius himself, not
Cleopatra, stars as the humorist in the Life: Plutarch mentions
several of his practical jokes, his love of players and jesters, 'his outrageous manner of railing' and of exchanging 'mocks' with all and
sundry, his Antonius being a comical, merry, happy-go-lucky fellow.[3]
In the play it is Cleopatra who rails and mocks, and Antony is always
at the receiving end, and not amused. She laughs, he glooms: and
even when the play refers back to earlier, happier times, Shakespeare
deftly changes a word or phrase for a similar effect. Cleopatra had a
salt fish attached to Antony's fishing-hook, and he 'thinking he had
taken a fishe in deede, snatched up his line presently. Then they all
fell a laughing. Cleopatra laughing also, said . . . this is not thy
profession . . . Nowe Antonius delighting in these fond and childish

pastimes, verie ill newes were brought him ...'⁴ It is clearly implied that a good time was had by all, and that Antonius laughed with the rest. Not so by Shakespeare:

> That time, – O times! –
> I laugh'd him out of patience; and that night
> I laugh'd him into patience ... (II. 5. 18ff.)

When Enobarbus speaks with Egyptian levity ('the tears live in an onion that should water this sorrow', I. 2. 156ff.), Antony also refuses to be jollied along. Only in the scene aboard Pompey's galley (II. 7), at a safe distance from Cleopatra, does Shakespeare permit his hero to enjoy himself (though this orgy proves a much tamer affair than others described by Plutarch): and here his mockery of Lepidus scarcely measures up to the 'outrageous' general behaviour of Plutarch's Antonius.

Shakespeare greatly accentuated the laughter at Antony's expense, in the play's opening scenes, and at the same time deprived his hero of the ability to laugh back. He almost suppressed Antony's delight in clever repartee, and as far as possible pushed out of view his fun-loving, playboy side, either having it reported by hostile witnesses (I. 4, II. 1, etc.) or somehow turning it to Antony's disadvantage. Even in the magnificent description of the first meeting with Cleopatra (II. 2. 195ff.: 'The barge she sat in ...'), where he followed Plutarch closely, he managed to introduce a touch of humour that cuts Antony down to size: the Roman, outshone by the Egyptian queen,

> Enthron'd i' the market-place, did sit alone,
> Whistling to th' air.

One of the several functions of the play's humour is to diminish Antony. Cleopatra out-thinks and out-smarts him, plays tricks on him to the very last (her pretended suicide), and often her humour is her deadliest weapon. 'Lord, what is a lover!' said Congreve's Millamant, in Mirabell's presence, implying that a lover is the most ridiculous animal: but Cleopatra even enjoys teasing Antony in his absence, almost without meaning to, when she sets out to praise him:

> Or does he walk? or is he on his horse?
> O happy horse, to bear the weight of Antony!
> Do bravely, horse; for wotst thou whom thou mov'st?
> The demi-Atlas of this earth ... (I. 5. 20ff.)

She partly smiles at herself, seeing herself in a horse, and then implies that though Antony bears the weight of half the earth, a horse goes one better, being another Atlas-figure in carrying him: not one of her wickedest jokes, as she misses Antony and therefore magnifies him, but it shows that even when well-disposed she can't resist laughing at him. Yet Antony's failure to snaffle Cleopatra and, while still alive, to exist unridiculed in her imagination, would not distinguish him from Shakespeare's grandest tragic heroes unsupported by other impressions. Iago, after all, treats Othello similarly. Only when we perceive how Shakespeare channels our response in other ways are we driven to conclude that, at the outset, he wished to *reduce* his hero.

Antony lacks not only humour but also high seriousness. Except for Coriolanus, the other tragic heroes very quickly recognise that they are under pressure, and respond with a passionate will to understand. Not so Antony, who waves away the messenger from Rome in his first scene, and thereafter may suffer from brief fits of thoughtfulness –

These strong Egyptian fetters I must break . . .
I must from this enchanting queen break off . . . (I. 2)

– but never, before his defeat at Actium, experiences tragic insight, never wishes to 'Rage, rage, against the dying of the light'.

Antony also differs from the other tragic heroes in lacking *spirit* (in various senses): 'I say again, thy *spirit*/Is all afraid to govern thee near him' (II. 3. 29: the Soothsayer to Antony, referring to Octavius); 'O'er my *spirit*/Thy full supremacy thou knew'st' (III. 11. 58: Antony, addressing Cleopatra). We gather, when Antony hears of Fulvia's death, that she too proved more than a match for him: 'There's a great *spirit* gone! Thus did I desire it . . .' (I. 2. 119). And throughout the play allusions to Julius Caesar remind us that a giant's robe now hangs upon a much smaller man. The other tragic heroes, though sometimes temporarily eclipsed by a Lady Macbeth or a Volumnia, are not dwarfed for so long and by so many stronger personalities.

His failure to control ordinary conversation brings out this general weakness. In his first scene he asks for the news from Rome, though almost grinding his teeth with irritation ('Grates me! The sum.'), but Cleopatra taunts him so cleverly that in the end he forbids the messenger to speak. In the second scene, when he tries to be serious,

Enobarbus' backchat impudently disregards Antony's mood, even after he hears of Fulvia's death, and the easy-going master has to struggle to assert himself. In the third he struggles quite pitifully, for Cleopatra breaks in on five of his first six speeches and, when he finally secures permission to speak, continues to interrupt and up-stage him. When we next see him (II. 2) he immediately loses the initiative to Octavius, to whose tart complaints Antony can only return evasive answers, a humiliation invented by Shakespeare.[5] And worse follows: Antony allows himself to be talked into marrying Octavia, a trap if ever there was one. According to Plutarch, be it noted, no single person or party proposed the marriage, 'which fortune offered' in that both Antony and Octavia had recently lost a spouse; and 'everie man did set forward this mariage'.[6] Agrippa's proposal in the play makes a very different impression. Just prior to it Antony twice ordered Enobarbus to 'speak no more', and twice suffered the indignity of being answered back. Octavius, with raised eyebrows, observes that he dislikes the 'manner' of Enobarbus' speech, the free and easy manner that goes with Antony's life-style, so different from his own. A proposal such as Agrippa's, it then dawns on us, must have been cleared by Octavius before the triumvirs met: it's a carefully rehearsed manœuvre, and Antony ('Whom ne'er the word of "No" woman heard speak'), encircled, capitulates. Even Enobarbus, by no means the play's sharpest mind, foresees that Antony won't give up Cleopatra (II. 2. 238: 'Never! He will not'), so we assume that Octavius could not fail to leap to the same conclusion. Long before Actium, therefore, Antony impresses us in scene after scene as a loser; Herculean, but still a loser; and his defeats in conversation, added by Shakespeare, distinguish him equally from Plutarch's Antonius and from the other tragic heroes.

As is well known, Shakespeare sometimes externalises a psychic drama in stage images: Lear, who divests himself of 'interest of territory, cares of state', wishes later to strip life of its pretences and tears off his own clothes (III. 4). To Antony Shakespeare also assigned a gesture and a pose, one closely connected with his other defeats, which acquires significance as the play proceeds. He appears before us, again and again, as a man bidding farewell. At first this happens quite naturally, and we pay little attention: he leaves Cleopatra (and she objects strenuously), sends back a pearl and a second farewell, leaves Octavius, sends away Octavia. After Actium, however, the farewell-scenes turn into extravaganzas, and, just in case we don't notice this, bystanders tell us so. Antony advises his friends to take a ship 'laden with gold' and make their peace with Octavius (III. 11): 'My treasure's in the harbour. Take it.' Quite madly, he seems to be offering his entire treasure, whereas Plutarch's Antonius 'toke one of his carects or hulks loden with gold and silver, and other rich cariage, and gave it unto his friends', the context suggesting that he had other resources, which makes the gesture less odd. And Plutarch's words, that 'Antonius very curteously and lovingly did comfort them, and prayed them to depart', could only be said to apply in a general sense to Shakespeare's scene, since Antony seems much more taken up with himself than with his friends, his love and courtesy impress us as partly a show, and we already guess at a motive that is later verbalised: 'What does he mean?' 'To make his followers weep' (IV. 2. 23–4). On hearing that Enobarbus has gone over to Octavius, Antony again strikes his characteristic pose:

> Go, Eros, send his treasure after; do it;
> Detain no jot, I charge thee; write to him –
> I will subscribe – gentle adieus and greetings. (IV. 5. 12–14)

Other notable farewells include Antony's emotionally charged scene with his servants (IV. 2), his speech to the absent and supposedly dead Cleopatra (IV. 14), and the longer leave-taking when he himself dies. It can happen, of course, that our attention swings round to someone else who takes leave of Antony, the god Hercules (IV. 3), or Eros:

> My dear master,
> My captain and my emperor, let me say,
> Before I strike this bloody stroke, farewell.
> Antony    'Tis said, man, and farewell.
> Eros    Farewell, great chief. Shall I strike now? (IV. 14. 89–93)[7]

Antony's curtness here confirms our uneasiness about *his* farewells: he has no time for Eros' emotion, though elsewhere very ready to indulge his own. He quickly recovers himself ('Thrice nobler than myself!'), but some damage is done. The overriding impression, however, as one farewell follows another, is that Antony retreats and fades from life, like Keats's joy – 'whose hand is ever at his lips/ Bidding adieu.'

Shakespeare, like other dramatists, was normally more interested in arrivals than departures. We watch Othello's coming before the

Duke, his arrival at Cyprus, at the night-brawl, his going with Iago
to Desdemona, the scene usually being carefully prepared to give the
greatest impact to the hero's entrances, whereas leave-takings pass by
quickly, with less effect. Antony's farewells accordingly intimate
something as fundamental as Lear's stripping gestures: indeed, they
affect us as a kind of stripping, one almost willed by Antony as his
friends peel off and leave him bare. After Actium he has to send a
mere schoolmaster as ambassador –

> An argument that he is pluck'd, when hither
> He sends so poor a pinion of his wing (III. 12. 3–4) –

but he continues to lavish gifts and love upon those who leave him
because he cannot help pouring himself away.

To give a balanced picture I should now describe a different man,
the Herculean hero, Antony the magnificent. Rather than repeat
what others have already said[8] I prefer to take it as known and more
or less agreed, and to leave the reader with a question. Must we
choose between the two, or could the heroic Antony and the per-
petual loser coexist in the same play?

*      *      *

Focusing repeatedly upon him from a particular angle the play
suggests a rigidity in Antony, as if he is held not only by strong
Egyptian fetters but by a psychic force that prohibits freedom of
movement. For Cleopatra, on the other hand, Shakespeare invented
an extraordinary range of special gestures, so that her physical
expressiveness intimates a corresponding emotional and intuitive
mobility. The loss of Shakespeare's stage-directions is above all regret-
table in *her* scenes, where they must often have been as character-
revealing as the four that happen to survive in the Folio within
thirteen lines of each other: 'Strikes him downe', 'Strikes him', 'She
hales him vp and downe', 'Draw a knife' (II. 5. 61ff.).[9] There are so
many descriptions of Cleopatra in an unusual pose, or flow of move-
ments, that Shakespeare might almost have seen her, in imagination,
as a choreographer. Immediately after Enobarbus' account of her
wonderfully stage-managed appearance in the barge, *lying* in her
pavilion (as in Plutarch), the royal statue springs to life in another
recollection (invented by Shakespeare):

> I saw her once
> Hop forty paces through the public street;
> And having lost her breath, she spoke, and panted . . .

The descriptions vary in length from the unhurried scene-painting of the 'barge' to Enobarbus' single-line admission that Apollodorus did indeed carry 'A certain queen to Caesar in a mattress' (II. 6. 70). The speakers, however, invariably admire Cleopatra (even Enobarbus should chuckle as he remembers the mattress, though actors sometimes bite off the words as if giving away a shameful secret): they admire not just her beauty but, more important, the originality of her several performances.

Shakespeare's interest in the infinite variety of Cleopatra's physical behaviour emerges also from the verbal pictures that describe neither what we see nor what others have seen but simply wishes, fears and other fumes of her imagination. Some of her wishes take shape in a leisurely fashion, as when, in borrowing the fishing-party episode (II. 5), Shakespeare improved it by making Cleopatra imagine herself one of the anglers (not so in Plutarch). Other wishes, as Tristram Shandy would say, come sideways in unexpected manner upon the listener:

> Help me away, dear Charmian, I shall fall . . .
> Cut my lace, Charmian, come!
> But let it be . . .                                          (I. 3)
>
> That I might sleep out this great gap of time . . .
> By Isis, I will give thee bloody teeth . . .
> Get me ink and paper . . .                          (I. 5)
>
> I have a mind to strike thee ere thou speak'st . . .
> Though I am mad, I will not bite him . . . (II. 5)

And so on. All such lines, I repeat, direct attention to Cleopatra's body, and to her brilliance as a performer. And since it soon transpires that she will do and say whatever comes into her head, a producer may regard all her wishes, even the negative ones, as oblique stage directions for other parts of the play, and call for the greatest possible variety of action from his Cleopatra: dancing, hopping, running, panting, leaning, falling, reclining, yawning, biting, pinching, fighting, and, above all, in her scenes with Antony, kissing, fondling, embracing.

Traditionalists will object that Cleopatra's physical contact with Antony should be reduced to the absolute minimum rather than stressed, on the ground that Shakespeare avoided love-scenes with amorous transports embarrassing to boy-actors, who took the female parts. The last point could be true in general without applying to *Antony and Cleopatra*, an exceptional play that presupposes a most exceptional boy. 'Pure rhetoric' said Granville-Barker of Antony's 'the nobleness of life/Is to do *thus*' (I. 1. 37), and, having deleted the play's first embrace, went on: 'Not till their passion deepens as tragedy nears does Shakespeare give it physical expression. Antony leaves her for battle with "a soldier's kiss" (it is the first the action shows) . . .'[10] A soldier's kiss (IV. 4. 30), presumably, would be chaste and unphysical, the merest flutter of lips? Be that as it may, Granville-Barker overlooked other, unequivocal directions for sensual contact:

> Fall not a tear, I say; one of them rates
> All that is won and lost. Give me a kiss;
> Even this repays me. (III. 11. 69–71)

And if Shakespeare trusted the Cleopatra-boy to carry off one kiss successfully, why not more? There are reasons for believing that Antony enters and leaves the play kissing and being kissed; just before his death he asks to lay upon Cleopatra's lips 'of many thousand kisses the poor last' – and this surely coincides with, rather than contradicts, our general impression of what has happened.

I insist on 'many thousand kisses', that is, on a dozen or so enacted upon the stage, because without number we cannot have variety, and it was the infinite variety of Cleopatra's sexual nature that Shakespeare celebrated in the familiar lines:

> Age cannot wither her, nor custom stale
> Her infinite variety. Other women cloy
> The appetites they feed on, but she makes hungry . . . (II. 2. 239ff.)

But her 'infinite variety' also alludes, at least partly, to the general range of Cleopatra's physical poses and performances that I have outlined, coming straight after descriptions of three of her greatest triumphs: the 'barge' scene, her victory over Caesar –

> Royal wench!
> She made great Caesar lay his sword to bed:
> He plough'd her, and she cropp'd –

and her hopping forty paces through the public street. The last of the three, indeed, ends with a line that, but for Maecenas'

interruption and a half-line of reply, should not be separated from
Enobarbus' summing-up; he says, in effect –

> And, having lost her breath, she spoke and panted,
> That she did make defect perfection,
> And, breathless, power breathe forth.
> Age cannot wither her, nor custom stale . . .

Cleopatra's infinite physical variety confirms that 'she is cunning
past man's thought' and at the same time breathes forth humour
and *power*.

\*          \*          \*

Though I have only scratched the surface in all that has been said so
far about Antony's weakness and Cleopatra's power, I must now
pause. Our response to the two principals changes so unmistakably
in the middle of the play that we must ask how it is done, and why.
And some of the answers are not far to seek. Half-way through,
Cleopatra's humour against Antony is damped down, almost extin-
guished; Antony's sense of shame ennobles him, despite his relapses,
and lifts him at last to seriousness; though defeated in battle, Antony
more readily imposes his will on Cleopatra. In their scenes together
Antony takes the lead, where previously Cleopatra had dominated.

Shakespeare, however, adjusts our response to prepare for this
when the principals are apart, and the transition-scenes therefore
repay special attention. Cleopatra's first interview with the messenger
from Italy (II. 5) probably achieves more than any other, since the
scene changes its mood at the exact mid-point ('For what good turn?'
'For the best turn i' th' bed') in a reversal as carefully planned as
'*Exit pursued by a bear*' in *The Winter's Tale*. Before hearing the
news Cleopatra gloats in her sexuality, basking so unashamedly in
self-admiration that she might well ogle a mirror and murmur
'music, moody food/Of us that trade in love' to her own reflection.
Her every second thought is of sex, and she utters it as if she and sex
are one, as if paying tribute to herself. Her puns and imagery convey
not merely delight in sex but also the confidence that she is sexually
all-powerful:

> As well a woman with an eunuch play'd
> As with a woman . . .

>                               I will betray
> Tawny-finn'd fishes; my bended hook shall pierce

Their slimy jaws, and as I draw them up
I'll think them every one an Antony
And say 'Ah ha! Y'are caught!' ...

Ram thou thy fruitful tidings in mine ears
That long time have been barren ...

... My bluest veins to kiss – a hand that kings
Have lipp'd, and trembled kissing.

Shakespeare pursues his lovers to their bedroom, in Cleopatra's joyous recollection of a sex-change that asserts her supreme self-confidence, just before the fateful messenger arrives:

Ere the ninth hour, I drunk him to his bed,
Then put my tires and mantles on him, whilst
I wore his sword Philippan.

Then, hearing that Antony has married, her defeat seems more stunning than Actium, since he receives several warnings of danger but Cleopatra thinks herself sexually secure. The messenger's line, 'For the best turn i' th' bed', treats her to the same kind of sexual brutality that she had enjoyed using against Mardian (I. 5. 9ff., II. 5. 5–6), and briefly lifts the speaker out of his role: as the words leap to his lips he is less a messenger addressing his queen than a man leering at a woman. This complicates what follows, subtly degrading Cleopatra (who had called herself 'a morsel for a monarch', I. 5. 31), for, though he quickly corrects himself ('Madam, he's married to Octavia'), her extravagant reaction seems to be partly triggered off by his manner, not just his matter. She reacts to him as a person: despite her violence, an element of sexual self-assertion creeps back into her speech (and becomes more manifest in the second interview, when she orders him to take note of her 'majesty': III. 3. 18). In effect she now acts out another sex-reversal, striking the man down, haling him up and down, threatening him with her knife. But whereas the recollected bedroom scene, in which she wore the sword Philippan, presented her as 'a most triumphant lady', when she crouches knife-in-hand upon the stage, hissing grotesquely 'Rogue, thou hast lived too long!', she makes a very different impression. All the humour of the scene, really *her* humour, contradicts her former claim to sexual supremacy, or even to respect. The messenger, an independent merchant (*not* a grovelling wretch),[11] reacts to her tantrums with a pleasing sense of what is his due, and she rages at him and at his rock-like persistence ('He's married', four times repeated) as a flock of small birds might scream at an owl: she dissipates her energy, she loses *power*. And in their second interview (III. 3), whilst the messenger adopts a humbler tone his willingness to let her think as she pleases about Octavia, and Cleopatra's retreat into fantasy, suggest an even greater loss of power, since hers depends so much on quickness of perception. Strangely enough, the impression that she wilfully deceives herself survives despite the fact that Enobarbus had twice prophesied that Antony would leave Octavia (II. 2. 238, II. 6. 112), despite Antony's saying, just before the first messenger-scene, 'I will to Egypt', despite his bidding farewell to Octavia just after the second one. Notwithstanding all these hints that Cleopatra reads the future correctly, she seems to lose herself in the messenger-scenes, and never fully recovers until Antony dies.

So much for two transition-scenes. When Antony rejoins Cleopatra their dialogues also affect us as transitions – coming between a scintillating first act and two grandly spectacular suicides – partly because we feel the play to be moving from comedy to tragedy, partly because Shakespeare never allows the principals to remain on-stage together for more than fifty lines at a stretch, or to build up momentum within the scene, except once (III. 13. 85–194). Moreover, their scenes are oddly repetitious, in that several of the more striking ones depict either a reunion after battle or a reconciliation, or both. I mention this not to accuse Shakespeare of a failure of inventiveness but to point out that these scenes have a serial relationship, and that each one channels our response to the next. In their first reconciliation, after Actium, Antony will not accept Cleopatra's plea

> Forgive my fearful sails! I little thought
> You would have followed (III. 11. 55–6),

insisting twice that she knew too well that he would follow. She doesn't deny it, sobs 'Pardon, pardon!' and, after a searching silence, he decides to make the best of things, and ostentatiously throws off his mood:

> Fall not a tear, I say; one of them rates
> All that is won and lost. Give me a kiss . . .

We are left feeling that much remains unexplained. The kiss deceives neither of them, and Antony immediately turns his back on it, his thoughts darting away:

> We sent our schoolmaster; is 'a come back?
> Love, I am full of lead. Some wine!

In their next reconciliation, the Thyreus-scene (III. 13), Antony's sense of betrayal carries all before it, exactly as Cleopatra's had done when Antony told her that he must return to Rome (in I. 3): in both scenes the 'betrayer' tries to interrupt the other's recriminations half a dozen times and only then succeeds in stating his case. Antony now listens to her promise of ever-enduring love, comments shortly 'I am satisfied', and changes the subject. In those three words, as in the kiss that patched up their earlier difference, he signifies that things do not bear looking into. A few lines later he shakes himself and tries to speak more cordially ('Where hast thou been, my heart? Dost thou hear, lady? . . .') but, as becomes increasingly obvious, without real conviction.

The third in the series, merely an attempted reconciliation-scene (IV. 12), presents Cleopatra even more damagingly as a betrayer, and Antony refuses to parley. MacCallum, to be sure, thought her 'in no way responsible' for her fleet's treachery,[12] and this is just possible; but the important point is that Antony believes her to be responsible. That is, we meet him in the fourth betrayal–reconciliation scene (IV. 14) convinced by the evidence of three previous betrayals, each more blatant than the last, that a right gipsy has incontrovertibly *sold* him. And what happens? Told that Cleopatra is dead, and that her last words were 'Antony! most noble Antony!', he discards his former suspicions and forgives her; or rather, accuses himself:

> I will o'ertake thee, Cleopatra, and
> Weep for my pardon.

Before long he hears, too late, that she still lives, and has therefore betrayed him once more. And yet, in the fifth and final reconciliation-scene (IV. 15), not a word of reproach. The scene's effect depends very largely, because of its serial placing, on his *not* acting as he acted earlier:[13] though the evidence against Cleopatra seems blacker than ever, from Antony's viewpoint, he magnificently forgives her. But – a point easily missed – he no longer fully believes her. For all her fine talk of 'Knife, drugs, serpents' he knows that she will negotiate with

Octavius and, despite her disclaimer, remains unshaken in his conviction.

>                                Antony   One word, sweet queen;
>    Of Caesar seek your honour with your safety. O!
>    Cleopatra   They do not go together. Antony   Gentle, hear me:
>    None about Caesar trust but Proculeius.

These lines tell us that although Antony forgives Cleopatra's recent betrayals, he has not forgotten them. He has achieved a new clarity of vision (at least, where Cleopatra is concerned), and therefore the value he places upon a parting kiss dignifies their love more than all previous pomps and pageants:

>    I am dying, Egypt, dying; only
>    I here importune death a while until
>    Of many thousand kisses the poor last
>    I lay upon thy lips.

                    *          *          *

When we move on to the play's ending, where all our earlier responses are put to the test, I find that I cannot agree with the very large number of critics who stress the 'glory' and 'triumph' of Cleopatra's death. Ernest Schanzer, who wrote so perceptively on the response to *Antony and Cleopatra*, saw that in accepting the majority-view of Cleopatra's triumphant death he also came close to disqualifying the play as a tragedy, and again I have misgivings.

>    If [Cleopatra] does not undergo an ennoblement (if we prefer to confine the word 'redemption' to religious contexts) which carries with it an increase in human kindness and a diminution of selfishness and pride . . . it is difficult to see what Shakespeare was doing in the last act.
>    Mingled with a sense of reconciliation there is in our response to Antony's death a strong feeling of 'the pity of it!' and 'would it were otherwise!' . . . At the death of Cleopatra this emotion seems to be entirely lacking . . . [and this] marks off *Antony and Cleopatra* from all the preceding tragedies.[14]

I react differently because I think of Cleopatra as in all things a performer, one who dramatises herself and those around her unashamedly, however serious the context. Unlike Shakespeare's other gifted actors (Richard III, Hamlet, Iago), she goes on performing to

he end, and this interferes, I believe, with the audience-response to
what she would like to make her most theatrical triumph, her
suicide.

Showmanship, we quickly learn, means as much to Cleopatra as
love. We often wonder whether she is interested in love for its own
sake, or whether she merely needs it as a pretext for posing in amusing new attitudes. In addition to the doubt expressed by hostile
witnesses, her own servants question 'if it be love indeed' ('Madam,
methinks *if you did love him dearly*', I. 3. 6), but are we ever
encouraged to doubt her total commitment to showmanship? Her
skills dazzle:

> If you find him sad
> Say I am dancing; if in mirth, report
> That I am sudden sick. (I. 3. 3–5)

Within seconds Antony approaches: she reads his mood at a glance,
and effortlessly slips into the appropriate routine – 'I am sick and
sullen.' The same alertness to others, and instantaneous adjustment,
astounds us at every turn.

> I know by that same eye there's some good news. (I. 3. 19)

> I have a mind to strike thee ere thou speak'st. (II. 5. 42)

Being an instinctive actress she attends to others' performances, not
just their words. In the very first scene she even anticipates Antony's
moods and seems to snatch away his role before he can put it on,
while he ('How, my love?') stands there like a man whose trousers
have been whipped off; and she still finds time to ham 'scarce-
bearded Caesar' and, probably, to mimic 'shrill-tongu'd Fulvia'.
Though aware that others admire her as a performer she pretends
that *they* are the performers, not very good ones, false where she is
true, but nevertheless blithely side-steps this secondary make-believe
to offer expert advice:

> I prithee, turn aside and weep for her,
> Then bid adieu to me and say the tears
> Belong to Egypt. Good now, play one scene
> Of excellent dissembling. (I. 3. 76–9)

I am not suggesting that acting and sincerity are necessarily incompatible, only that Cleopatra's ineradicable love of pose and
spectacle generates doubts not hitherto attempted in Shakespearian

tragedy when she finally stages her suicide. Shakespeare nudges u
towards this position by making her mind dwell on alternative way
of playing out her part:

> I shall see
> Some squeaking Cleopatra boy my greatness
> I' th' posture of a whore. . . .
>
> Show me, my women, like a queen. Go fetch
> My best attires. I am again for Cydnus . . . (v. 2. 218ff.)

In all that follows she continues to think in theatrical terms. Prepar
ing to repeat her greatest triumph she casts her attendants in th
role of dressers, and in imagination converts her surroundings into :
star's dressing-room (or the Egyptian or Elizabethan equivalent)
The performance completely fills her mind: she pays no heed to th
Clown's well-meant compliments, replies distractedly, adjustin;
mentally to the role she is about to assume, half herself and hal
someone else. When her 'best attires' arrive she sees herself as abou
to go on-stage ('Give me my robe, put on my crown'), her stag
being the afterworld, where her co-star awaits her. Our minds at thi
point switch back to Antony's parallel thoughts before death:[15]

> Where souls do couch on flowers we'll hand in hand,
> And with our sprightly port *make the ghosts gaze.*
> Dido and her Æneas shall want troops
> And all the haunt be ours. (IV. 14. 51ff.)

Much more than Antony, she hopes to make the survivors and th
ghosts *gaze,* admiringly of course; but whereas he imagines an un
divided future, she wants a spotlight for herself: 'I am again fo
Cydnus', 'Give me my robe', 'I see him rouse himself/*To praise m*
*noble act.*'

'Why fuss about a little feminine vanity?' I now hear the reade
say. 'After all, she promised Antony to die, and she dies. She sel
lessly chooses death – doesn't that count for more than all her cravin;
for effect?' In the fifth act, unhappily, what seemed a free choic
dictated by grief for Antony turns into something less disinterested
She goes on negotiating with Octavius, reactivating the audience'
lingering half-belief that she 'sold' Antony, as he had so passionatel
asserted, and 'pack'd cards with Caesar' (IV. 12. 15; IV. 14. 19): sh
sends to the conqueror to ask for 'instruction' (V. 1. 54), receives hi
messenger and tells him

> I hourly learn
> A doctrine of obedience and would gladly
> *Look him i' th' face.* (V. 2. 30–2)

She said the same once before, to the messenger Thyreus (III. 13. 73ff.), kissing his hand 'in deputation' and permitting him to kiss hers. Interrupting this telecoquetry just as she mused aloud that 'your Caesar's father' had often 'bestow'd his lips on that unworthy place', Antony interpreted it:

> I found you as a morsel cold upon
> Dead Caesar's trencher. Nay, you were a fragment
> Of Cneius Pompey's . . .

Pompey, Caesar, Antony . . . and Octavius? When Cleopatra, 'a morsel for a monarch', asks a second time to 'look him i'th' face', our earlier impressions suggest that she, 'a boggler ever', still believes in that old Egyptian magic, and hopes to make another conquest; at least, hopes until Octavius appears, for his failure to identify her ('Which is the Queen of Egypt?') intimates that her *power* has gone.[16]

It would be wrong not to mention that Cleopatra's behaviour after Antony's death has been much debated, and that some readers prefer to think of her as unwaveringly resolved on suicide. Mac-Callum, acutely though he wrote on Shakespeare's 'elliptical treatment' of impressions, held that when Proculeius surprises Cleopatra in the monument 'there is no question of the genuineness of her attempt at self-destruction'; and many have believed, with Kenneth Muir, that in the Seleucus-episode (V. 2. 137ff.), exactly as in Plutarch, 'Cleopatra had fully determined on suicide: she pretended about the treasure to make Caesar believe she wished to live'.[17] This reading of the Seleucus-episode seems to me neither more nor less compelling than the traditional alternative, that Cleopatra tried to mislead Octavius about her finances because she hoped to go on living; as Reuben Brower has said, 'it is pretty hard to decide who in this scene has cheated whom'.[18] The point of the episode, as presented by Shakespeare, may therefore lie in its obscurity, and critical clarifications of the either–or kind could then be equally misleading. Of Cleopatra's attempt to stab herself when captured (V. 2. 40) I prefer, again, to speak less positively than MacCallum. Did she not draw her dagger once before (II. 5. 73), and threaten to kill, without using it? True, she now invokes death ('Where art thou, death?'), and grandly abjures life ('Sir, I will eat no meat . . .') and *may* mean all she says. She *may*; on the other hand, when she imagines her own death and describes Antony she works herself into a rhetorical frenzy which seems to become an end in itself, a self-indulgence:

> *Rather* a ditch in Egypt
> Be gentle grave unto me! *Rather* on Nilus' mud
> Lay me stark-nak'd, and let the water-flies
> Blow me into abhorring! *Rather* . . .
>
> His legs bestrid the ocean; his rear'd arm
> Crested the world. His voice was propertied . . .

It is one of her most beautifully controlled performances, gathering momentum until she soars; but it is fuelled on hyperbole, and the higher she flies the less literally we can take her. Her attempt to stab herself and, when foiled, her repudiation of life, whether convincing or not as we witness them, both acquire a 'hyperbolical' colouring as the scene moves on, and lose some authenticity. But, though some such doubts ought to flit through our minds, if only 'the lady doth protest too much', a much simpler point has still to be made, reinforcing all that went before. *La donna è mobile*: whatever her motives in this episode or that, Cleopatra personifies infinite variety and mystery, the serpent of old Nile. A Roman fixity of purpose would contradict her nature: she may mean all she says, though this is not what we have come to expect of her, and yet still waver; she may repeat what she said, and mean it, and waver again. To tidy up Cleopatra is to turn her into a different person.

Though Cleopatra's choice of death seems unconditional when Antony dies, she has time to think again, and her final decision affects us differently. She learns that Octavius will lead her in triumph, and that he can resist her charms, and again her vanity comes into play. Her actions, not necessarily all of a piece, suggest that she *may* still wish to live. The precise mix remains uncertain, but we observe a shift from Antony-centred to self-centred motives. And something similar happens to her notion of suicide. She had wanted it to be 'after the high Roman fashion' (IV. 15. 87), and refers to it several times as *noble*, a word that points back to Antony, 'noblest of men' (IV. 15. 55, 59), yet two suicides could not be more unlike than his and hers. His – unplanned, messy, a man alone; hers

– a basket of figs prepared with asp, supported by her women, thrillingly beautiful. The difference is brought home to us by Antony's unbearable physical pain, succeeded by her death 'As sweet as balm, as soft as air, as gentle'.

Within the perspective of the play Antony's pain devalues the death of one who had 'pursu'd conclusions infinite/Of *easy ways to die*' (v. 2. 352–3). And his end obliquely affects our response to hers in other ways. He, gasping for breath, still thinks of life continuing after him, and of the wellbeing of the survivors; she, on the other hand, slips back into a familiar attitude ('Melt Egypt into Nile!') and thinks only of herself. A pardonable weakness, in the circumstances? Perhaps; but Shakespeare must have wished to jolt us when she, disregarding what Octavius had so explicitly spelt out a couple of minutes before, that he would destroy her children if she took her life, holds the asp to her breast murmuring –

> Peace, peace!
> Dost thou not see *my baby at my breast*
> That sucks the nurse asleep?

Nobility, all the same, may look like vanity or self-centredness when we apply our magnifying-glass to selected blemishes, and yet remain nobility if we keep at a proper distance. Whereas 'one fire drives out one fire, one nail one nail', Cleopatra's little weaknesses don't crowd out larger impressions, they merely nag at the periphery of consciousness. The real reason why I question her 'ennoblement' is that she tries too hard. She strains after 'what's brave, what's noble' – especially to 'be noble to myself' – therefore undertakes 'a noble deed', imagines Antony rousing himself 'to praise my noble act', and the idea of the noble so fills her universe that some of it rubs off on 'noble Charmian' and her 'noble girls'. She not only gives the performance, she writes the programme-notes. Now a human being can certainly discover his 'inner self' during a performance (as Pirandello quite splendidly demonstrated in *Henry IV*); character and role can sometimes melt into one. Cleopatra's performance in the suicide-scene, however, raises doubts because the scornful antagonist of Roman virtues changes so completely: the Egyptian turns Roman, she performs an 'Antony' and his large gestures, imitating his camaraderie and his emotional appeals to his followers and, above all, his self-dramatised nobility.

Little as we know about Shakespeare and his private thinking, we may confidently claim that he distinguished between the wish to be noble and the thing itself, since he wrote several tragedies with precisely this point. It will help to turn back to *Othello*, and to the rather similar discussion of the Moor's *bovarysme* or 'will to see things as they are not'.[19] T. S. Eliot, noting the 'attitude of self-dramatisation assumed by some of Shakespeare's heroes at moments of tragic intensity', refused to read Othello's suicide-speech as it is usually taken, at face value, 'expressing the greatness in defeat of a noble but erring nature'.[20] I react even more sceptically to Cleopatra's self-dramatised nobility, since she showed no signs of a noble nature in earlier scenes. As she launches into the suicide-speech its willed exaltation finally confirms that she retreats into fantasy, and this feeling about her style is matched by our response to the speech's content, since we were reminded of other, less agreeable ways of looking at death not long before:

> To rush into *the secret house of death* ... (IV. 15. 81)

> Finish, good lady; the bright day is done,
> And *we are for the dark.* (V. 2. 192–3)

When Cleopatra imagines an Antony who calls, rouses himself, praises her, mocks Caesar and kisses her in the afterworld we admire her as she speaks but we no more believe in her curled Antony as lover-in-waiting than we believe in Cordelia's breathing, willed with an equal intensity by King Lear. She strains to deceive herself, and we can identify the exact moment when she surrenders to illusion; namely, when 'Methinks' and '[Methinks] I see him' and '[Methinks] I hear him' give way to direct address:

> Methinks I hear
> Antony call. I see him rouse himself
> To praise my noble act. I hear him mock
> The luck of Caesar, which the gods give men
> To excuse their after wrath. *Husband, I come!*

She immediately draws back ('Now to that name my courage prove my title!'), then returns to the illusion, a process repeated several times, as in *King Lear*. In short, *Antony and Cleopatra* has much in common with at least one of the earlier tragedies in its definitive moments, just before the heroine dies; and the tragic effect, I believe, partly depends on Cleopatra's wish to escape reality, and on her conviction that another reality of her own choosing awaits her.

And yet, in spite of all that I have said about Cleopatra's fluctuating intentions after Antony's death, her showmanship and her retreat into fantasy, there comes a point, as we are swept along by her performance, when we wonder whether she has indeed transcended 'baser life'. Ennoblement remains a possibility. Cleopatra, though she reminds us of other Shakespearian heroes who die tragically self-deceived, also differs from them: whereas the others look back, and surrender to wishful thinking as they try to explain away facts about which the audience has already made up its mind, she looks forward, to her death. Before the event an audience cannot be so sure that she deceives herself, and after it she makes no false claims. Again, she differs from Othello and Lear and the rest in being a self-conscious performer, as opposed to their unconscious self-dramatisation, which means, very nearly, that she is a conscious self-deceiver, therefore not a self-deceiver. Shakespeare built so many contrary impressions into the fifth act that Cleopatra's motives and self-awareness are much harder to assess than those of the typical tragic hero, or of Antony. Ennoblement remains a possibility, though not one that we can fully believe in. It is merely a possibility – and *Antony and Cleopatra* differs from the other tragedies in leaving this all-important point unresolved.

# The Clarity of *Coriolanus*

What could have moved Shakespeare to write as strange a play as *Coriolanus*? A play where he made no attempt to engage the audience as in his earlier tragedies, where he dispensed with many of the essentials of tragedy as he himself had come to see it, the inward-looking hero, the metaphysical interest, the supernatural, the spiritualised emotions. Instead of continuing to work in this success-ful framework he tried out a different kind of tragedy, one that includes the most difficult crowd-scenes in the canon (plebeians, soldiers, citizens, senators, Volscians, all 'crowds' with their own identities), more tumult and sheer brute-human noise than perhaps accords with tragic thoughtfulness, and, strangest of all, an entirely new tragic tone.

Many different answers have been given. Shakespeare could have been inspired by the social unrest of 1607–8, when prices were rising and the dearth of grain provoked rebellions in the Midlands; he could have disliked the peace policy of James I, as did others, and have written the play to encourage a more aggressive nationalism.[1] I agree with J. Dover Wilson that 'what chiefly fascinated him as a dramatist, and moved him as a man, was the encounter between son and mother when she pleads for Rome',[2] and consequently think that there may be a connection between the play and the last illness of Shakespeare's mother (who was buried on 9 September, 1608).[3] Mary Arden, unlike Shakespeare's father, was related to an aristo-cratic family, the Ardens of Park Hall, and, like other mothers of genius, must have had an important influence on her son. But, despite the coincidence that Shakespeare created his most interesting mother–son relationship just before or just after his own mother died, I am not suggesting that the patrician Volumnia is Mary Arden, nor even that Mary Arden's son wanted us to admire the Roman matron.

If we wish to explain why Shakespeare attempted a tragedy so fundamentally different from all that he had done before we must not attach too much significance to the public and private griefs of 1607–8, but look instead at his dramatic development. *Coriolanus* seems to have been his last tragedy. Immediately after it (or perhaps

even before he had completed it) he tried his hand at romantic tragi-
comedy, probably following Beaumont and Fletcher, two younger
writers who were soon to be widely admired. This suggests that his
interest in tragedy had exhausted itself, a point that may be con-
firmed by *Coriolanus* itself. Of the seven mature tragedies *Coriolanus*
appears to stand at the farthest possible remove from the Shakespearian centre, being more positively influenced by other dramatists
than its six predecessors.[4] The tragic hero, for all that he has in
common with Lear and Mark Antony, follows in the tradition of
Chapman's *Bussy D'Ambois* (printed 1607), a Herculean hero in
whom pride and an extravagant sense of honour are similarly mixed;
and the tragic tone owes something to Jonson's satiric invective.
*Coriolanus* itself thus suggests that Shakespeare had come to the end
of the road in tragedy. Like its immediate predecessor, *Antony and
Cleopatra*, it contains scenes that lack tragic urgency and, more than
that, we are also tempted to talk of a decline – or at least a contraction – of the author's powers.

We must not go too far, however, in distinguishing *Coriolanus*
from the other mature tragedies. Some of the essential features of
'Shakespearian tragedy' still survive, including the all-important
sense of tragic mystery, which is sometimes denied the play. 'Its
clarity is the clarity of full daylight', said Harold Goddard, 'and only
rarely does it give us that sense of the unfathomable that most of the
Tragedies impart.'[5] *Coriolanus* gives a false impression of daylight,
as I shall try to show by glancing first at a short episode closely
modelled upon Plutarch.

*    *    *

When he has led the attack against Rome's enemies and refused a
special reward, Coriolanus remembers a *poor man*, once his host in
Corioli, and asks for his freedom (I. 9. 79ff.). In Plutarch the host
figured as 'an honest *wealthie man*', so M. W. MacCallum and
others have thought that in Shakespeare's version Coriolanus'
humanity acquired a wider range.[6] But the incident can also give an
entirely different impression. According to Plutarch, 'the souldiers
hearing Martius wordes, made a marvelous great showte among
them' (which suggests a happy outcome), whereas Shakespeare
concluded thus:

*Lartius* Marcius, his name? *Coriolanus* By Jupiter, forgot!
I am weary; yea, my memory is tir'd.
Have we no wine here?

MacCallum took the favourable view that after his heroic exertions Coriolanus 'rallies his strength for a last effort, and is just able to intercede for his humble guest-friend ere he succumbs.' But is it not equally probable that, as we never hear of the poor host again, Coriolanus was content with a noble gesture and left it at that? The callousness of 'Have we no wine here?', dismissing all that went before, seems to me the Shakespearian touch that transforms the whole episode: or rather, it introduces an 'unfathomable' element, since potentially noble and callous gestures are juxtaposed and neither can be regarded as definitive.

*          *          *

The central mystery, of course, is the character of Coriolanus and his development – if develop he does. Some think that 'there is no . . . journey towards painful discovery in *Coriolanus*. The Coriolanus of the first scene is the same Coriolanus at the end of the play', or that the hero 'is almost an absolute constant';[7] others believe in 'psychological change' but are puzzled by the mystery that when Coriolanus decides to revenge himself against Rome and when he later reverses his decision (IV. 4. 12ff., V. 3. 182ff.), the play provides 'no explanation':[8] the first 'psychological change' takes place off-stage, the second in total silence, as he listens to his mother, without a hint to the audience. We shall have to return to these contradictory impressions. For the time being I shall merely add that both were recorded as self-evident, impressions that were not expected to provoke dissent.

And the hero is not only a mystery in himself, he is also unfathomable in his two most important relationships. That with Virgilia Shakespeare chose to present as a feeling above words, an extraordinary dramatic achievement. Husband and wife are never alone together and address each other very rarely – but when they do every phrase flashes light into the depths. 'My gracious silence, hail!', 'Nay, I prithee, woman –', 'O, a kiss/Long as my exile, sweet as my revenge!'[9] Not even Cordelia's relationship with Lear suggests so much with such economy. That very economy, however, and the intensity of a feeling that is never fully expressed, guards the privacy of Virgilia's relationship with her husband from the audience and lifts it out of the realm of the wholly known.

The hero's relationship with his mother seems mysterious for different reasons. Goddard, though he wrote perceptively about it as a 'not wholly normal mother–son relationship', took a wrong turning when he guessed that 'she was far more father than mother to him'.[10] Consider Volumnia's second sentence in the play: '*If my son were my husband*, I should freelier rejoice in that absence wherein he won honour than in the embracements of his bed . . .' (I. 3. 3). The same idea slips from her when she urges her son to temporise:

> I would dissemble with my nature where
> My fortunes and my friends at stake requir'd
> I should do so in honour. *I am in this*
> *Your wife*, your son, these senators, the nobles . . . (III. 2. 62–5)

A figure of speech, but a revealing one. And there is a similar hint when Volumnia exclaims 'my boy Marcius approaches; *for the love of Juno*, let's go!' (II. 1. 92) and describes herself as '*Juno-like*' (IV. 2. 53). For Coriolanus, though also associated with other gods,[11] is seen throughout the play as a Jupiter-figure: he swears 'by Jupiter' and 'by Jove',[12] the nobles bow to him 'as to Jove's statue' (II. 1. 255), he has a voice of thunder,[13] and Volumnia knows of the comparison.

> Speak to me, son.
> Thou hast affected the fine strains of honour,
> To imitate the graces of the gods,
> To tear with thunder the wide cheeks o' th' air,
> And yet to charge thy sulphur with a bolt
> That should but rive an oak. (V. 3. 148ff.)

Others, too, think of Jupiter when they speak of Coriolanus: his wife ('His bloody brow? O Jupiter, no blood!' I. 3. 37), Menenius,[14] and Aufidius:

> If Jupiter
> Should from yond cloud speak divine things
> And say ''Tis true', I'd not believe them more
> Than thee, all noble Marcius. (IV. 5. 103–6)

Plutarch had painted a very different picture of Volumnia, who plays a much smaller part in his story until she goes to the Volscian camp to plead with her son. A more feminine woman, Plutarch's Volumnia is found 'weeping, and shreeking out for sorrowe'[15] when Coriolanus has been banished, whilst Shakespeare's Volumnia, glorying in the thought of her son's wounds or honourable death,[16] was I believe modelled on Plutarch's Spartan mothers: 'the parents and friends of them that were dead met in the market-place, looking

cheerfully of the matter, and one of them embraced another . . . The
mothers of them that were slain, went friendly to visit one another,
to rejoice together'.[17] Spartan heroism, however, has a strange effect
in Rome, where Shakespeare placed beside Volumnia a completely
un-Spartan Virgilia, tender and sensitive, a living contradiction of all
that her mother-in-law stands for. Volumnia, so clear-cut in her
opinions, therefore seems far from clearly-defined in her inmost
being: a Juno to her son's Jupiter, and oddly masculine in her relations with Virgilia, there is a hint of ambivalence in much that she
says.

> *Methinks I hear* hither your husband's drum;
> See him pluck Aufidius down by th' hair;
> As children from a bear, the Volsces shunning him.
> Methinks I *see him* stamp thus, and call thus . . . (I. 3. 29ff.)

The accent of Cleopatra, and a vision like hers of the irresistible
male![18] 'I tell thee, daughter, I sprang not more in joy at first hearing
he was a man-child than now' (I. 3. 15): this must mean that she
sprang for joy immediately after her son was delivered. It is odd, too,
in a play where family-relationships are important, that Volumnia
thinks 'There's no man in the world/More bound to's mother'
(V. 3. 158) and never refers to her son's father: here silence again
generates mystery.

Volumnia can be very easily sentimentalised, as Eternal Mother
or *madame Mère* or the Roman equivalent. She saves the state – yet
we must not forget that she herself, more than any other person,
destroys her son and deserves a place with Lady Macbeth and
Cleopatra in the gallery of Shakespeare's most destructive women.
(All three dominate the man they love and ask too much of him,
thus driving him to his death; but of course they do so in entirely
different ways.) She could be regarded as the villain of the tragedy
since she implanted ideas in her son from which he could not
emancipate himself, particularly his idea of honour, so extravagant
because a man's code has been romanticised by a woman. He, a 'most
absolute sir', grows 'too absolute' even for her,[19] yet the urge to be
uncompromisingly oneself, to 'honour mine own truth' (III. 2. 121),
points back to the play's three ladies, upholders of an all-or-nothing
morality – to Virgilia, who will not budge from home till her husband returns (I. 3), to Valeria, the moon of Rome, chaste as the icicle
(V. 3. 65), and above all to Volumnia, who may advise her son to

temporise (III. 2. 39ff.) but remains at heart the most inflexible
'absolutist'. Volumnia, in brief, while she spends all her time telling
others exactly what to do, herself exists in a strange haze of motives
and relationships, a man–woman and a wife–mother who loves
and destroys, whose own impulses we can only dimly apprehend,
and to whom we respond far less decisively than she responds to
others.

*     *     *

It was once taken for granted that the fable of the belly (I. 1. 87ff.)
clarifies all the political subtleties that follow in the play. Before I try
to explain the fable's function differently I must comment on the
dramatic speaker, Menenius. Readers have always happily sentimentalised 'that pleasant and wise old gentleman Menenius, whose
humour tells him how to keep the peace while he gains his point,
and to say without offence what the hero cannot say without raising
a storm. Perhaps no one else in the play is regarded from beginning
to end with such unmingled approval.'[20] 'A perfecter giber for the
table than a necessary bencher in the Capitol' (II. 1. 76), the pleasant
and wise old gentleman is an honorary member of every Senior
Common Room, and perhaps that helps to explain his popularity.
Yet, although he is hailed by a citizen, when he first enters, as
'worthy Menenius Agrippa, one that hath always lov'd the people',
we must remember that the stage-response often distorts in this play.
He gains his point in I. 1 by telling his pretty tale, but his opportunism is not pretty to watch: John Palmer, who said that 'there is
good-natured chaff on both sides',[21] forgot about the smiler with the
knife beneath the cloak. First Menenius flatters the mutineers, then
he picks on one as whipping-boy, when he thinks it safe to do so,
and finally he jeers at the plebeians, while pretending that he
criticises only one man. He addresses them as 'my countrymen' (or
equals), then as 'masters, my good friends, mine honest neighbours'
(a note of condescension), turns on 'this fellow' (I. 1. 118), who
becomes 'the great toe of this assembly', a 'rascal' who leads 'Rome
and her rats'. His ascendancy is such that, though physically out-
numbered, he seems to play a cat-and-mouse game, an experienced
politician who has fooled a crowd of simple but (in their plight) not
unreasonable fellow-citizens.

That is the first impression, soon to be modified by more attractive
behaviour: yet a flatterer he remains to the end, in a play that makes
much of the evils of flattery. For the play deals with two parallel

problems, the political immaturity of Rome and the emotional immaturity of Coriolanus, the one exploited by two unscrupulous tribunes, the other manipulated by a too determined mother, who boasts 'my praises made thee first a soldier'.[22] No wonder that Coriolanus reacts, in such a corrupting moral atmosphere, with an almost obsessive horror of flattery: 'No more of this, it does offend my heart'.[23] And Menenius, though Coriolanus seems unaware of it, might be regarded as a source of this corruption, being the only man in the play who flatters both sides, the only one who delights in the ignoble art.

In a few scenes Menenius even seems something of a go-between. In the very first one the actor sometimes arrives as if by chance, an elderly gentleman lost in thought who slowly wakes up to the fact that he has wandered into a mutiny. 'What work's, my countrymen, in hand?' he enquires, amazed. 'Where go you?' One day, perhaps, he will enter with a little dog on a lead, even though nothing could be wider of the mark. For Menenius always knows what he is about, and can only have made for the mutiny's storm-centre with a purpose, as First Citizen immediately takes for granted: 'Our business is not unknown to th' Senate; they have had inkling this fortnight what we intend to do . . .' First Citizen treats Menenius as an emissary of the Senate, not as a mere passer-by; and, though Shakespeare's Menenius never defines his role explicitly, this was also how Livy and Plutarch had introduced him: 'So it was thought good and agreed upon, that one *Menenius Agrippa* . . . should be sent as an Orator to treat with them'.[24]

From first to last Menenius plays roles that are left strangely half-defined, a peace-maker without portfolio, a shadowy father-figure to Coriolanus, a patrician 'that hath always lov'd the people' and calls them 'rats' (I. 1. 49, 160). He hangs loose upon society, insinuates himself where he wishes, and pays his way with words. At the very end, however, he acquires a defined role as his 'country's pleader', one that ought to suit him perfectly (he himself thinks so, when he reveals that he has his plan of campaign ready, V. 1. 47ff.) – and fails in it miserably. He fails with the audience even before Coriolanus makes a sign, because the scene is so arranged that sheer technique seems to conjure forth the pleader's feeling, which thus verges on the dishonest. Shakespeare achieved this effect by introducing a sudden stylistic break, when Menenius stops crowing over the Guards who would not let him pass and sails into his speech to Coriolanus. It is as if an actor stops chatting with a colleague and steps on to the stage to perform.

> . . . you shall perceive that a Jack guardant cannot office me from my son Coriolanus. Guess but by my entertainment with him if thou stand'st not i' th' state of hanging, or of some death more long in spectatorship and crueller in suffering; behold now presently, and swoon for what's to come upon thee. – (*To Coriolanus*) The glorious gods sit in hourly synod about thy particular prosperity, and love thee no worse than thy old father Menenius does! O my son! my son! thou art preparing fire for us; look thee, (*dabbing his eyes*) here's water to quench it . . .
>
> (V. 2. 61ff.)

'Away!' cries Coriolanus, and the guards snigger at the orator's *débâcle*. And a similar anti-climax follows two scenes later, where Menenius confidently reiterates that the ladies will not persuade Coriolanus to spare Rome ('there is no more mercy in him than there is milk in a male tiger', v. 4. 28), which the audience knows to be wrong, having just seen the ladies succeed in v. 3. 'Good news, good news!' interrupts a messenger. Menenius listens in silence, then makes his last speech in the play.

> This is good news.
> I will go meet the ladies. This Volumnia
> Is worth of consuls, senators, patricians,
> A city full; of tribunes such as you
> A sea and land full. You have pray'd well to-day:
> This morning for ten thousand of your throats
> I'd not have given a doit. Hark, how they joy!

O lame and impotent conclusion to a politician's career! The speech picks up as it goes along, just as Menenius managed to pull himself together after the anti-climax in v. 2, but in saying 'This is good news' he has to swallow a bitter pill. A 'humorous patrician' in his own eyes, a 'giber' to Brutus,[25] he suffers a discomfiture in v. 2 and v. 4 not unlike that of the Shakespearian jester-villain in the fifth act elsewhere (Falstaff, Parolles, Pandarus, Pistol in *Henry V*), except that his is less humiliating.

Yet, as I have hinted, there is much to say on the other side. I have focused on Menenius' first and last scenes where he probably appears at his worst, as a flatterer and go-between. But this is not to argue

that we ought to see him as a thinly disguised Pandarus. Quite the
contrary: the commonest mistake has always been to simplify him as
one type or another, either 'a pleasant and wise old gentleman'
(A. C. Bradley), or a buffoon (O. J. Campbell), or 'a hypocrite, a fool,
and a snob' (Harold Goddard).[26] He is all or most of these things, a
perfect mixture of three separate characters in *Troilus and Cressida*,
Pandarus – Ulysses – Nestor. In the play's middle scenes he continues
to sprinkle flattering phrases in all directions,[27] yet he also repri-
mands Coriolanus, he takes risks, genuine feeling breaks through,
and he emerges as a complicated human being. Not quite as he sees
himself, nor as admirable as Bradley thought him when he said that
no one else in the play deserves 'such unmingled approval' (I would
award that honour to Virgilia or Cominius): but, significantly, as a
man who can make mistakes, as Shakespeare stressed in the closing
scenes.

\*         \*         \*

We are now ready to return to the fable of the belly, which was
placed at the very forefront of the play, it is so often alleged, 'since it
expressed the point of view of all right-minded persons in his audience about the issue between populace and nobility in general, a
point of view in fact that held the field in political economy down to
the nineteenth century'.[28] The 'advantage of responding to political
feeling in the play', countered A. P. Rossiter, 'is that we need not
freeze it to a rigid Tudor-myth pattern of order':

> That is, we need not narrow it to what it doubtless showed to
> many c. 1607–8: an exposition of the evils which arise in the
> God-ordained microcosmic State when degree is neglected . . . That
> is by far the easiest way to systematize or pattern the play. Make
> the Fable of the Belly the key; turn all to Tudor-political moral
> allegory; throw in all the images of the body, disease, physic; and
> it all comes out pat. But you will have lodged the play back in
> Tudor distances, stopped all live political feeling . . .[29]

Who, in the 1970s, will care to deny the gap between 'a rigid Tudor-
myth pattern of order' and 'live political feeling' as *we* experience
the play? That feeling, however, need not be thought a purely
modern one, sharply distinct from what the play 'doubtless showed
to many c. 1607–8.' It may well be influenced by extra-dramatic
factors but, I believe, could and should be explained from within the
play, a response conditioned by the author himself.

Take, first, the dramatic context, to which I have already referred. Menenius tells the fable of the belly for a purpose. The theatre-audience, though it may have heard the pretty tale before and recognised it as a traditional apologue of 'order', cannot fail to realise that Menenius uses it as a political sedative, to get the better of a simple stage-audience: even a spectator who believed in a rigid political order should feel that Menenius' insinuating manner, as he weaves his web of words round First Citizen, subtly discredits the fable (without, however, proving or disproving its argument). In addition it is relevant that Shakespeare made Menenius, who speaks for 'your most grave belly' (I. 1. 126), into a devotee of belly-cheer, 'one that loves a cup of hot wine with not a drop of allaying Tiber in't' (II. 1. 44). Although the explicit evidence as to his character follows later,[30] in the theatre the opening scene necessarily gives an immediate impression of the *bon-vivant's* life-style, from his deportment and the tone of his voice. Sleek and well-fed, he addresses the plebeians, who are famished. The contrast, accentuated by Shakespeare,[31] influences the political feeling of the scene, placing the fable of the belly in a human context that challenges its impersonal social theory.

Shakespeare also brings the fable's theory into question in another way. Arguing that 'all the body's members' should work together for the common good, Menenius takes it for granted (with other 'order' apologists) that all must accept their 'degree, priority, and place' in the body politic.[32] All the members have their own function – to see or hear, the vigilant eye, the counsellor heart, the arm our soldier (I. 1. 100, 113) – and yet they can all think and talk as well, participating in each other's functions. The fable begins to break down as soon as the body's members are humanised beyond the conventional Aesopian minimum (attributing mere speech to animals and so on), for it then comes close to conceding that social roles are interchangeable, that one can do the work of another: and Shakespeare chose to go beyond Plutarch in this respect. Plutarch introduced a human touch in passing ('the bellie, all this notwithstanding, *laughed at their follie*, and sayed: It is true . . .'),[33] to which Shakespeare gave a special, attention-tangling emphasis:

> Sir, I shall tell you. With *a kind of smile*
> *Which ne'er came from the lungs, but even thus –*
> *For look you, I may make the belly smile*
> *As well as speak – it tauntingly replied . . .*

Another significant twist follows when Menenius *applies* the fable. 'The senators of Rome are this good belly', he explains, as in Plutarch. Then, suddenly pouncing on First Citizen, he adds (not so in Plutarch) –

> What do you think,
> *You, the great toe of this assembly?*
> 1 Citizen    *I the great toe? Why the great toe?*
> Menenius    For that, being one o' th' lowest, basest, poorest,
> Of this most wise rebellion, thou goest foremost . . .

Lightly but pertinently Shakespeare raises a question about social roles. Why the great toe? How can we know our own place in the 'order', and who determines it? The fable urges that each man's place is fixed, an arm cannot substitute for a leg, and, as I have suggested, Shakespeare's version blurs these social boundaries. And before the first scene ends a very different social theory has been propounded: Sicinius wonders that Coriolanus has consented to serve under Cominius, and Brutus explains that 'a place below the first' suits Coriolanus, whether Cominius wins or loses.

> Half all Cominius' honours are to Marcius,
> Though Marcius earn'd them not; and all his faults
> To Marcius shall be honours, though indeed
> In aught he merit not. (I. 1. 271–4)

According to this alternative theory, with which Sicinius immediately agrees, a member of the body politic can choose his place in the 'order', and will do so for purely selfish reasons.

Not so very long ago the fable of the belly was still seen as the key to an anti-democratic play. It was assumed that Shakespeare states a political axiom and then demonstrates how it works, as in *Henry V* and *Troilus and Cressida*, where the 'honey-bee' and 'order' speeches have a similar function.[34] Such an interpretation overlooks an interesting common factor – that each of the three speeches is given to a wily politician (Canterbury, Ulysses, Menenius) each of whom tries to manipulate a situation to gain an advantage, using traditional ideas as a verbal smoke-screen. In all three plays Shakespeare generates uneasiness about the speaker and thus makes the audience vaguely suspicious about his ideas: not, I believe, because he planned the plays to discredit 'order' politics but because political stories drew him into the realm of ideas, the probing of which at second-hand, through his dramatic characters, brought its surprises. The fable of the belly served him well in one respect: the assumption that members of a commonwealth must live and die together as 'incorporate friends' (I. 1. 128) remains valid and points forward directly to Coriolanus' error, the belief that a man can renounce kith and kin,

> As if a man were author of himself
> And knew no other kin.[35]

On the other hand, the deeper the play penetrates into character the farther it moves away from the fable's assumptions about social roles and obligations. What qualifications has Coriolanus to be the body's 'head', or consul? What right has his mother to ask him to be consul? How justified is he in turning 'dragon' and leading an army against ungrateful Rome? Raising such questions the play outgrows the fable, substituting for it a very different vision of society.

*    *    *

All is not 'daylight' in *Coriolanus*, and this partly explains why there are so many comment-scenes, a fact that has been often noticed. Yet *Coriolanus* can hardly be called Shakespeare's most obscure tragedy, so we must look farther to account for its exceptionally active stage-response. As in *Antony and Cleopatra*, the only other tragedy in which comment seems to become an end in itself, it could be urged that a political play must include 'public opinion' – but is that the explanation? Shakespeare had written other political plays, and yet had never felt it necessary to mount a stage-response on such an elaborate scale.

*Coriolanus* differs from the other political plays and tragedies in being an essay in response-brinkmanship. In almost every scene the hero can be viewed in one of two ways – as either magnificently true to his ideal of honour or insufferably proud. Stage-commentators mostly adopt one attitude or the other but they alternate so rapidly that the audience soon settles for the middle ground between them, identifying all he says or does as proud honour or honourable pride. Whereas the audience-response to Lear lurches in many directions (difficult to define, but progressing from hostility in I. 1 towards undiluted pity in IV. 7), *Coriolanus* goes through the same proudly honourable motions until V. 3. 182, when he decides to spare Rome, and the audience responds all the time in essentially the same way, teetering on the brink of dislike and admiration: the response grows in complexity but remains fixed between the same two emotions.

Shakespeare, therefore, had good reasons for what may at first appear to be the over-active stage-response in *Coriolanus*, and for adopting a similar technique in *Antony and Cleopatra*, where the hero occupies the emotional no-man's-land between love and lust, polarities that can be as far apart or as close as honour and pride. Confining the audience-response within clearly defined boundaries while at the same time preventing it from adopting either of the two expressed attitudes, he drove every spectator to a tantalisingly divided response and yet ensured that this would never go wildly astray. And he avoided monotony, an eternal ding-dong of the same two attitudes, by changing his speakers wherever possible, and also their style. He starts with short prose exchanges by two citizens, one of whom is hostile (I. 1. 25ff.), switches to admiring exclamations from the patricians ('worthy Marcius', 'O true bred!', 'Right worthy!', 'Noble Marcius!', I. 1. 234ff.), then the two tribunes continue the hostile comment, more venomously, in verse (I. 1. 250ff.) –

Was ever man so *proud* as is this Marcius? . . .
                     Such a nature,
Tickled with good success, *disdains* the shadow
Which he treads on at noon. But I do wonder
His *insolence* can brook to be commanded . . .

The ladies see Coriolanus differently, gossiping about his *honour* and about his son, 'a noble child', quietly convinced of their own point of view (I. 3). The battle-scenes then exhibit Coriolanus as Volumnia has just described him, with brief exclamatory comments from fellow-soldiers: one refuses to follow him into Corioli ('Fool-hardiness; not I', I. 4. 45: a rough-and-ready attempt to define the middle ground between pride and honour, a word that sticks), but the key-note is praise: 'O noble fellow', 'Worthy sir', 'Bold gentleman', 'Thou worthiest Marcius'. When the two attitudes collide they do so glancingly (II. 1. 1ff.), Menenius referring to 'noble Marcius', the tribunes briefly stating their different view ('He's poor in no one fault, but stor'd with all.' 'Especially in pride.') – and the patrician's banter gains an easy advantage. The Herald's short, formal speech of praise confirms the now dominant attitude (II. 1. 153–7), and the tribunes' third comment-sequence fails to dislodge it (II. 1. 195–260).

At this point Shakespeare inserts the first undisguised comment-scene, the first one assigned to speakers introduced in only one scene, who exist only to guide the audience-response. '*Enter two Officers to lay cushions, as it were in the Capitol'* (II. 2. 1). For the first time the two attitudes to Coriolanus meet in a genuine discussion, and the man who starts as an opponent gives way. We soon see why: within fifty lines Cominius launches into his formal speech of praise (II. 2. 80ff.), carrying the feeling for Coriolanus as high as it will go. The ups and downs continue thereafter, artfully regulated by the dramatist. I shall not enumerate them all but turn at once to the most extraordinary comment-scene, the one usually headed 'A *highway between Rome and Antium. Enter a Roman and a Volsce, meeting'* (IV. 3). Two dramatic characters, hitherto unknown, have to cross the open platform-stage, identify themselves, and are then free to exchange news and views, which at first seems to be the only reason for their appearance. What could be clumsier? To avoid giving this impression producers sometimes have the scene played as if it comes from *The Bald Prima Donna* ('What a coincidence!'), the two actors passing each other, pausing, turning back, a Tweedledum and Tweedledee going through precisely the same motions; or they angle for more subdued laughter, and the two men start back, hesitate, two dogs that sniff each other nervously as they meet, until a slow light dawns – 'Nicanor? No!' The dialogue, however, offers little verbal support for comic relief, and should not be regarded as merely an undistinguished exercise in information-giving. This is a comment-scene that looks forward as well as back. The audience already knows the facts, and the stage-response adds nothing new: the scene really exists to tell us that a Roman may choose to work for the Volscians, obliquely preparing us for Coriolanus' decision to do the same. More important, it suggests that a Roman and a Volsce who belong to the same social class may think and feel alike, matching sentence for sentence, courtesy for courtesy – a verbal embrace that points forward to Aufidius' welcome to his former enemy ('Let me twine/Mine arms about that body . . .', IV. 5. 106). The scene also marks the passage of time, and helps to change the mood of the play (somewhat like the 'bear' scene in *The Winter's Tale*, though not so obviously). In short, the scene serves as a bridge between the play's two parts, and, coming where it does, it steadies the audience-response before Shakespeare jolts this again at Antium. Since the two speakers think alike, and view Coriolanus from an emotional distance, and at a distance in time and place, they carry the audience with them.

\*    \*    \*

The death of Coriolanus has provoked less discussion than that of any other of Shakespeare's tragic heroes, although there are problems of staging and response that remain unsolved. Everyone observes that Aufidius 'draws' Coriolanus by calling him traitor, exactly as did the tribunes in III. 3. 66, and that Aufidius' taunt, 'Name not the god, thou boy of tears' (V. 6. 101), overwhelms Coriolanus because a half-truth can be more unbearable than a lie. But the words *traitor* and *boy*, rapier-thrusts to which Coriolanus reacts with sharply defined emotion, merely prepare for and lead towards the tragic climax which, when it comes, consists of two separate actions that the text leaves oddly undefined. The producer, accordingly, may give whatever definition he thinks appropriate to the final audience-response, and the opportunities open to him deserve careful scrutiny.

By the two actions of the climax I mean the killing of Coriolanus and the treatment of his body immediately afterwards. A single stage-direction describes both in the Folio – '*Draw both the Conspirators, and kils Martius, who falles, Auffidius stands on him.*' Consider, first, the final humiliation of the lifeless body, which was added by Shakespeare (Plutarch has no hint of it), though not as a last-minute afterthought. He was already looking ahead to it in V. 3, where he prepared the audience's imagination for what was to come.

> . . . thou shalt no sooner
> March to assault thy country than to tread –
> Trust to't, thou shalt not – on thy mother's womb
> That brought thee to this world. *Virgilia*  Ay, and mine,
> That brought you forth this boy to keep your name
> Living to time. *Boy*  'A shall not tread on me!
> I'll run away till I am bigger, but then I'll fight. (v. 3. 122–8)

If, however, we ask why Coriolanus had to die as he does (and each of Shakespeare's tragic heroes dies in his very own way, just as each one speaks his own language) we must go back farther, to some of the play's central scenes.

When '*Aufidius stands on him*' attention is focused on a body. Shakespeare had previously aroused curiosity about this same magnificent body with its 'large cicatrices to show the people when he shall stand for his place', its twenty-seven wounds, every gash an enemy's grave,[36] an elaborately conditioned response that he chose to disappoint. Now Plutarch's Coriolanus, standing for the consulship, had observed custom and publicly exhibited 'many woundes and cuttes apon his bodie';[37] Shakespeare's, though persuaded against his will to

put on the gown of humility, pretends not to understand when
Fourth Citizen says 'You have received many wounds for your
country' (II. 3. 104), and no one sees his twenty-seven good-conduct
marks.

> He should have show'd us
> His marks of merit, wounds receiv'd for's country.
> *Sicinius*   Why, so he did, I am sure.
> *All*   No, no; no man saw 'em. (II. 3. 159–62)

And no man or woman in the theatre saw 'em either.

Shakespeare had required the audience to take a special interest in
his Herculean hero's physical existence (the fable of the belly and the
play's generalised body-imagery both point towards it, among other
things). He gave what support he could to the actor, magnifying
Coriolanus by means of the stage-response – usually in his absence,
so that the gap between praise and reality is not too noticeable – and
suggesting in various ways that in his physical pre-eminence he
seems more than a mere mortal:

> His bloody brow
> With his mail'd hand then wiping, forth he goes
> Like to a harvest-man that's task'd to mow ... (I. 3. 34ff.)

We think of Death and his scythe. We see Coriolanus, with
Menenius, as one who 'wants nothing of a god but eternity' (V. 4.
23) – and suddenly the impossible happens, he is struck down, life
stops, Aufidius stands on him. How are the mighty fallen! The very
vision of Volumnia, ironically reversed –

> He'll beat Aufidius' head below his knee
> And tread upon his neck.[38]

Indeed, something worse may be implied, for Aufidius could have
been told to stamp on his enemy as he stands on him, as the
murderers stamp on the Duke in *The Revenger's Tragedy* (1607), to
express his fury in a once traditional manner.[39] And there is poetic
justice in such a treatment of the Herculean body, meting unto
Coriolanus as he had measured unto others. As Chateaubriand said
of the order 'Bonaparte was to be disarmed' when Napoleon was on
the way to St Helena, alone, a prisoner on board ship – 'what a
lesson from Heaven to men who abuse the sword!'[40] Coriolanus had
shown very little respect for human dignity, and now his turn has

come. 'Hence, rotten thing! or I shall shake thy bones/Out of thy garments!' he had shouted at Sicinius, no doubt giving the old man a foretaste of what he might expect (III. 1. 178); he had turned the Volscian servant about with his finger and thumb 'as one would set up a top' (IV. 5. 152); and it is conceivable that in the fury of an earlier battle-scene he had himself kicked at or stood on a human body, just after Volumnia had imagined him stamping: 'Methinks I see him stamp thus, and call thus: /"Come on, you cowards!" '[41]

The humiliation of the Herculean body may be dramatically necessary but how, precisely, should the killing be staged? Can such an indestructible warrior go down without a fight? There are several possibilities. First – 'As he turns on Aufidius, the conspirators rush upon him, and in a moment, before the vision of his glory has faded from his brain, he lies dead.' So Bradley, who nevertheless conceded that 'the instantaneous cessation of enormous energy (which is like nothing else in Shakespeare) strikes us with awe, but not with pity', and that 'some readers, I know, would like Coriolanus to die fighting'.[42] Yet the stage-response suggests that Shakespeare wanted the audience to feel some pity,[43] and Bradley possibly argued from a mistaken premise. 'If Coriolanus were allowed to fight at all', he said, 'he would have to annihilate the whole assembly.' Only, we must reply, if Coriolanus were as well armed as in Act I: and though he may manage to draw his sword and defend himself, he would be doomed without a shield.[44] A second possibility would be to have a desperate last duel, Aufidius throwing himself upon Coriolanus with the words 'Insolent villain', battling it out alone and perhaps very nearly beaten, until the Conspirators surge forward to his aid. Such a man-to-man encounter and rescue would bring back memories of I. 8, and would give an added poignancy to the lesser man's revenge – 'Aufidius stands on him'. A third possibility to consider is that in V. 6 we still see the Coriolanus of V. 3, 'the new man created by Virgilia's kiss and the love of his child' who, as Harold Goddard believed, 'presents his own body to the swords of others'.[45]

As Goddard recognised, we cannot explain the death-scene without accounting for the hero's development. We must therefore look more closely at the two revelations of 'psychological change' to which I have already referred.[46] The first occurs when Coriolanus arrives at Aufidius' house 'in meane Apparrell' (IV. 4. 1, Folio), in clothes that are probably travel-stained and tattered as well ('thy tackle's torn', IV. 5. 61). Can we doubt that his 'meane Apparrell' bears a marked resemblance to the cloak of humility, which had so offended Coriolanus that he felt that he could not 'know himself again' until he changed his garments (II. 3. 143ff.)? Now, at Aufidius' house, he throws back his cloak, stands silent, for the first time asks to be looked at, and a few at least of those tremendous cicatrices are on show. A stunning stage-effect, combining a visual and a psychological surprise: he wears his mean apparel proudly, he proclaims his military achievements, he humbles himself before a fellow-being – the very things he could not stoop to when he stood for the consulship.

And yet he remains at heart the same man, too 'absolute' in his vengefulness as earlier in his other emotions. He had despised the cowardly plebeians, now he scorns 'our dastard nobles' as well (IV. 5. 75). He gambles with his life against the odds, entering an enemy city alone on an all-or-nothing mission, as he had once dared to enter Corioli. His clothes and 'outer behaviour' are different but his 'inner behaviour' – particularly the conviction of his own rightness, and the resolve to assert it against the world – continues as before. The more fundamental change appears in v. 3, though this also can be exaggerated.

> the most eloquent stage-direction in Shakespeare is that which follows Volumnia's appeal – *Holds her by the hand, silent*. During this silence Coriolanus grows up, comes to know himself and to understand the meaning of life for the first time; and his reply when he speaks is his first calm, thoughtful, adult utterance in the play.[47]

I prefer to see the hero's development as more gradual – a journey from action to reflection, from noise to silence – which makes his surrender in v. 3 the more meaningful. The 'thunder-like percussion' of his voice (I. 4. 60) gives way in Act IV to a much quieter tone, he scolds less readily, we hear that ''Twas very faintly he said "Rise"' to Cominius (v. 1. 66), and v. 3 includes a series of silences all of which point towards Coriolanus' growing up into self-knowledge. The others are not marked in the text but are almost as important as '*Holds her by the hand, silent*' – the pauses that drag on painfully when Volumnia says 'Speak to me, son' and 'Why dost not speak?'[48] We must not imagine them to be hostile silences; the audience knows, from Coriolanus' words before the ladies begin to plead, that he will be unable to resist.

What is that curtsy worth? or those doves' eyes
Which can make gods forsworn? I melt, and am not
Of stronger earth than others ... (v. 3. 27ff.)

Like Isabella in *Measure for Measure*, Coriolanus develops from
loudly affirmed convictions that are self-centred and life-denying to a
new thoughtfulness that culminates in silence and self-sacrifice.
Isabella, the novice, asked to leave her religious order and marry the
Duke, makes her choice silently; Coriolanus, asked to save Rome,
silently decides on a course that will be, he fully understands, 'most
mortal to him' (v. 3. 189). It matters little whether we ascribe the
victory to his wife, his 'gracious silence' (II. 1. 166), whose mere
presence influences him profoundly, or to his mother – for in effect
he wins a victory over himself.

The tragedy, however, moves on from this moment of perception
and self-mastery, and the final twist comes when the new Coriolanus
relapses in v. 6 into his former self, reliving his greatest military
exploit in imagination, rejoicing in it and taunting those he despises.
For the first time since his expulsion from Rome we hear again the
thunder of his voice, the accent of the earlier Coriolanus, and this in
itself contradicts the view that he 'presents his own body to the
swords of others'; his very last words, indeed, belie such a spiritual
victory by uncannily echoing the contemptuousness of Volumnia.

O that I had him,
With six Aufidiuses, or more – his tribe,

I would my son
Were in Arabia, and thy tribe before him,
His good sword in his hand! (IV. 2. 23–5)

If Coriolanus achieves a new self-knowledge in v. 3, as I have
argued, his relapse in the death-scene will seem the more pitiful.
Bradley, I must now repeat, felt little pity at the end,[49] and explained
v. 3 differently – not as Coriolanus' victory over himself but as a
mere submission to his mother. His will gives way, said Bradley,
because 'deliberately to set it against hers is beyond his power.'[50]
Such a reading still has its supporters, even though it deprives the
ending of tragic impact.

And what has Volumnia learnt from it all? She makes no reply
when her son surrenders, and has another difficult silence in v. 5. on

her triumphant re-entry into Rome, 'passing over the stage' as the mob unshouts 'the noise that banish'd Marcius'. Is she to walk with head held high, proud of having won 'a happy victory to Rome'? Or angrily, despising those who welcome her? Or without expression, refusing to reveal her thoughts? Her bearing in this six-line scene has a connection with that of her son in the death-scene, but the text provides no clue and we can make of it what we will.

*          *          *

While it seems possible to adjust the impact of Coriolanus' death, rendering it more pitiful or less, we have still to ask whether the play as a whole calls for pity at the close. Of all the mature tragedies *Othello* and *King Lear* have without doubt the most heart-rending final scenes: and it can be no accident that earlier scenes in both dwell on 'the pity of it',[51] nourishing the emotion that finally engulfs the play. Pity, in short, grows out of pity, and may fail in its effect if conjured forth too suddenly from an emotional void. In *Coriolanus* the ladies appeal to the hero's compassion –

> How more unfortunate than all living women
> Are we come hither (v. 3. 97–8)

– yet the scene's emotional pressure cannot compare with that of the most moving scenes in *Othello* and *King Lear*, if only because Volumnia talks of pity from afar and scarcely understands it. Apart from this one late scene very little in the play elicits the audience's pity or points inexorably forward to a pitiful catastrophe.

If, as is often assumed, a play has a characteristic tone, and if that tone helps to determine the impact of individual scenes, it should be possible to see how Shakespeare prepares for the death of Coriolanus. Bradley, who believed that 'a Shakespearean tragedy, as a rule, has a special tone or atmosphere of its own' and described that of *Macbeth* and *King Lear* so admirably,[52] failed, I think, to do justice to the complexities of *Coriolanus*. Its many amusing touches, he thought, help 'to produce the characteristic tone of this tragedy.'

> When the people appear as individuals they are frequently more or less comical . . . Again, the talk of the servants with one another and with the muffled hero, and the conversation of the sentinels with Menenius, are amusing. There is a touch of comedy in the contrast between Volumnia and Virgilia . . . What is amusing in [the play] is, for the most part, simply amusing, and has no tragic

tinge. It is not like the gibes of Hamlet at Polonius . . . or that humour of Iago which for us is full of menace . . . Even that Shakespearean audacity, the interruption of Volumnia's speech by the hero's little son, makes one laugh almost without reserve.[53]

This may be more or less true, without getting at the heart of the matter. Comical touches abound, yet they are confined to transition-scenes or serve merely as brief interruptions. The tone of a play depends much more on the upward than on the downward surge of the scene: climactic moments count for more than loose chat, and those of *Coriolanus* have so narrow an emotional range that they affect the play's tone to an unusual degree. O. J. Campbell came nearer the truth when he called it a tragedy 'full of the spirit of derision' (though not when he went on to say that it 'can be understood only if it be recognized as perhaps the most successful of Shakespeare's satiric plays').[54] Derision, then, must be understood to include related forms of feeling and speech: on the one side, jeering, gloating over the misfortunes of one's enemies, or raging at them, insulting them; on the other, tut-tutting or scolding one's friends, or dismissing them callously (V. 1. 66, V. 2. 76).

Seen thus, the play has much the same tone in a great variety of episodes. Its physical battles mirror a ceaseless verbal and emotional attack, a hacking and hewing that continues in one form or another in almost every scene. The hero pours forth contempt as if for sheer pleasure: he scolds the plebeians, curses his own soldiers, jeers at the citizens, shakes off the tribunes, denounces 'our dastard nobles' and finally derides Aufidius, 'who wears my stripes impress'd upon him' (V. 6. 108). These, some of the play's more important tone-setting passages, are not 'simply amusing' but (*pace* Bradley) have something in common with the gibes of Hamlet at Polonius. They function as the emotional main-stream, into which flow the quite similar emotions of most of the secondary characters – as, for instance, Menenius' contempt for the rats of Rome,[55] his many acidulous side-swipes at the tribunes, and his exchanges with the Volscian guards (which are not 'simply amusing' because impregnated with the play's potent class-feeling: 'You guard *like men*, 'tis well; but, by your leave,/ I am *an officer of state*', V. 2. 2–3). And the same tone and emotions are repeated even in the decorative detail: the belly 'tauntingly replied' (I. 1. 108), Coriolanus' son with the butterfly 'did so set his teeth and tear it' (I. 3. 63), Aufidius' servants recall with barely disguised satisfaction that Coriolanus 'was wont to thwack our general', 'he scotch'd him and notch'd him like a carbonado' (IV. 5. 178ff.).

A play's dominant tone must not be confused, however, with its characteristic tone. In *Coriolanus* the 'derisive' passages are counterpointed by others, speeches of praise, and the two together and in interaction give the tragedy what Bradley called its 'special tone or atmosphere'. Volumnia and Cominius speak of Coriolanus in the heroic strain, and because he himself echoes their tone in the death-scene we are prevented from taking as narrow a view as the one proposed by O. J. Campbell.

> His automatic response to the artfully arranged provocation has at last entrapped him to his death. His end is the direct result of an over-stimulated reflex mechanism. The catastrophe of such an automaton is not tragic. It is so completely devoid of grandeur and dignity that it awakens amusement seasoned with contempt.[56]

This view of Coriolanus' development and death seems as improbable as the opposite one, that 'Virgilia's kiss and the love of his child' change him so completely that he refuses to defend himself in Antium.[57] After all, a death-scene that swings the audience too decisively in one direction or the other would really contradict all that had gone before, in a play that never permits a favourable or unfavourable response to the hero to continue unchallenged for long. Too much 'daylight' at the end must be avoided – as it was also avoided at crucial turning-points earlier, when Coriolanus determined on revenge and when he abandoned the siege of Rome.

# Conclusion

Although I have discussed only selected problems it will be clear by now that Shakespeare gave his unremitting attention to audience-response in each of the tragedies. The question 'What should Hamlet do or say next?' must have been inseparable for the dramatist from the question 'How will it affect the audience?' As he shaped each play its response problems seem to have been in the forefront of his mind, together with character and plot, at a more conscious level of decision-making than when he settled on its appropriate mood or imagery. While it would be wrong to suggest that its response problems are the only avenue of approach to a tragedy (I have admitted this already) we cannot explain how it 'works' without taking them into account at every turn.

As I said at the outset, my purpose was to describe the astonishing variety of response problems in Shakespeare and his technical resourcefulness in solving them. The reader will have noticed that I looked for what was unique in each play but at the same time chose to return often to Shakespeare's standard devices, which were invariably adjusted to the play's special needs. In particular I returned to the dramatic use of blurred impressions: different kinds of mixed response, the zigzagging of response, the interweaving of contrary impressions, the strategy of confusing the audience, compelling it to suspend its judgement. A second recurring interest was the audience's relationship with the dramatic hero, its access to his mind, and the different effects of soliloquy. Thirdly, we may group together large-scale response regulators: the stage-response, comment scenes, rehabilitation-scenes, transition-scenes. Fourthly, the use of 'serial' effects: the impact of characteristic gestures and of paradigmatic situations; the scene that 'inoculates' the audience against the one that follows, and its opposite, the retroactive effect; repeated words that acquire new overtones or cue the audience. Fifthly, the manipulation of stock-responses and stock ideas. Sixthly, the importance of dramatic perspective.

Although the approach differs in every chapter it was necessary to glance in each one at a few of Shakespeare's standard devices. I thought that it would be useful to examine at least one in more detail, and therefore return repeatedly to the 'tragic effect'. What is meant by this term? I have tried to describe the responses elicited by seven plays called 'tragedies', each of which has an observable emotional 'effect' at the close: that is as near as I shall venture to theory. Aristotle's catharsis, with its emphasis upon pity *and terror*, seems inappropriate to Shakespeare, but I would happily subscribe to his own definition of the tragic effect in *Hamlet*:

What is it you would see?
If aught of *woe or wonder*, cease your search.

Having drawn up a list of some of the standard devices that called for our attention again and again – and, as already stated, it is by no means complete – I must now add several warnings. To suggest that the dramatist forever adjusts the response by nudging the audience this way and that could be dangerous unless we remember, in addition, that there is a steady deepening of the spectator's relationship with at least some of the tragic heroes. The dramatist sometimes merely nudges the 'surface' of our response, without greatly troubling the depths. Let us remember, too, that we respond simultaneously to a play's quite different interests: although we may choose to distinguish between the response to ideas, rhythm, scenic effects and so on for critical purposes, all such responses flow together and interpenetrate while we read or watch a play, as do our impressions. I have perhaps dwelt too much on responses channelled through character – but only as a point of critical convenience, without wishing to imply that we always put character first.

Indeed, the 'mix' and quality of our response changes in every play from scene to scene. Even in one as centrally concerned with character as *Othello*, insistently teasing us with questions of motive, we find that after a time our interest partially disengages itself from character. Here, and in all of the tragedies, our response becomes detached and intellectual towards the end, in that we contemplate the inexorable necessities of character and story as they work themselves out; and the intellectual interest interferes with our capacity for sympathetic 'identification', if we are properly attentive to the shape of the play and its formal appeal. We stand back from the tragic hero and contemplate him from outside, in woe and wonder, as one might marvel at a splendid storm spending itself. And this, the distancing of the audience from the play, was just another controlled effect – another response problem to which Shakespeare certainly gave expert attention.

# Notes

(The place of publication is London unless otherwise specified; customary abbreviations are used for periodicals.)

A NOTE ON DATES AND DEFINITIONS
1 For most of the dates I have followed E. K. Chambers, *William Shakespeare*, 2 vols (Oxford, 1930).
2 Compare also A. C. Bradley, *Shakespearean Tragedy* (1904) pp. 79ff.; Maurice Charney, 'The Roman Plays as a Group', in *Shakespeare's Roman Plays* (1961); and J. L. Simmons, *Shakespeare's Pagan World: the Roman Tragedies* (Charlottesville, Va., 1973), ch. 1.
3 *'Timon of Athens'*, *Shakespeare Quarterly*, XII (1961) 3-20.

CHAPTER 1: INTRODUCTION: SHAKESPEARE AND THE STUDY OF RESPONSE
1 See, for example, S. L. Bethell, *Shakespeare and the Popular Dramatic Tradition* (1944); J. V. Cunningham, *Woe or Wonder: The Emotional Effect of Shakespearian Tragedy* (University of Denver Press, 1951); William Rosen, *Shakespeare and the Craft of Tragedy* (Harvard University Press, 1960); Maynard Mack, 'Engagement and Detachment in Shakespeare's Plays', in *Essays on Shakespeare and Elizabethan Drama in Honor of Hardin Craig*, ed. R. Hosley (1963); J. R. Brown, *Shakespeare's Plays in Performance* (1966); Norman Rabkin, *Shakespeare and the Common Understanding* (1967); Stephen Booth, 'On the Value of Hamlet', in *Reinterpretations of Elizabethan Drama*, English Institute Essays, ed. N. Rabkin (1969); B. Beckerman, *Dynamics of Drama* (New York, 1970); Arthur C. Kirsch, *Jacobean Dramatic Perspectives* (University of Virginia, 1972).
2 *Johnson on Shakespeare*, ed. Walter Raleigh (1908 ed.) pp. 201, 177.
3 See Maurice Morgann's *Essay on the Dramatic Character of Sir John Falstaff* (1777). In Daniel A. Fineman's splendid edition of Morgann's *Shakespearian Criticism* (Oxford, 1972), Morgann's pioneer work on the audience's response to dramatic 'impressions' is carefully explained.

CHAPTER 2: IMPRESSIONS OF 'CHARACTER'
1 Compare J. I. M. Stewart, *Character and Motive in Shakespeare* (1949); S. L. Goldberg, *An Essay on "King Lear"* (Cambridge, 1974) ch. 2; Michael Black, 'Character in Shakespeare', *The Critical Review*, XVII (Melbourne, 1974) 110-19.
2 Una Ellis-Fermor explained the 'inwardness' of Shakespeare's characters in *Shakespeare the Dramatist* (1961) pp. 21-59. See also Michael Goldman on the 'unsounded self', *Shakespeare and the Energies of Drama* (Princeton, N.J., 1972) and Lionel Trilling, *Sincerity and Authenticity* (1972).
3 A. J. A. Waldock, *Hamlet A Study in Critical Method* (Cambridge, 1931) p. 98.
4 Compare Chapter 6.

5 See also Una Ellis-Fermor, 'The Revelation of Unspoken Thought in Drama', in *The Frontiers of Drama* (1945).
6 J. W. Mackail, *The Approach to Shakespeare* (Oxford, 1933 ed.) p. 25.
7 Compare Gilbert Ryle, *The Concept of Mind* (1949) 'Self-knowledge'; Sydney Shoemaker, *Self-Knowledge and Self-Identity* (Ithaca, N.Y., 1963).
8 Compare p. 88; also Peter Ure, 'Shakespeare and the Inward Self of the Tragic Hero', 'Character and Role from *Richard III* to *Hamlet*', in *Elizabethan and Jacobean Drama* (Liverpool, 1974).
9 Montaigne, *Essayes*, trans. J. Florio, 3 vols (Everyman ed., 1910) III, ch. x.
10 David Hume, 'Of Personal Identity', in *A Treatise of Human Nature*, I.
11 *Song of Myself*, xvi.
12 Compare Panofsky's view that the typical *figura serpentinata* of Mannerist art 'seems to consist of a soft substance which can be *stretched* to any length and *twisted* in any direction': *Studies in Iconology* (1962 ed.) p. 176; my italics.
13 See *Hamlet* III. 2. 71, *Othello* IV. 2. 58ff.; also *Hamlet* V. 1. 251: 'This is I,/Hamlet the Dane', *Antony and Cleopatra* III. 13. 92: 'I am/Antony yet'. In Greek drama the hero sometimes asserts his 'sense of self' by naming his ancestors: 'Agamemnon's son am I, the son of one/Held worthy to rule Greece'. *The Tragedies of Euripides*, trans. A. S. Way, 3 vols (1898) III, 158.
14 Harley Granville-Barker, *Prefaces to Shakespeare*, 4 vols (1927-45) III, 307-312.

## CHAPTER 3: RESPONSE AND DRAMATIC PERSPECTIVE

1 Boswell's *Life of Johnson*, 19 October 1769; my italics. Joseph Baretti, with whom Johnson had been friendly for fifteen or so years, was arraigned at the Old Bailey for murder, and Johnson gave evidence as to his good character.
2 Raleigh (ed.), *Johnson on Shakespeare*, pp. 187, 193, 158.
3 See p. 2.
4 Lamb, 'On the Artificial Comedy of the Last Century', *The Works* (1904 ed.) p. 419.
5 Macaulay, 'Leigh Hunt', *Essays and Lays of Ancient Rome* (1902 ed.) p. 574.
6 W. Raleigh, *Shakespeare* (1950 ed.) pp. 151-2.
7 Robert Langbaum, *The Poetry of Experience* (New York, 1971 ed. pp. 164, 169, 179.
8 Ibid., pp. 163, 167.
9 Compare Helen Gardner, *The Business of Criticism* (Oxford, 1959) p. 34; W. Sanders, *The Dramatist and the Received Idea* (Cambridge, 1968); R. Ornstein, *A Kingdom for a Stage* (Cambridge, Mass., 1972). I return to the Elizabethan World Picture on pp. 123-4.
10 Langbaum, *Poetry of Experience*, p. 3.
11 T. S. Eliot, 'Dante', *Selected Essays* (1951 ed.) p. 257.
12 R. B. Heilman has said that, to explain our relationship with a criminal tragic hero, we perhaps 'need a new term like "consentience" to suggest more than "sympathy" but less than "identification" or "empathy"': 'The Criminal as Tragic Hero', *Shakespeare Survey*, XIX (1966) 24. I use the word 'sympathy' to suggest *community of feeling*: it may be comparatively disengaged or close to 'identification', as the context usually indicates.
13 Arthur Sewell, *Character and Society in Shakespeare* (Oxford, 1951) p. 76.
14 A. Harbage, *As They Liked It* (1947) p. 6.

15 Compare p. 18.

16 J. Keats, *The Letters*, ed. M. B. Forman (1942 ed.) pp. 69, 227–8. Keats was probably indebted to Coleridge, who had described Shakespeare as 'darting himself forth, and passing himself into all the forms of human character and human passion'. Coleridge's comparison of Milton and Shakespeare also seems to lie behind Keats' thoughts about 'the wordsworthian or egotistical sublime'. See S. T. Coleridge, *Shakespearean Criticism*, ed. T. M. Raysor, 2 vols (1960 ed.) II, p. 66.

17 Wyndham Lewis, *The Lion and the Fox* (1927) p. 178. Compare John Holloway, *The Charted Mirror* (1960) p. 202: 'There is no simple sense in which our desires are frustrated when Desdemona is killed or Oedipus found out, or satisfied when the traitor Macbeth is beheaded. We do not "side with" Lear in that we "wish good" for him in the shape of military victory or the rescue of Cordelia. So far as these things go, our sympathy for the characters somehow co-exists with a detachment in which we accept – no, more than that, we demand – whatever is brought by the fable in its entirety.' Also Heilman, 'The Criminal as Tragic Hero', p. 21.

18 Madeleine Doran, *Endeavors of Art* (Madison, Wisconsin, 1954) p. 320. For *Richard II* as tragedy see Chapter 4 n.1.

19 W. Hazlitt, *Characters of Shakespeare's Plays* (1895 ed.) pp. 13, 225.

20 E. E. Stoll, *Shakespeare Studies* (New York, 1927) p. 331.

21 E.g. *Twelfth Night* II. 4. 114, *All's Well* V. 3. 32–4, *Lear* IV. 3. 16–19.

22 Samuel Richardson, *Clarissa Harlowe*, vol. 2, letter 9; D. H. Lawrence, *Women in Love*, ch. 11 (my italics).

23 A. P. Rossiter, *Angel with Horns* (1970 ed.) pp. 52, 54. The passage quoted comes from a lecture delivered in 1951.

24 Compare E. Schanzer, *The Problem Plays of Shakespeare* (1963) Introduction.

25 Compare E. Honigmann (ed.), *Twelfth Night* (1971) pp. 17ff. and *Shakespearian Tragedy and the Mixed Response* (Newcastle upon Tyne, 1971).

26 A. C. Sprague, *Shakespeare and the Audience* (Cambridge, Mass., 1935) p. 243.

## CHAPTER 4: SYMPATHY FOR BRUTUS

1 *Richard III* and *Richard II* were described as tragedies on the Quarto title-pages. Though the authorship of *Titus Andronicus* has been much debated, there is now a tendency to accept it as immature but authentic Shakespeare.

2 See pp. 26–7.

3 Raleigh (ed.), *Johnson on Shakespeare*, p. 179.

4 M. W. MacCallum, *Shakespeare's Roman Plays and their Background* (1910) pp. 233–7.

5 *Julius Caesar*, ed. T. S. Dorsch (New Arden ed., 1955) p. xxxix.

6 *Narrative and Dramatic Sources of Shakespeare*, ed. Geoffrey Bullough, 8 vols (1957–75) V, p. 90. (Hereafter cited as Bullough, *Sources*.)

7 Ibid., pp. 92, 107, 116.

8 *Julius Caesar* V. 1. 100ff., IV. 3. 143–4.

9 I. 2. 295, V .5. 26.

10 Dorsch (ed.), *Julius Caesar*, p. xl.

11 Bullough, *Sources*, p. 97.

12 In Plutarch the conspirators 'were every man of them bloudied' as they killed Caesar (ibid., p. 102).

13 Compare Cassius' *then* ('Stoop *then*') here and elsewhere when he gives way to Brutus: '*Then* leave him out' (II. 1. 152.), '*Then*, with your will, go on' (IV. 3. 222).

14 See p. 32.
15 See p. 33.
16 I. 2. 314–19, II. 1. 36–58.
17 MacCallum, *Shakespeare's Roman Plays*, p. 201.
18 Dorsch (ed.), *Julius Caesar*, p. 33.
19 MacCallum, *Shakespeare's Roman Plays*, p. 264.
20 See Harold C. Goddard, *The Meaning of Shakespeare* (1965) I, 325. J. Dover
   Wilson (ed.), *Julius Caesar* (1949) p. 176, has argued that Cassius was
   suspected of taking bribes (IV. 3. 10–12) but not of extorting money, 'a
   very different thing. Nowhere does Shakespeare say that the money Brutus
   asks to share had been got "by vile means" '. But this is mere hair-splitting,
   for Brutus knows that the money Cassius might have lent him was acquired
   corruptly (line 15), i.e. by vile means.
21 Compare p. 38.
22 Bullough, *Sources*, p. 120.
23 Dorsch (ed.), *Julius Caesar*, p. xl.
24 IV. 3. 67–8, V. 1. 110–12 (compare p. 36). Brutus, of course, intends *great
   mind* as 'great spirit', but Shakespeare's irony seems as unmistakable as
   when Caesar talks of his constancy.
25 IV. 3. 201. Compare III. 1. 225, 238, III. 2. 7.
26 Bullough, *Sources*, p. 83.
27 Ibid., p. 85.
28 See Bullough, p. 102n.
29 Compare pp. 33–4. A. C. Sprague (*Shakespeare and the Actors* (1660–1905)
   (Cambridge, Mass., 1945, p. 321) mentions one Brutus who shrank from
   touching Caesar's hand, and adds that on the stage the conspirators did
   not often 'stoop and wash' in Caesar's blood.
30 MacCallum, *Shakespeare's Roman Plays*, p. 240.
31 Bullough, *Source*, p. 86 (from the *Life of Julius Caesar*).
32 Compare Dover Wilson's stage direction (*Julius Caesar*, p. 45), which is
   nevertheless much closer to Plutarch than that in most modern editions.
   Notice that there is no support in Plutarch or Shakespeare for the common
   stage direction that Brutus strikes 'the last blow'. Plutarch says (in the
   *Marcus Brutus*) that when Caesar had cast his gown over his face the
   conspirators, 'thronging ... to have a cut at him', accidentally hurt each
   other, Brutus being wounded in the hand (Bullough, *Sources*, p. 102);
   Marcus Brutus seems to have struck Caesar 'about his privities' in the
   general *mêlée*, his one and only blow; and Shakespeare may well have
   intended the same.
33 Editors describe Lucius as one of Brutus' *servants*. Though the Folio gives
   no indication of his exact status, it is reasonable to suppose that the boy
   who has to serve his master at all hours, and to follow him to the wars,
   will be a slave, a point that could be made visually by his costume and
   bearing. The lower his status, the more considerate is Brutus' treatment
   of him.
34 Bullough, *Sources*, p. 96.
35 Ibid., p. 98.
36 How was the quarrel-scene staged at the Globe? Dover Wilson thought that
   the 'inner stage' served as tent (*Julius Caesar*, p. 175). But there is no
   certainty that an inner stage existed, and there are two other possibilities:
   either the main stage itself becomes the inside of a tent, or a real tent was
   erected on the stage (as in *Richard III* V. 3, and several other plays of the
   period). If a real tent or mansion was used, the guards would be clearly

visible to the audience; if not, the audience could still be made aware of the physical presence of the guards, just off-stage, by anxious glances from either Brutus or Cassius as the other speaks too loudly.

37 Bradley, *Shakespearean Tragedy*, p. 60.
38 See Ernest Schanzer, *The Problem Plays of Shakespeare* (1963) p. 65.
39 Dorsch (ed.), *Julius Caesar*, p. xli.
40 Granville-Barker, *Prefaces*, I, 58–60.
41 Bullough, *Sources*, pp. 268–9.
42 Dorsch (ed.), *Julius Caesar*, p. li.
43 IV. 2. 47, IV. 3. 16, 20.
44 Bullough, *Sources*, pp. 114–15.
45 Granville-Barker, *Prefaces*, I, p. 60.
46 Kenneth Muir, *Shakespeare's Tragic Sequence* (1972) p. 51, believed that 'Shakespeare intended the duplicate revelation to stand'; Dorsch (*Julius Caesar*, p. 106) took the opposite view.
47 MacCallum, *Shakespeare's Roman Plays*, pp. 275ff. Compare Dorsch (ed.), *Julius Caesar*, pp. xlivff.; Muir, *Shakespeare's Tragic Sequence*, p. 53.
48 *The Devils* (Penguin ed., 1971), part II, section 6, p. 388, section 8, p. 420.
49 Dorsch (ed.), *Julius Caesar*, p. xxx.
50 II. 1. 165, 158ff.
51 Bullough, *Sources*, p. 260.
52 Ibid., p. 263.

CHAPTER 5: HAMLET AS OBSERVER AND CONSCIOUSNESS

1 Friend and foe think of Hamlet as *sweet* (i.e. sweet-natured): ' 'Tis sweet and commendable in your nature, Hamlet' (Claudius, I. 2. 87); 'words of so sweet breath compos'd' (Ophelia, III. 1. 98); 'No more, sweet Hamlet' (Gertrude, III. 4. 96); 'Good night, sweet prince' (Horatio, V. 2. 351). For 'gentle Brutus' see above, p. 41.
2 See Coleridge's *Table Talk* (1917 ed.) p. 65, and Hazlitt's *Characters of Shakespeare's Plays* (1895 ed.) p. 74.
3 By Shakespeare's tragic heroes I mean an exclusive men's club; one heroine, Cleopatra, may be said to rival Hamlet as a humorist. Perhaps we should also except King Lear, some of whose mad or nearly-mad speeches have the grotesqueness and cutting edge of humour (e.g. 'Get thee glass eyes...', IV. 6. 170; 'and hear poor rogues/Talk of court news...', V. 3. 13–18).
4 Compare Lear's 'Thank you, *sir*' at the very end of *King Lear* (below, p. 121).
5 Compare pp. 34ff.
6 Macbeth has his suspicions about the Weird Sisters, but fails to suspect Lady Macbeth (see also p. 131).
7 R. A. Foakes, '*Hamlet* and the Court of Elsinore', *Shakespeare Survey*, IX (1956) 38. Compare also Granville-Barker, *Prefaces*, III, 62.
8 See Caroline F. E. Spurgeon, *Shakespeare's Imagery* (Boston, 1958 ed.) p. 316; G. Wilson Knight, *The Wheel of Fire* (1960 ed.) p. 28.
9 II. 2. 180, IV. 3. 27–9. For the generalised sense of inward corruption in the play compare Spurgeon, *Shakespeare's Imagery*, p. 133.
10 I. 4. 24, II. 2. 255, 302, 306.
11 These are not hard and fast distinctions, I should add. Claudius pounces on Hamlet when he asks 'Now, Hamlet, where's Polonius?' (IV. 3. 17); yet it is not a 'moral' test and he learns nothing from it, whereas Hamlet springs his surprises to better effect.
12 Muir, *Shakespeare's Tragic Sequence*, pp. 67–8.

NOTES 199

13 *Twilight in Italy* (1916): 'The Theatre'.
14 Bradley, *Shakespearean Tragedy*, p. 147.
15 'Hamlet', in *Selected Essays* (1953 ed.) p. 145.
16 See G. Wilson Knight, 'The Embassy of Death: an Essay on *Hamlet*', first published in 1930, and '*Hamlet* Reconsidered (1947)'. Both essays are in *The Wheel of Fire* (1960 ed.).
17 L. C. Knights, *An Approach to 'Hamlet'* (Peregrine ed., 1966) pp. 202, 210–14.
18 Ibid., p. 212.
19 Compare H. Granville-Barker: 'He seems indeed to have Claudius beaten ... he scourges him from the field' (*Prefaces*, III, 96).
20 Granville-Barker thought less well of Hamlet's judgement at the critical moment when he kills Polonius. 'Is Hamlet meant to think that the eavesdropper is the King, and the actor to show this? I believe not; for we are aware that he has just come swiftly from the King's closet where he has left him on his knees ... He is not, surely, meant to think at all. He ... is so excited as to be "beyond himself" ... His "Is it the King?" is the unreasoningly hopeful question of the imaginative man' (*Prefaces*, III, 113n.). To which we may reply as follows. (i) It is misleading to say that Hamlet 'has just come swiftly from the King's closet' since he goes to Gertrude's room with obvious reluctance. She has to send for him twice (III. 2. 322, 365); he stalls for time ('I will come by and by' – 'By and by is easily said'); he pauses as Claudius prays, and then there follows another scene-change during which, for all we know, he may lose more time. (ii) Even though excited, why should Hamlet wish to kill a mere eavesdropper, unless he thought Claudius the man? Compare his behaviour in the previous eavesdropping-scene, where he was also excited (III. 1. 130ff.) (iii) The Queen had just threatened to hand Hamlet over to Claudius ('Nay then, I'll set those to you that can speak'), and had thus aroused his suspicions. (iv) I cannot see why we should disbelieve 'I took thee for thy better' – Hamlet, having been summoned to discuss delicate family affairs (III. 2. 290ff.), quite naturally assumed that the only person the guilty Queen would want to eavesdrop would be the King.
21 Compare p. 60.
22 Compare p. 60.
23 Knights, *An Approach to 'Hamlet'*, p. 200. Notice that there is a similar repetition a moment later, when Gertrude says 'These words like daggers enter in my ears', unconsciously echoing Hamlet's 'I will speak daggers to her, but use none' (III. 2. 386): this reinforces the audience's feeling that Hamlet has accomplished exactly what he set out to do.
24 Bradley held that in the closet-scene 'we cannot suppose the Ghost to be meant for an hallucination', yet admitted that precisely this has been supposed (*Shakespearean Tragedy*, p. 139). I believe that there is no conclusive evidence either way, but that the audience is first inclined to take the Ghost as an hallucination (because of Hamlet's hysterical condition before it appears, and because the Queen cannot see it), then veers to the other view, without feeling certain of it. Elizabethan demonologists held that a ghost could show itself to one person while remaining invisible to others, so the Ghost of III. 4 (invisible to Gertrude) could have been thought as 'real' as the Ghost of Act I (attested by several pairs of eyes).
25 The Ghost, I. 5. 55ff.; Hamlet, III. 4. 92ff. Notice that *nasty* was a much stronger, richer word than today: it meant 'filthy, to a disgusting degree' (OED).

26 Compare n.20, above, and also Knights, *An Approach to 'Hamlet'*, p. 213.

27 II. 2. 542ff., IV. 4. 32ff.

28 II. 2. 431, 492, III. 2. 1ff.

29 I. 2. 150, IV. 4. 35, etc.

30 H. D. F. Kitto, *Form and Meaning in Drama* (1956) p. 330; quoted by Knights, *An Approach to 'Hamlet'*, p. 177.

31 I. 2. 140, 153; III. 4. 56ff. Since Hamlet twice talks of his father as 'Hyperion' it is interesting to compare the Ghost's similar image, 'a radiant angel' (I. 5. 55).

32 Compare p. 180.

33 Peter Alexander, whose lectures I was privileged to hear at Glasgow, 1944–1948, always stressed the importance of the gentlemanly ideal in *Hamlet*.

34 Hamlet does not mean what he says in some earlier scenes, a trick that adds to our confusion in the prayer-scene. Compare 'it cannot be/But I am pigeon-liver'd ...' (II. 2. 571ff.), 'I never gave you aught', 'I loved you not' (III. 1. 96, 119), 'Now could I drink hot blood ...' (III. 2. 380).

35 C. S. Lewis, 'Hamlet: The Prince or the Poem?', in *Studies in Shakespeare*, British Academy Lectures, ed. Peter Alexander (1964) p. 210.

36 When Hamlet says 'I'll call thee Hamlet,/King, father, royal Dane' (I. 4. 44) this is a provisional identification, not one that he at this point subscribes to. Significantly, he speaks of the Ghost in Act I as 'it', not 'he', and addresses it as poor ghost (twice), boy, old mole, perturbed spirit, etc., never explicitly as his father's ghost.

37 V. 2. 63ff., 211ff.

38 See also Nicholas Brooke on Hamlet's *conscience* in *Shakespeare's Early Tragedies* (1968) pp. 166, 195ff.

39 Eleanor Prosser, *Hamlet and Revenge* (1967) pp. 102, 103.

40 Ibid., pp. 122, 138.

41 Ibid., pp. 98, 119.

42 Ibid., pp. 121–2.

43 *Ibid.*, pp. 133ff.; compare pp. 108ff.

44 Ibid., p. 140.

45 Miss Prosser was not impressed by the Ghost's Christian doctrine. 'The Ghost urges Christian forbearance for Gertrude. Admitted. But that is what we are warned the Devil will do' (ibid., p. 137). Well: if you are determined to find a devil you will find a devil. I believe that the Ghost's Christian *feeling* will affect the audience more decisively than its *doctrine*, but that even its predominantly Christian feeling fails to satisfy us completely – i.e. it remains ambiguous.

46 In this chapter I am indebted at several points to Nigel Alexander's *Poison, Play and Duel* (1971). Compare also Stephen Booth, 'On the Value of *Hamlet*', in *Reinterpretations of Elizabethan Drama*, English Institute Essays, ed. N. Rabkin (1969).

CHAPTER 6: SECRET MOTIVES IN *Othello*

1 Compare pp. 5ff.

2 Helen Gardner, ' "Othello": A Retrospect, 1900–67', *Shakespeare Survey*, XXI (1968) 3.

3 See Coleridge's *Shakespearean Criticism*, I, 44, Bradley (*Shakespearean Tragedy*, p. 228n.) thought that Coleridge could not have meant motiveless love of evil, but rather 'that Iago's malignity does not spring from the causes to which Iago himself refers it.' Strangely enough, Wordsworth thought it possible in 1795 to explain 'those tendencies of human nature,

which make the apparently motiveless actions of bad men intelligible to
careful observers' (referring to Oswald in *The Borderers*, whose connection
with Iago is obvious). Coleridge could also have known E. H. Seymour's
*Remarks...upon the Plays of Shakspeare*: 'there are no sufficient
motives apparent [in Iago] for this excess of malignity' (1805 ed. II, 320).
See also E. S. Shaffer, 'Iago's Malignity Motivated' (*Sh. Q.*, XIX (1968) 195–
203).

4 Bradley, *Shakespearean Tragedy*, p. 226; Gardner, '"Othello": A Retrospect', p. 3.

5 Bradley, *Shakespearean Tragedy*, p. 227.

6 Ibid., pp. 222–32.

7 Ernest Jones, quoted by J. I. M. Stewart, *Character and Motive in Shake-
speare*, p. 143. So too F. L. Lucas (*Literature and Psychology*, 1951, p. 76).
See also S. E. Hyman, *Iago Some Approaches to the Illusion of his
Motivation* (New York, 1970) ch. 4.

8 M. Rosenberg, *The Masks of Othello* (Berkeley and Los Angeles, 1961) p.
158.

9 L. C. Knights, 'The Question of Character in Shakespeare', in *More
Talking of Shakespeare*, ed. John Garrett (1959) p. 62n.

10 I. 3. 301ff., II. 1. 211ff.

11 II. 3. 12ff.

12 II. 1. 290, 301.

13 Bradley, *Shakespearean Tragedy*, p. 232.

14 Ibid., p. 230.

15 R. B. Heilman, *Magic in the Web* (Lexington, Kentucky, 1956) pp. 204–5.

16 I. 1. 68ff.; II. 1. 215ff. (here Iago seems quite intoxicated by his own
fantasies); II. 3. 12ff., etc.

17 See p. 87.

18 Bradley, *Shakespearean Tragedy*, pp. 213–14.

19 W. Empson, *The Structure of Complex Words* (1964 ed.) pp. 219, 222n.
Notice that in *Clarissa* the servant Joseph Leman objects to being called
'honest Joseph' (II, 51).

20 V. 1. 73ff.

21 Compare p. 94.

22 Bradley, *Shakespearean Tragedy*, p. 225.

23 Ibid., pp. 227, 229, 213.

24 Rosenberg, *The Masks of Othello*, pp. 124, 128.

25 Coleridge, *Shakespearean Criticism*, I, 41. Compare Bradley, *Shakespearean
Tragedy*, p. 227.

26 For Emilia see II. 1. 100ff., III. 3. 307ff., V. 2. 234 ('Filth, thou liest').
Whereas Iago's contempt for Othello and Roderigo shows from the start,
his attitude to Emilia only reveals itself gradually.

27 IV. 1. 44–5. Compare II. 3. 334–7.

28 Bradley, *Shakespearean Tragedy*, p. 225; Heilman, *Magic in the Web*, p. 31.

29 I. 3. 380ff.; IV. 2. 146ff.

30 'Diabolic Intellect and the Noble Hero' in F. R. Leavis, *The Common
Pursuit* (1952).

31 Compare Leavis's essays on Milton in *The Common Pursuit* and his remarks
on Arnold in *Education and the University* (1943) pp. 73ff.

32 A. W. Schlegel, *Lectures on Dramatic Art and Literature* (1889 ed.) p. 402.
I think it was a little unfair of Kenneth Muir to urge against Leavis that
he had the backing of only two or three modern critics and that he
disagreed with 'three hundred years of stage tradition' (*Shakespeare's

*Tragic Sequence*, pp. 103–4). Muir nevertheless makes some telling points against Leavis.

33 Quoted by Rosenberg, *The Masks of Othello*, p. 103; my italics.

34 *The Brothers Karamazov*, Book VIII section 3; also quoted by Muir, *Shakespeare's Tragic Sequence*, p. 97.

35 Compare also Heilman, *Magic in the Web*, pp. 139, 147.

36 Gardner, ' "Othello": A Retrospect', p. 8.

37 See G. Wilson Knight's classic essay, 'The Othello Music', in *The Wheel of Fire*.

38 I. 3. 283ff., II. 1. 199ff. Compare I. 3. 294ff., II. 3. 1ff., etc.

39 Muir, *Shakespeare's Tragic Sequence*, p. 102.

40 I. 3. 76ff., 128ff., III. 3. 351ff.

41 'Shakespeare and the Stoicism of Seneca', in *Selected Essays* (1951 ed.) p. 130.

42 I. 2. 62ff., I. 3. 59ff., 98ff.

43 Bradley, *Shakespearean Tragedy*, p. 187; Heilman, *Magic in the Web*, pp. 138–9; Leslie A. Fiedler, *The Stranger in Shakespeare* (1973) p. 173; for a different view see G. K. Hunter, 'Othello and Colour Prejudice', *Proceedings of the British Academy*, LIII (1967); K. W. Evans, 'The Racial Factor in Othello', *Shakespeare Studies*, V (1970) 124–40.

44 *Othello* III. 3. 455; *King Lear* IV. 6. 188.

45 III. 3. 435, IV. 1. 140, 196. Compare IV. 1. 42, 'noses, ears, and lips'.

46 *Coriolanus* V. 6. 101. Compare Iago's 'gentlemen' (above, p. 83), Lear's 'Thank you, *sir*' (below, p. 121), Cleopatra's *Husband*, I come' (V. 2. 285).

47 V. 2. 204, 257. Observe a similar effect, though not so arresting, when Othello calls himself Iago's *friend* (III. 3. 146, V. 1. 32).

48 The *turban'd Turk* is sometimes said to stand for malignant Iago. Othello's repeated action, the smiting of the Turk and the similar thrust against himself, inclines me to identify the Turk with Othello – who at this point perceives the 'split' in his personality, the Turk-and-Venetian, the smiter and the smitten (compare also p. 13). I assume that Othello was not *born* a Christian, which is suggested by the play though it cannot be proved. His mother received the fateful handkerchief from an Egyptian, it was dyed in mummy, the work of a sibyl (III. 4. 55ff.): this conjures forth a pagan background for Othello's parents. There are other hints, e.g. his tendency to lapse into a polytheistic view ('Amen to that, *sweet powers*', II. 1. 193; 'Had it pleas'd heaven/To try me with affliction, had *they* rain'd . . .', IV. 2. 48): but Elizabethan usage was lax, and we must not make too much of it. Notice that the Moorish ambassador who visited London in 1600 naturally wore a *turban*: Bernard Harris, 'A Portrait of a Moor', *Shakespeare Survey*, XI (1958) 89–97.

49 *The Golden Bowl* (1963 ed.) ch. 31, p. 382.

50 Helen Gardner, 'The Noble Moor', *Proceedings of the British Academy*, XLI (1955) 197. Compare 'Iago ruins Othello by insinuating into his mind the question, "How do you know?" ' (ibid.).

51 Granville-Barker, *Prefaces*, IV, 15ff.; M. R. Ridley, *Othello* (New Arden ed., 1958) p. 54.

52 'She'll find a white that shall her blackness hit', 'But does foul pranks which fair and wise ones do' (II. 1. 133, 142). Compare p. 80.

53 Compare also p. 83.

54 Empson (*Structure of Complex Words*, p. 228) writes of Desdemona's 'giggling at the jokes of Iago.' I see no excuse for giggling.

55 For Vandenhoff and Wilson Knight see Sprague, *Shakespeare and the Actors*, p. 206; G. Wilson Knight, *Shakespearian Production* (1964) p. 102.

56 Goddard, *The Meaning of Shakespeare*, II, 94–9.
57 Bradley, *Shakespearean Tragedy*, p. 197.
58 v. 2. 237, 290, 359.

## CHAPTER 7: LEAR'S MIND

1 Lamb, 'On the Tragedies of Shakespeare', *The Works* (1904 ed.) p. 568.
2 Bradley, *Shakespearean Tragedy*, p. 273. For the play's bleakness and unpleasantness see also Nicholas Brooke's excellent *Shakespeare: King Lear*,
Studies in English Literature, no. 15 (1963).
3 J. Keats, *The Letters*, ed. M. B. Forman (1942) p. 71.
4 It has been suggested that the mock-trial of Goneril and Regan was
omitted from the Folio text because the Jacobean audience laughed at it.
See Kenneth Muir (ed.), *King Lear* (1952) p. xlviii.
5 III. 2. 7, IV. 6. 188, V. 3. 284–5.
6 Carol J. Carlisle, *Shakespeare from the Greenroom* (Chapel Hill, N.C., 1969)
p. 294.
7 See Coleridge, *Shakespearean Criticism*, I, 49–54, and William Frost, 'Shakespeare's Rituals and the Opening Scene of *King Lear*', in *Shakespeare's
Tragedies An Anthology of Modern Criticism*, ed. Laurence Lerner (Pelican
ed., 1963) p. 165. Compare Granville-Barker, *Prefaces*, I, p. 146; H. S. Wilson,
*On the Design of Shakespearian Tragedy* (Toronto, 1957) p. 182; and
Maynard Mack on the play's 'combination of parable and parable situations
with acute realism', *King Lear In Our Time* (1966) p. 56.
8 Compare p. 120.
9 II. 4. 163–4, III. 4. 66–7, III. 6. 15–16.
10 *King Lear* III. 2. 51, IV. 6. 109, 118. Compare *Timon* IV. 1. 1ff., IV. 3. 1ff.
11 Margaret Webster, *Shakespeare Today* (1957) p. 218.
12 Henry James, *The Art of the Novel*, ed. R. P. Blackmur (1934) p. 62.
13 II. 4. 277–82, III. 4. 17, V. 3. 8. Compare Lear's insistent negation when he
finds Kent in the stocks (II. 4. 14ff.), and II. 4. 224ff., III. 2. 16ff. – I return
to Lear's inwardness on p. 115, and to 'Never, never . . .' on p. 121.
14 We read of two Gonerils who *shrieked* when cursed by Lear (Sprague,
*Shakespeare and the Actors*, p. 287), one of whom also *fainted*: I find this
utterly wrong.
15 III. 4. 28ff., IV. 6. 160. Compare J. C. Maxwell on Lear's invocation of Nature:
'Shakespeare presents the precise degree of anthropomorphism that suits
Lear's state of mind', 'The Technique of Invocation in "King Lear"', *MLR*,
XLV (1950) 144.
16 III. 2. 67, III. 4. 21, IV. 6. 129.
17 I. 4. 237, II. 4. 155.
18 See I. 4. 49, 95, 187.
19 I. 4. 62, II. 4. 138.
20 A. L. French, *Shakespeare and the Critics* (Cambridge, 1972), p. 179.
21 'Are you our daughter?' 'Your name, fair gentlewoman?' (I. 4).
22 III. 2. 51ff., III. 6. 20ff., IV. 6. 108ff.
23 Bradley, *Shakespearean Tragedy*, p. 263.
24 I. 1. 178, II. 4. 20.
25 Compare Tourneur's crude imitations (*The Revenger's Tragedy*, ed. R. A.
Foakes, 1966, IV. 2. 199, V. 3. 41). In Peter Brook's film it was 'impossible to
tell how much [the storm] is the real world undergoing this epic convul-
sion, how much the landscape is the inside of Lear's mind', M. Rosenberg,
*The Masks of King Lear* (1972) p. 184.
26 III. 1. 30, IV. 3. IV. 7.

27 Bradley, *Shakespearean Tragedy*, pp. 312–13. Others see the Fool as a 'disinterested truthteller' (Rosen, *Shakespeare and the Craft of Tragedy*, p. 13). I have followed Empson, *Structure of Complex Words*, pp. 132–133.

28 *King Lear*, ed. Russell Fraser (Signet Classic ed., 1963) pp. xxxff. The wish to defend Cordelia is of course widespread (compare John F. Danby, *Shakespeare's Doctrine of Nature: A Study of 'King Lear'*, 1949, p. 132).

29 V. 3. 212, I. 1. 165.

30 Bradley, *Shakespearean Tragedy*, p. 292; Raleigh (ed.), *Johnson on Shakespeare*, p. 162.

31 Bradley, *Shakespearean Tragedy*, p. 291; J. Stampfer, 'The Catharsis of *King Lear*', in Lerner (ed.), *Shakespeare's Tragedies*, p. 151.

32 II. 4. 258. Compare also IV. 7. 71: 'Be your tears wet? Yes, faith.' Garrick and later Lears touched Cordelia's cheek at this point; Irving touched her cheek and 'carried his finger to his lips', Sprague, *Shakespeare and the Actors*, p. 295.

33 'I have seen the day . . .' and 'This is a dull sight . . .'

34 See Muir (ed.), *King Lear*, p. 217.

35 'Pray, do not mock me', 'I pray, weep not', 'Pray you now, forget and forgive' (IV. 7. 59ff.). Lear also used the weaker form, *prithee* (II. 4. 217, III. 4. 23).

36 Lear's usual form of address had been *sirrah*, but he had also used *sir* threateningly (I. 4. 76–7, 257–8).

37 Bradley, *Shakespearean Tragedy*, p. 293.

38 Stampfer, 'Catharsis of *King Lear*', p. 150.

39 See Danby, *Shakespeare's Doctrine of Nature*, pp. 20ff.

40 Theodore Spencer, *Shakespeare and the Nature of Man* (Cambridge, 1943 ed.) pp. 146–7.

41 Webster, *Shakespeare Today*, pp. 98, 222.

42 I. 4. 275ff., II. 4. 263ff.

43 Danby, *Shakespeare's Doctrine of Nature*, pp. 31ff., 46–7.

44 Bacon, 'Of Cunning', a passage added in 1625; modernised spelling. The essay is 'traditional' at the start ('We take cunning for a sinister or crooked wisdom') but Bacon's true attitude betrays itself when he writes 'It is *a good point of cunning*, for a man, to shape the answer he would have, in his own words . . .'

45 Compare pp. 70, 180.

46 Rosen, *Shakespeare and the Craft of Tragedy*, p. 21; but compare also p. 29. Danby (*Shakespeare's Doctrine of Nature*, p. 174) noted that Lear 'includes both sides of the argument in himself.'

CHAPTER 8: *Macbeth*: THE MURDERER AS VICTIM

1 Thomas De Quincey, 'On the Knocking at the Gate in *Macbeth*', in *Shakespeare Criticism*, ed. D. Nichol Smith, World's Classics, no. 212 (1961).

2 II. 2. 12–13, V. 1. 49–50.

3 Sprague, *Shakespeare and the Actors*, p. 243.

4 Bradley, *Shakespearean Tragedy*, p. 341.

5 The theatre-audience might well suspect the Weird Sisters of being witches but could not be certain of it – not, at least, in Act I, where it matters most. Though they are called witches in the Folio stage-directions (which are the work of a copyist, not necessarily Shakespeare's own words), the audience had no access to this text and could not be misled by it. Nor would it be misled by the rump-fed ronyon who allegedly addressed one of

the Weird Sisters as 'witch' (I. 3. 6), since this was a common term of
abuse, not always used discriminatingly. More significant is the fact that
Macbeth and Banquo never identify them as witches, and that Simon
Forman, who saw the play at the Globe in 1611, called them not witches
but '3 women feiries or Nimphes.'

6 Dover Wilson (ed.), *Macbeth*, p. xxi.
7 J. M. Murry, *Shakespeare* (1948 ed.) p. 326.
8 W. Moelwyn Merchant, in *Shakespeare Survey*, XIX (1966) 75.
9 Carlisle, *Shakespeare from the Greenroom*, p. 346.
10 See Dover Wilson (ed.), *Macbeth*, pp. xxxivff.
11 Bradley, *Shakespearean Tragedy*, p. 480.
12 I. 5. 23.
13 D. Bartholomeusz, *Macbeth and the Players* (Cambridge, 1969) p. 199.
14 Quoted ibid., p. 144.
15 Quoted by Sprague, *Shakespeare and the Actors*, pp. 233–4.
16 'My thought, whose murder yet is but fantastical' (I. 3. 138), 'Let not light
   see my black and deep desires' (I. 4. 51).
17 Bradley, *Shakespearean Tragedy*, p. 358.
18 *Hamlet* II. 2. 577, 584. Compare the effect of 'Must I remember?', 'Let me
   not think on't' (I. 2. 143, 146).
19 V. 5. 19, III. 1. 92ff.
20 See pp. 2, 21–3.
21 Carlisle, *Shakespeare from the Greenroom*, pp. 363, 369.
22 E. E. Stoll, *Poets and Playwrights* (University of Minnesota Press, 1930)
   p. 28.
23 Wayne Booth, 'Shakespeare's Tragic Villain', in Lerner (ed.), *Shakespeare's
   Tragedies*, pp. 180–90.
24 Richard David, 'The Tragic Curve', *Shakespeare Survey*, IX (1956) 131.
25 An exit normally refers to the last speaker, unless a different person is
   clearly indicated.
26 Bradley, *Shakespearean Tragedy*, p. 336.
27 At this point I quote and paraphrase Rosen, *Shakespeare and the Craft of
   Tragedy*, pp. 53–7.
28 III. 1. 67, I. 7. 20, II. 2. 31–3. Claudius is another 'religious' villain, but,
   reflecting about prayer rather than praying (*Hamlet* III. 3. 36ff.), he lacks
   Macbeth's passionate Christian intensity.
29 I confess that my feeling about Macbeth in this scene may be excessively
   influenced by one weak speech, 'That will never be...' (IV. 1. 94ff.). Since
   two other bits of dialogue in this very scene are widely thought to be
   interpolations (IV. 1. 39–43, 125–32), the same might be true of this curious
   rhymed speech, where Macbeth so oddly refers to himself as 'our high-
   plac'd Macbeth'.
30 Heilman, 'The Criminal as Tragic Hero', pp. 12–24.
31 'Filthy hags!', 'Let this pernicious hour/Stand aye accursed...', 'Infected
   be the air whereon they ride!'
32 Compare p. 92.
33 W. Macready (quoted by Bartholomeusz, *Macbeth and the Players*, pp.
   135–6), who admired Kemble's rendering.
34 III. 4. 129, I. 7. 45.
35 After IV. 1 we never again see Macbeth on-stage with his earlier com-
   panions, until he faces Macduff in V. 7. No other tragic hero is so
   completely severed from his past at the end – an effect that is destroyed if
   we recognise Seyton, when he first appears in V. 3, as the Bleeding Sergeant

or as an attendant seen earlier in Macbeth's entourage, as we do in some productions.

36 Rosen, *Shakespeare and the Craft of Tragedy*, p. 102.

37 V. 7. 10, 14, 25.

38 A. C. Sprague notes that 'the critics disagreed sharply as to the propriety of showing the head', *Shakespeare and the Actors*, p. 279.

39 Compare pp. 2, 25.

40 See Bartholomeusz, *Macbeth and the Players*, pp. 100, 201.

41 Bradley, *Shakespearean Tragedy*, pp. 366ff.

42 Ibid., p. 378.

43 I. 5. 38. *Tend on* = wait upon, serve, follow.

44 II. 2. 35, IV. 3. 140ff.

45 'The kingdom of heaven is likened unto a certain king, which would take account of his servants...' (*Matthew* xviii. 23ff.) Notice that Malcolm says, just before the sleep-walking scene begins, that Macbeth 'Is ripe for shaking, and *the powers above/Put on their instruments*' (IV. 3. 238–9).

46 Bradley, *Shakespearean Tragedy*, p. 395.

## CHAPTER 9: ANTONY VERSUS CLEOPATRA

1 Dover Wilson (ed.), *Antony and Cleopatra* (Cambridge, 1950) p. xxx.

2 French, *Shakespeare and the Critics*, p. 214.

3 A. P. Riemer, *A Reading of Shakespeare's 'Antony and Cleopatra'* (Sydney, 1968) p. 15, surveying 'the traditional body of attitudes that had accumulated around the lovers', declared that Shakespeare's 'passages of comedy...find no sanction at all in these traditions.' Shakespeare's passages are largely his own, of course, but Plutarch told him that jesting had an important place in Antony's life.

4 Bullough, *Sources*, V, 277.

5 According to Plutarch, 'when Antonius landed in Italie, and that men saw Caesar asked nothing of him, and that Antonius on the other side layed all the fault and burden on his wife Fulvia: the frendes of both parties would not suffer them to unrippe any olde matters, and to prove or defend who had the wrong or right, and who was the first procurer of this warre, fearing to make matters worse betwene them: but they made them frendes together...' (Bullough, *Sources*, V, 278). Shakespeare, on the contrary, after disposing of Fulvia's war, chose to 'unrip old matters'.

6 Ibid.

7 Compare Plutarch, who says nothing about farewells: 'His man drawing his sworde, lift it up as though he had ment to have striken his maister: But turning his head at one side, he thrust his sword into him selfe, and fell downe dead' (ibid., V, 309).

8 Compare Eugene M. Waith, *The Herculean Hero* (1962); Reuben A. Brower, *Hero & Saint: Shakespeare and the Graeco-Roman Heroic Tradition* (Oxford, 1971); Dover Wilson (quoted above, p. 150); and, as an example of a mixed response, Riemer, *A Reading of Shakespeare's 'Antony and Cleopatra'*.

9 I am not suggesting that Shakespeare wrote many more stage-directions than those that have come down to us in the Folio text. But we may assume that he will have given some personal directions to the actors.

10 Granville-Barker, *Prefaces*, II, 125–6, 203–6.

11 The messenger's undismayed expostulations persuade me that though Cleopatra 'strikes him down' he quickly collects himself, and that when she hales him up and down (by the arm, or by his clothes) he, physically

much the bigger, allows her to tug at him without being too intimidated. She draws her knife because her other attempts to shake him have failed. and he still takes time to announce 'Nay, then I'll run', reasoning with her to the last. The scene has something in common with the later episode of the Clown (v. 2. 240–77), Cleopatra being quite unable to move either man from his purpose; and the messenger, I believe, should appear almost as imperturbable as the Clown, thus heightening Cleopatra's comical ineffectiveness.

12 MacCallum (*Shakespeare's Roman Plays*, p. 424) also urged that Cleopatra's one line in the scene, 'Why is my lord enrag'd against his love?' expresses 'genuine amazement rather than assumed innocence'. As she usually speaks to Antony more directly when her emotion is genuine, the double use of the third person ('my lord . . . his love') surely suggests 'posing', as does the sense of the line: how, after all, can she fail to know the answer to her own question?

13 The death-scene, of course, also concludes the series of Antony's farewells (cf. pp. 153–4), and repeats his earlier magnanimous gestures to friends who had betrayed him, his speeches about Fulvia (I. 2. 119) and Enobarbus (IV. 5. 6ff.).

14 Schanzer, *Problem Plays of Shakespeare*, pp. 148, 181–2. Compare also Goddard, *The Meaning of Shakespeare*, ch. 31, and, for a reading closer to mine, Rosen, *Shakespeare and the Craft of Tragedy*, pp. 152–60.

15 Though Cleopatra didn't hear Antony's words, *we* heard them and we make the connection. Schanzer (*Problem Plays of Shakespeare*, pp. 134ff.), who noted some of 'the lovers'' echoes of each other's words and sentiments', could have cited the following: 'I *come*, my queen', 'Husband, I *come*'; 'Thrice nobler than myself', 'This proves me base' (referring to the servants who die before them); Antony's wish to '*run into*' death 'as to a *lover's bed*', and Cleopatra's 'To *rush into* the secret house of death', and her later line, 'The stroke of death is as as a *lover's pinch*'; both imagine themselves humiliated in a Roman triumph, and so on (IV. 14, 15; V. 2). These are all echoes for the audience, since Cleopatra heard none of the lines that she appears to echo.

16 The two lines after Octavius' entry (v. 2. 112–13) represent a sex-duel as fascinating as any in the play. No one else can be mistaken for Cleopatra, so Octavius' question, 'Which is the Queen of Egypt?', sounds like a studied insult. She, always so quick, must recognise him instantly, if only from the bearing of his *entourage*, but stares haughtily, challenging him to recognise her, until Dolabella whispers 'It is the Emperor, madam.' She kneels, but doesn't give up, for when he speaks, impersonally, of injuries 'written in our flesh' she takes this literally, confesses 'like frailties' that have 'sham'd our sex', twisting his words and manifestly inviting a compliment.

17 MacCallum, *Shakespeare's Roman Plays*, pp. 428, 432–3; Muir, *Shakespeare's Sources*, I, 205.

18 Brower, *Hero & Saint*, p. 341.

19 I am indebted to William Rosen (*Shakespeare and the Craft of Tragedy*, pp. 158ff.) for several points in my reading of Act v.

20 Compare p. 92.

## CHAPTER 10: THE CLARITY OF *Coriolanus*

1 See Bullough, *Sources*, V, 456ff.

2 J. Dover Wilson (ed.), *Coriolanus* (New Shakespeare ed., 1960) p. xviii.

3 See Bullough, *Sources*, V, 453.

4 *Timon* may have preceded *Coriolanus*, and went even farther from the 'centre': so far, in fact, that I am reluctant to regard it as a tragedy (see p. viii).

5 H. C. Goddard, *The Meaning of Shakespeare*, II, 209. Compare A.C. Bradley, '*Coriolanus*', in A Miscellany (1929) p. 75.

6 MacCallum, *Shakespeare's Roman Plays*, pp. 581–2; compare John Palmer, *Political and Comic Characters of Shakespeare* (1962 ed.) p. 264; and Bullough, *Sources*, V, 515.

7 Rosen, *Shakespeare and the Craft of Tragedy*, p. 187; Rossiter, *Angel With Horns*, p. 250.

8 Dover Wilson (ed.), *Coriolanus*, p. xxxvi.

9 II. 1. 166, IV. 1. 12, V. 3. 44.

10 Goddard, *The Meaning of Shakespeare*, II, 212–13.

11 The other important association is with Mars (IV. 5. 118, 192; V. 6. 100, etc.).

12 I. 9. 90, III. 1. 86, 107.

13 I. 4. 60, I. 6. 25.

14 'Take my cap, Jupiter, and I thank thee. Hoo! Marcius coming home!' (II. 1. 98).

15 Bullough, *Sources*, V, 526.

16 I. 3. 1–44.

17 *The Life of Agesilaus* (spelling modernised, from North's translation); compare also Plutarch's *Life of Pyrrhus*.

18 '*Methinks I hear*/Antony call. *I see him* rouse himself...' (*Antony and Cleopatra* V. 2. 281).

19 IV. 5. 136, III. 2. 39.

20 Bradley, '*Coriolanus*', p. 96.

21 John Palmer, *Political and Comic Characters*, p. 254. Compare William Rosen, who described Menenius in I. 1 as 'calmly good-humored, reasoning, friendly' (*Shakespeare and the Craft of Tragedy*, p. 178).

22 III. 2. 108. Compare I. 9. 15: 'my mother ... When she does praise me grieves me'; I. 1. 36: 'he did it to please his mother.'

23 II. 1. 159. Compare I. 9. 42, II. 2. 67, II. 3. 93, etc.

24 Bullough, *Sources*, V, 497, and 510: 'Menenius Agrippa was he, who was sent for chief man of the message from the Senate.'

25 II. 1. 43, 76.

26 See p. 175, above; and O. J. Campbell, *Shakespeare's Satire* (1943) pp. 204ff.; Goddard, *The Meaning of Shakespeare*, II, 225. I am indebted to Goddard for several points in my discussion of Menenius.

27 II. 2. 120, 127; III. 2. 31, 69; III. 3. 38.

28 Dover Wilson (ed.), *Coriolanus*, p. xx.

29 Rossiter, *Angel with Horns*, pp. 241–2.

30 Some of the key-passages are cited by M. W. MacCallum (*Shakespeare's Roman Plays*, p. 562) and by Harold C. Goddard (*The Meaning of Shakespeare*, II, 226), who pointed out that the speaker's character makes the fable of the belly 'both highly appropriate and fatally ironic on Menenius' lips'.

31 Shakespeare added Menenius' allusions to food and drink (other than the fable of the belly) to Plutarch's story. Plutarch's Menenius has a much smaller role.

32 Compare *Troilus and Cressida* I. 3. 85ff.

33 See Bullough, *Sources*, V, 510.

34 See *Henry V* I. 2. 183ff., and *Troilus and Cressida* I. 3. 85ff.

35 V. 3, 36–7. Compare V. 2. 78: 'Wife, mother, child, I know not.'

36 II. 1. 147.
37 Bullough, *Sources*, V, 518.
38 I. 3. 46–7. Compare Maurice Charney, *Shakespeare's Roman Plays* (Cambridge, Mass., 1963) p. 179.
39 See *The Revenger's Tragedy*, III. 5. 157; also Heywood's *The Rape of Lucrece* (1608) sig. B$_2$ᵇ, where 'Tulla treades on her father', and Marlowe's *Edward II* (the king's death). The victor who stands on his enemy is a commonplace of Renaissance art (e.g. Donatello's David). Stamping on one's enemy, however, was not only a theatrical convention. The dramatist George Wilkins was accused in 1612 of having 'outragiously beaten one Judyth Walton & stamped upon her so that she was Caried home in a Chayre' (*Shakespeare Survey*, XXV (1972) 147).
40 Chateaubriand, *The Memoirs* (Penguin ed., 1965) p. 324.
41 I. 3. 32. Volumnia's words prepare for I. 4. 30ff. At I. 4. 37 Coriolanus could turn over a body with his foot.
42 Bradley, 'Coriolanus', p. 95 (my italics).
43 'Thou hast done a deed whereat valour will weep', 'I am struck with sorrow'.
44 Compare the murder of Hector, *Troilus and Cressida* V. 8. 5ff.
45 Goddard, *The Meaning of Shakespeare*, II, 240.
46 Compare p. 172.
47 Dover Wilson (ed.), *Coriolanus*, p. xxxiv.
48 V. 3. 148, 153.
49 Compare p. 186.
50 Bradley, 'Coriolanus', p. 100.
51 See *Othello* IV. 1. 191ff., IV. 2. 42ff., IV. 3. 22ff., *King Lear* III. 6. 57ff., IV. 6. 85, 206, IV. 7. 44ff.
52 Bradley, *Shakespearean Tragedy*, pp. 333ff., 247, 303.
53 Bradley, 'Coriolanus', pp. 96–7.
54 O. J. Campbell, *Shakespeare's Satire* (1943) p. 199.
55 I. 1. 160. Notice that Shakespeare needed this preliminary gesture from Menenius to modulate directly into Coriolanus' extraordinary first speech.
56 Campbell, *Shakespeare's Satire*, p. 215.
57 Goddard, *The Meaning of Shakespeare*, II, 240.

# Index of Names

Alexander, Nigel, 200
Alexander, Peter, viii, 200
Arden, Mary, 170
Aristotle, 193
Auden, W. H., 78, 97

Bacon, Francis, 3, 122, 123, 204
Barnes, J. H., 134
Bartholomeusz, D., 205
Beaumont and Fletcher, 171
Beckerman, B., 194
Bernhardt, Sarah, 54
Bethell, S. L., 194
Bible, 11, 206
Black, M., 194
Booth, Edwin, 84
Booth, S., 194, 200
Booth, Wayne, 134–6, 138, 205
Boswell, J., 16
Bradley, A. C., 10, 12, 46, 60, 77, 79,
   81–2, 84, 94, 96, 100, 115–16, 119,
   121, 130, 133, 137, 145, 148, 178,
   186, 188–91, 194, 199, 200, 208
Brook, Peter, 203
Brooke, Nicholas, 200, 203
Brower, Reuben, 165, 206
Brown, J. R., 194
Bullough, Geoffrey, 196ff., 206ff.
Burbage, R., 4
Burns, Robert, 23

Campbell, O. J., 178, 190–1, 208–9
Carlisle, C. J., 203
Chambers, E. K., 194
Chapman, G., 171
Charney, M., 194, 209
Chateaubriand, 185, 209
Chekhov, A., 14
Cinthio, G., 97
Coleridge, S. T., 1, 54, 78, 85, 88, 96,
   104, 117, 196, 198, 200–1
Congreve, W., 151
Cunningham, J. V., 194

Danby, J. F., 123, 204

David, Richard, 137 n.24
De Quincey, Thomas, 126 ff., 134, 138,
   204
Dickens, Charles, 147–8
Diderot, D., 12
Donatello, 209
Donne, John, 90
Doran, M., 196
Dorsch, T. S., 31–2, 35 n.18, 37 n.23,
   47 n.39, 48, 196ff.
Dostoyevski, F., 51, 90

Eliot, T. S., 19, 61, 64, 91–3, 168, 195
Ellis-Fermor, Una, 194, 195
Empson, W., 82, 201, 202
Euripides, 195
Evans, K. W., 202
Fichte, J. G., 1
Fiedler, L. A., 202
Fineman, D. A., 194
Foakes, R. A., 57, 203
Forman, S., 205
Forrest, E., 133
Fraser, Russell, 117 n.28, 204
French, A. L., 150, 203, 206
Freud, S., 12, 26
Frost, W., 203

Gardner, Helen, 78, 91, 95, 195, 202
Garrick, D., 204
Gentleman, F., 134
Goddard, H. C., 99, 171–3, 178, 186,
   197, 207
Goldberg, S. L., 194
Goldman, M., 194
Granville-Barker, H., 14, 42, 47, 50,
   78, 97, 157, 195, 198–9, 202–3, 206
Guthrie, Tyrone, 131

Harbage, A., 21, 195
Harris, Bernard, 202
Hazlitt, W., 25–6, 54, 79, 134, 196,
   198
Heilman, R. B., 82, 91, 139, 195–6 201,
   205

*Macbeth,* vii, 2, 6, 8, 11, 15, 19–22,
  37, 49, 69, 73, 104–6, 126–49, 152,
  174
*Measure for Measure,* vii, 25, 188
*Merchant of Venice, The,* 25
*Merry Wives of Windsor, The,* vii
*Midsummer Night's Dream, A,* 21
*Othello,* vii, 2–3, 5, 9, 10, 12–16, 18,
  20–3, 27, 29, 60, 69, 77–100, 121–
  122, 131–2, 152, 154, 168, 189,
  193, 195, 209
*Richard II,* 24, 25, 30, 196
*Richard III,* 30, 77, 196
*Romeo and Juliet,* vii, 16, 30
*Taming of the Shrew, The,* 13
*Tempest, The,* 13
*Timon of Athens,* vii, viii, 105, 110,
  203, 207
*Titus Andronicus,* 30, 196
*Troilus and Cressida,* vii, viii, 4, 70,
  178, 180, 208–9
*Twelfth Night,* vii, 5, 196
*Winter's Tale, The,* 9, 79, 158, 183
Shaw, G. Byam, 136
Shoemaker, S., 195
Siddons, Sarah, 145
Simmons, J. L., 194
Spencer, Theodore, 122–3, 204

Sprague, A. C., 27, 196–7, 202–6
Spurgeon, C. F. E., 198
Stampfer, J., 120 n. 31, 121 n. 38, 204
Stewart, J. I. M., 194, 201
Stoll, E. E., 25, 134, 196, 205
Strindberg, J. A., 12
Swinburne, A. C., 79

Terry, Ellen, 145
Theobald, L., 137
Tourneur, C., 56, 185, 203, 209
Trilling, L., 194

Ure, Peter, 195

Vandenhoff, J., 99

Waith, Eugene M., 206
Waldock, A. J. A., 5 n. 3, 194
Webster, John, 14
Webster, Margaret, 106 n. 11, 122–3
Whiter, W., 12
Whitman, Walt, 12
Wilkins, George, 209
Wilson, H. S., 203
Wilson, J. Dover, 130, 150, 170, 172
  n. 8, 187 n. 47, 197, 205–6, 208–9
Wordsworth, William, 200

# Index of Technical Terms

(*This is an index of technical or unusual terms. It refers the reader to pages where these terms are defined, or to passages where they are used. It is not a complete index.*)